A gift from
Howard County
Genealogical
Society

(via Duane Smith)

THE MAYFLOWER DESCENDANT

Volume XVIII

THE MAYFLOWER DESCENDANT

1620 1920

A QUARTERLY MAGAZINE OF
PILGRIM GENEALOGY AND HISTORY

VOLUME XVIII

1916

PUBLISHED BY THE

MASSACHUSETTS SOCIETY OF
MAYFLOWER DESCENDANTS
BOSTON

Editor

GEORGE ERNEST BOWMAN

Committee on Publication

REV. FREDERICK B. ALLEN   ALVIN P. JOHNSON
ARTHUR PERRY   FREDERICK FOSTER
GEORGE ERNEST BOWMAN

A Facsimile Reprint
Published 1995 by

HERITAGE BOOKS, INC.
1540E Pointer Ridge Place
Bowie, Maryland 20716
1-800-398-7709

ISBN 0-7884-0378-8

INDEX OF SUBJECTS

THE MAYFLOWER

Approaching the Land

(See page 64)

THE MAYFLOWER DESCENDANT

Vol. XVIII JANUARY, 1916 No. 1

THE "MAYFLOWER"

By Mr. R. G. Marsden

[In the following pages we re-print in full, by permission of the author and the publishers, an important article by Mr. R. G. Marsden about the Pilgrims' ship, the "Mayflower", and Christopher Jones, her captain. This article was printed in the October, 1904, issue of "The English Historical Review", published by Messrs. Longmans, Green and Co., of London.—*Editor.*]

More than one writer upon New England history has attributed the landing of the Pilgrim Fathers at Plymouth, instead of in Virginia, whither they intended to go, to the evil doings of the master of the "Mayflower." It has been suggested that he was instigated either by the Dutch of New Amsterdam or by Sir Robert Rich, who was at variance with the Virginia Company, to plant the colonists upon a shore far removed from that to which he was employed to carry them. These suggestions are founded mainly upon the assumption that the master, who we know from Bradford's History was a "Mr." Jones, was a certain Captain Thomas Jones, of whose character and connections enough is known to make such a suggestion credible. The identity of the master of the "Mayflower" is therefore a matter of some historical importance, and of more than local or antiquarian interest. The object of the present paper is to bring forward, from a source that has not hitherto been explored, some evidence to show that the master of the Pilgrim Fathers' ship was not Captain Thomas Jones; but that he was one Christopher Jones, against whose character nothing is known; and that the theory of a conspiracy to deposit the Pilgrim Fathers at Cape Cod, under color of a contract to land them elsewhere, so far as it rests upon the supposed evil character of "Mr." Jones, has no foundation in fact. The mistake which has been committed in identifying "Mr." Jones with Captain Thomas Jones has arisen in consequence of the supposed absence of any evidence as to the history and career of the Pilgrim Fathers' ship before and after she made the historic voyage. No serious attempt has hitherto been made to identify her with any one of the many "Mayflowers" that are known to have been afloat in and about 1620. When a ship named "Mayflower" occurs in a document of the period, it is commonly assumed that probably she is the Pilgrim Fathers' ship. The facts stated below will show that conjecture resting only upon identity of name is of very slight value.

The name "Mayflower" was, in fact, very common in the sixteenth and seventeenth centuries. Besides Scotch and Irish "Mayflowers," of which there were several, there were "Mayflowers" belonging to almost every port in England. There were "Mayflowers" of Aldeburgh, Brightlingsea, Bristol, Chester, Dover, Grimsby, Looe, Lyme, Lynn, Maidstone, Millbrook, Newcastle, Plymouth, Portland, Rye, St. Ives, Sandwich, Scarborough, Shoreham, Southwold, Stockton, Stonehouse, Swansea, York, Weymouth, and Whitby. And although the same ship is not always described as belonging to the same port, some of the larger ports, such as Ipswich, London, Newcastle, and Yarmouth, possessed two or even several "Mayflowers" apiece. There cannot have been fewer than forty or fifty "Mayflowers" existing between A.D. 1550 and 1700. There were "Mayflowers" trading to Virginia and New England, to the East and West Indies, to Africa, the Levant, and the Mediterranean, to Greenland, Norway, Spain, Portugal, Scotland, and Ireland. There were "Mayflowers" in the service of the king, and "Mayflowers" in the service of parliament; "Mayflowers" East Indiamen, men-of-war, privateers, whalers, slavers, colliers, and fishermen; "Mayflowers" of all sorts and sizes, from 15 to 400 tons. In the autumn of 1620, while the Pilgrim Fathers' ship was on her outward voyage, at least two other seagoing "Mayflowers" were under way, one in Eastern seas and one in the Thames. So fruitful in "Mayflowers" are the records that it is very difficult to distinguish them, and still more difficult to identify any one of them with the Pilgrim Fathers' ship. The task would indeed be impossible were it not for a mass of records which, to all appearance, have never been systematically searched for this or any other purpose, the records, namely, of the High Court of Admiralty. It is not possible here to describe these records, which have only recently been thrown open to the public. It is enough to state that during the Elizabethan and Stuart periods much of the shipping business of the country came before the Admiralty court, and that there is no class of records which contains so many references to the ships of that period as the records of that court. They are very voluminous, but are almost wholly without calendar or index, and a great part of them are in the utmost confusion. An exhaustive search of them would be the work of a lifetime; and it is probable that some documents relating to the subject before us have escaped the notice of the present writer.

The constant occurrence in these records of ships bearing the name of "Mayflower" is confusing. Nevertheless it is not difficult, by collecting a large number of references, to reduce the number of possible Pilgrim Fathers' "Mayflowers" to some half-dozen ships; for many craft bearing the name may be at once dismissed as impossible; such, for example, are all "Mayflower" pinks, hoys, fishermen, and small craft, and all "Mayflowers" built after or lost before the year 1620.*

The first step towards identifying the Pilgrim Fathers' ship with a "Mayflower" mentioned in the records is to collect all the facts bearing upon her identity which are to be gathered from outside sources. These are scanty and may be summed up in a few lines. Bradford, Mourt, Winthrop, Prince, Neill, and Hazard are our authorities. From them we learn that between 1620 and 1630 a "Mayflower," or "Mayflowers," crossed the seas three times. One in 1620 carried the Pilgrim Fathers to New Plymouth; one in 1629 carried Higginson's party to Salem; and one in 1630 carried Winthrop's party to Charlestown. It has generally been assumed that these three voyages were made by the same ship; but the strong probability is that the voyages of 1629 and 1630 were not made by the ship that sailed in 1620. Our reasons for arriving at this conclusion are given below. In this connection it may be stated that besides the three "Mayflower" voyages above mentioned at least three and probably more voyages were made by other "Mayflowers" to America during the first half of the seventeenth century.

As to the Pilgrim Fathers' ship, the historians give us the following particulars. First, as to her name: this we should expect to find in Bradford's history, but it is not there; nor is it

* A large number of references cannot be made use of, because no fact stated in any one of them enables us to identify the "Mayflower" to which it relates.

mentioned by Mourt: it occurs in the records of the Old Colony, of the year 1623; and "A Note of the shipping, men, and provisions sent and provided for Virginia by the Right Honorable the Earl of Southampton and the Company this year 1620," preserved among the duke of Manchester's papers,* mentions "the May-Flower of 140 tuns, sent in August 1620, with 100 persons." This, it would seem, must be the Pilgrim Fathers' ship; but the note is not accurate, for she was not "sent and provided" by Lord Southampton's Virginia Company, but by the Plymouth Adventurers. As to the tonnage of the "Mayflower," Bradford says that her burden was "about nine score." This has universally been interpreted to mean nine score tons; but it is possible that Bradford meant nine score lasts (about 340 tons); and, if that be so, the ship of the Manchester papers would not be Bradford's ship. The "last" was the Dutch unit of measurement, and when Robert Cushman wrote to Bradford about a ship which he was inclined to charter for the Leyden Company he described her as of sixty lasts. The probability, however, is that the traditional interpretation of Bradford's phrase is correct. The Pilgrim Fathers' ship had two decks. This we know from Mourt, who tells us that her shallop, a boat able to carry twenty-five persons under sail, was with some difficulty stowed "betwixt the decks." As to her age in 1620, it would seem that she was not then a new ship. This may be inferred from several facts. Bradford tells us that on the voyage out one of the beams in the midships was "bowed and cracked," and that her condition was so critical that, had she not been halfway out to New England, her master would have abandoned the voyage. The passengers lay wet in their berths, and continual caulking failed to keep the decks staunch. She was, says Captain John Smith, "a leaking, unwholesome ship." But her master, who knew her well, had faith in her; and after straining the buckled beam into its place with a screw-jack the crew shored it up and decided to continue the voyage. They were obliged, however, to keep the ship under small sail, and to ease her as much as possible.

Her master, we know from Bradford, was a "Mr." Jones. Unfortunately we are not told his Christian or first name. The records supply us with a "Mayflower" of 1609–1624, whose master and part owner was a Christopher Jones; and it is this connection of a "Mayflower" with a master whose name was Jones that enables us to identify the Pilgrim Fathers' ship, and to follow her career in the records for at least thirteen years.

* No. 291; not fully set out in *Hist. MSS. Comm.: 8th Report*, pt. ii. App. p. 37b.

The master of our ship being for the present assumed (though hereafter, it is submitted, he is proved) to be Christopher Jones, it is perhaps superfluous to show that he cannot have been the Captain Thomas Jones above mentioned. Inasmuch, however, as Captain Thomas Jones was undoubtedly trading to New England in 1620, and has for this reason been supposed by more than one writer to have been the master of the Pilgrim Fathers' ship, it may be well to state that the Admiralty court records show that Captain Thomas Jones was in Virginia, in command of the "Falcon," in September, 1620, at the time when "Mr." Jones was on his outward voyage to New Plymouth in the Pilgrim Fathers' ship, and that in April, 1621, Captain Thomas Jones was being sued in England by some of the "Falcon's" crew for their wages, when "Mr." Jones was on his voyage home from New Plymouth to England.* The historians do not tell us the names of any of the owners of the Pilgrim Fathers' ship. This is unfortunate, because the identity of the ship in the records can frequently be traced by owners' names. Nor do they tell us to what port she belonged. All we can gather from them is that she was chartered, probably in London, in July, 1620.

As to the date and place of her sailing, we know that she sailed from London, some days before 19 July, 1620, for Southampton, and that she arrived at the latter port on that day. She sailed from Southampton on 5 August, and soon afterwards put into Dartmouth. Thence she sailed on 23 August, but had again to put back to Plymouth. From Plymouth she sailed on 6 September, and arrived at her destination in New England on 11 November. She lay in New Plymouth harbour through the winter of 1620–1, and sailed back for England about 5 April, arriving on the 5th or 6th of May. During the voyage she had on board, besides her crew, 104 passengers.

These are nearly all the facts to be gathered from contemporary writers which will assist us in our search for the Pilgrim Fathers' ship among the records. They are set forth here at some length because, if any one of them were inconsistent with any fact stated in the records touching the ship in this paper called Christopher Jones's "Mayflower," the conclusion at which we shall arrive as to her identity with the Pilgrim Fathers' ship would be wrong. It is necessary, therefore, to state here that, so far as the writer is aware, there is nothing stated in the records about Christopher Jones's ship which is inconsistent with what the chroniclers tell us about the Pilgrim Fathers' ship.

* For the authorities for this and other statements see the note at the end of this article.

There is a passage in Mourt's "Relation" which is of some importance in connection with a "Mayflower" whaler mentioned in the records, about which ship something will be said below. The passage is as follows. Speaking of whales seen by "Mr." Jones and the crew of the Pilgrim Fathers' ship on the New England coast during the winter of 1620–1, Mourt says:

Our master and his mate and others experienced in fishing professed we might have made £3,000 or £4,000 worth of oil. They preferred it before Greenland whale fishing, and purposed the next winter to fish for whale here.

From this passage it would seem reasonable to infer that previously to 1620 "Mr." Jones, or some of his crew, had either been on a whaling voyage themselves or had some acquaintance with whale fishery. Now the records of the Admiralty court show that in 1624, and again in 1626, a "Mayflower" of Yarmouth (or of Hull) was whaling in Greenland. And although the whaler of 1624 probably was not Christopher Jones's "Mayflower" it will be seen below that there is reason to think that at least two of the owners of Jones's ship were part owners of the whaler of 1624. Further, Purchas in his *Pilgrims* (iii. 565) tells us that a Master Jones was whaling at Cherrie Island * in 1609, the year in which we first find Christopher Jones's name as master of the "Mayflower" in northern seas. Purchas tells us also (iii. 560, 561) that whalers sailed from Harwich; and it will be shown below that both Christopher Jones and his ship are described as "of Harwich" in a document of 1611. There are other indications pointing to the conclusion that Jones's "Mayflower" may have been a whaler before 1620. The whaling fleet of 1624, of which the "Mayflower" of Yarmouth (or of Hull) was one, was fitted out by merchants of York and Hull; and this fleet had been whaling in Greenland for several years before 1624. Aldeburgh has always been closely connected with the neighbouring fishing port of Yarmouth; it is distant from Yarmouth only about 30 miles, and it was at this date a member of the port of Yarmouth. At Aldeburgh, it will be seen below, there was built in or about the year 1624 a new "Mayflower," and the master of this new "Mayflower" was part owner of Christopher Jones's "Mayflower." Since, as is stated above, there is reason to think that the new "Mayflower" built at Aldeburgh was the whaler of 1624, it seems reasonable to conjecture that she was built to supply the place of the old (Christo-

* This probably was one of the ships set out by Roger Jones, Henry Jones, John Jones, and James Duppa, merchants; Admiralty Court Exam. 40, 4 and 13 Oct. 1609; Exam. 108, 6 Oct. 1609; Acts 27, 15 Sept., 7 Oct., 25 Oct., 21 Nov. 1609.

pher Jones's) "Mayflower," and that the old "Mayflower" had also been a whaler.

To return to the historic ship, we have gathered from the chroniclers her name and tonnage, her occupation from July, 1620, to May, 1621, and the surname of her master. We now turn to the Admiralty court records for information about Christopher Jones and his "Mayflower." Only those documents are here quoted which certainly relate to the same ship, her identity throughout being assured by statements as to her owner's or master's name and as to her tonnage. Upon the last point it is necessary to state that the records cannot be relied upon for accuracy in their statements as to a ship's tonnage. The same ship is found to be described as of 200, 240, 250 tons; and sometimes the figures vary more than this. Nor is it safe to rely upon the description of a ship as belonging to a named port as evidence of identity. The same ship is frequently described as belonging to different ports. Christopher Jones's "Mayflower" is described sometimes as "of London" and twice as "of Harwich." She may nevertheless have been owned in Aldeburgh, Ipswich, or elsewhere. As regards her connection with Harwich, that port is much frequented by ships bound either to Ipswich or to Aldeburgh. It is, in fact, the entrance to the Ipswich river, and many ships bound into Orford Haven (the entrance to the Aldeburgh river, about 7 miles distant) bring up at Harwich, in order to wait there until the tide serves to cross the bar at Orford Haven. The Aldeburgh river is very difficult to enter, and the bar can be crossed only at the top of high water. Consequently at the present day Aldeburgh cod smacks, and other vessels of any draught, are constantly in and out of Harwich harbour.

Christopher Jones first appears in the records as master of a "Mayflower" in a document of 1609. Two years before this he is stated to have been owner and master of the "Josan" (or "Jason") of London. In her he made a voyage to Bordeaux in 1606 or 1607, and brought prunes to London. He sued James Campbell for freight of the prunes, and the suit was stayed by prohibition from the Common Pleas on 22 May, 1611. Of the history of Jones's "Mayflower" before 1609 nothing can be stated for certain. Her name does not appear in the report of the Historical Manuscripts Commission upon the Ipswich records, and the present writer has not succeeded in finding it amongst the (unpublished) records of the Harwich corporation. It is possible, however, that a more careful search at one of these places, or at Aldeburgh, or Yarmouth, or Hull, may discover further facts as to her ownership and history. The records of the Admiralty court and other sources contain a good deal of information about "Mayflowers" of an earlier date, but no fact is stated about any one of them which enables us to identify her with Jones's ship. We are told of a "Mayflower" of Dover, which had wine on board in 1603, and some years later was in Barbary; a "Mayflower" or "Mayflowers" of Hull, referred to in documents dated between 1573 and 1582; a "Mayflower" of Ipswich of 120 tons, built after 1571, and mentioned again (or another "Mayflower" of Ipswich) in 1598; a "Mayflower" of Lynn of 150 tons, which fought the Spaniards under Lord Edward Seymour in 1588; a "Mayflower" of London of 250 tons, owned by John Vassall and others, fitted out by the Londoners for the queen in 1588, and mentioned in documents until 1594; a "Mary Floure" of Newcastle, of 140 or 160 tons, which was captured from the Scots in 1558, rebuilt in 1566, and was trading in 1582; another "Mayflower" of Newcastle (or possibly the same ship) trading to Africa in 1601–2; a "Mayflower" of Southwold that was fishing at Iceland in 1593 · and a "Mayflower" of Yarmouth of 120 tons, of the year 1593. No evidence has been found of the loss, capture, or breaking up of any of these ships; and Christopher Jones's "Mayflower" may be any one of them.

The records give the following particulars of the doings of Christopher Jones's ship from 1609 to 1624. In August, 1609, Andrew Pawlinge chartered the "Mayflower," Christopher Jones master, Robert Childe, Christopher Jones, and probably also Christopher Nicholls and Thomas Shorte, being her owners, for a voyage from London to Drontheim, in Norway, and back to London. Her cargo on the return voyage consisted wholly or in part of tar, deals, and herrings. She met with bad weather, lost an anchor and cable, and made short delivery of her herrings. Litigation followed, and was proceeding in 1612. Another suit arose out of this voyage which is of more interest. In 1609, when the "Mayflower" was lying in the Thames, goods on board were arrested, at the suit of the king, for a crown debt owing by Pawlinge. Richard Nottingham claimed to be then owner of the goods under an assignment from Pawlinge. On behalf of the crown it was alleged that the assignment was fraudulent, and made for the purpose of evading payment of Pawlinge's debt to the crown. Application was made to the court by Nottingham that the goods should be released on bail. The judge of the admiralty, Sir Richard Trevor, doubted whether he could take bail in a crown suit, and refused to release the goods. Subsequently Nottingham procured the opinion of Sir Henry Hobart, attorney-general, that the goods might be released. This opinion was submitted to the court, and upon the strength of it the goods were released. In the course of this suit the "Mayflower's" charter-party and a receipt by Christopher Jones for payment by Nottingham of freight and other charges on the goods were produced as evidence of Nottingham's ownership of the goods. These documents were filed in the registry of the Admiralty court, but apparently they have been lost.

In January, 1611, Christopher Jones was probably at London in the "Mayflower." In the Thames estuary he had picked up at Gore End some wreckage, sails and other ship's gear, which were presented as admiralty droits and claimed on behalf of the lord high admiral. In the appraisement of their value, dated 14 Jan. 1610–1, Christopher Jones is described as of Harwich, and his ship is called the "Mayflower" of Harwich. In 1613 the "Mayflower," Christopher Jones master, was twice in the Thames, once in July and again in October and November. Export duties upon stockings, bayes, and coney skins, part of her outward cargoes, were paid in London. In 1614 Christopher Jones was again party to an Admiralty suit. There are several other references to a "Mayflower" in the years 1613, 1614, and 1615, but the particulars given are not sufficient to identify the ship. The next reference, which certainly relates to Christopher Jones's ship, is in 1616. In that year John Cawkin came on board her in the Thames, and there, according to Jones's statement, misconducted himself by inciting the crew to mutiny, abusing Jones, and drinking from the cargo of wine. For these matters he was sued by Jones in the Admiralty court, with what result does not appear. Cawkin was an officer of the court, and he may have been on board the "Mayflower" in connection with the death of Edward Baillie, who was drowned from a "Mayflower" in the Thames about this time. The claim of the Admiralty coroner to hold an inquest upon bodies found in the Thames not infrequently led to trouble at this date. The mention of wine on board suggests that the "Mayflower" had recently been on a voyage to France, Spain, Portugal, the Canaries, or some other wine country.

After 1616 no record has been found which certainly relates to Jones's "Mayflower" until the year 1624. This is remarkable, for a ship trading to London does not usually disappear for so long a time from the records. No Admiralty court document relating to the Pilgrim Fathers' voyage of 1620 has been found, and no litigation arose out of the voyage. Perhaps the hurry and secrecy with which the transfer of the Pilgrims from Leyden to New England was arranged may account for this. Moreover the business of the Admiralty court at this period was at a low ebb, owing to the vigorous attack which had recently been made upon its jurisdiction by Lord Coke; and paucity of business was accompanied by neglect and dilapidation of its records, many of which belonging to this period have been lost. There is another possible explanation of the silence of the records touching Jones's "Mayflower" from 1616 to 1624. If the suggestion made above as to the whaling career of the ship is correct, there are reasons why she would not be likely to have come to London during those years. The Muscovy Company were now taking active measures to stop interlopers from Hull and Yarmouth, who were trespassing upon the Company's patent monopoly of whaling in the Northern seas. If Jones's "Mayflower" was, in fact, one of the Hull and Yarmouth whalers, she would not be likely to have come within reach of the officers of the Admiralty court in London. Had she done so, she would probably have been arrested, and proceedings taken against her as an interloper. There is evidence to show that the east coast whalers carried their oil cargoes to Scotland and Hull; and this, Jones's ship, if she was a whaler, may have done.

The next appearance of Christopher Jones in the records of the High Court is in 1618. In that year he was plaintiff in an Admiralty suit, and is described as of Redrith (Rotherhithe), mariner. In another suit of the same year he was arrested as defendant, and was released upon bail. The name of the "Mayflower" does not occur in either of these suits. Before 26 August, 1622, Christopher Jones died. The books at Somerset House tell us that on that day administration on his effects was granted to Joan, his widow.* He must have died between the spring of 1621, when he was in the "Mayflower" in New England, and 26 August, 1622. It is possible that he made whaling voyages in the "Mayflower" in the summers of 1621 and 1622, but the absence of any whaling gear in the inventory of the "Mayflower," made in 1624, and mentioned below, makes this improbable.

About two years after the death of Christopher Jones, on 4 May, 1624, Robert Childe, John Moore, and [Joan,] widow of Christopher Jones, owners of three-fourths of the "Mayflower," obtained a decree in the Admiralty court for her appraisement. She was then probably lying in the Thames; for the commission of appraisement issued to four mariners and shipwrights of

* "Prerogative Court Books."

Rotherhithe. The appraisement is extant. It is a significant document, as regards her age and condition. Her hull was valued at £50; her five anchors at £25; her one suit of worn sails at £15; her cables, hawsers, and standing rigging at £35; her muskets, arms, pitchpots, and 10 shovels at £3, 8s. It does not appear for what purpose the appraisement was made, nor has any other document or reference to the suit, if there was a suit, been found among the Admiralty court records. It is possible that the owner of the remaining one-fourth of the ship was unwilling to contribute to the cost of repairing her, or of fitting her out for a new voyage, and that the other co-owners took proceedings to compel him to contribute; or, possibly, the appraisement was made to fix the value of the widow Joan Jones's one-fourth, for purposes of administration of Christopher Jones's estate. A total value of £160 for a ship of 180 tons seems a low value; but we know that she was at least thirteen years old, and possibly she had been laid up since Christopher Jones's death in 1622, and had been allowed to get out of repair. In the suit of 1609 she was bailed for £800.

The next document * which may relate to Christopher Jones's "Mayflower" is a certificate made by the mayor and bailiffs of Aldeburgh of the losses which that town had suffered by wreck and capture of their ships; and the object of the petition, to which it was probably attached, was doubtless to obtain relief from naval assessment. The certificate gives a list of ships lost and captured, and first amongst them is a "Mayflower" of Aldeburgh of 160 tons, which is stated to have been owned in Aldeburgh and to have been worth £700. The names of the owners are not given. She was captured on 5 March, 1626, by Dunkirkers, while on a fishing voyage to Iceland. As compared with £160, the appraised value of Christopher Jones's "Mayflower" in 1624, £700 seems to be excessive, and to point to her being a different ship. But it is certain that the certificate would put the value of the captured ship at the highest possible figure, which would include the value of stores, provisions, fishing gear, and possibly some cargo. Unless the captured ship was ransomed (and there is no evidence that she was ransomed), it is not possible that she was the new ship next mentioned, which was trading for her owners of 1626 in the year 1630. In 1626 Robert Child, John Totten, Michael (or Myles) White, and others not named were owners of a "Mayflower" of about 200 tons, which had been built at Aldeburgh "about a year since," John

* *S. P. Dom.* Chas. I, cxxvi. no. 55. For this reference I am indebted to the kindness of Mr. M. Oppenheim.

Moore being designed her master. It will be remembered that Robert Child was a part owner of Christopher Jones's "Mayflower" in 1609, and that he and John Moore were part owners of her when she was appraised in 1624. Myles White is perhaps the Myles White of London, grocer and rope-seller, who in 1625 owned the "William and Mary" of Ipswich. The fact that Child and Moore named their new ship "Mayflower" makes it unlikely that their old "Mayflower" (Christopher Jones's "Mayflower") was still afloat and owned by them. If, as is possible, their old ship was the ship that had been captured by Dunkirkers, they would not be unlikely to call their new ship by the old name. The new ship may be the whaler of 1626, which is in that year described as a new ship.

It has been stated above that the voyages made by "Mayflowers" to New England in 1629 and 1630 were probably not made by the Pilgrim Fathers' ship. Apart from the probability that the "Mayflower" captured by Dunkirkers in 1626 was the Pilgrim Fathers' ship there are other reasons for distinguishing the ships of 1629 and 1630 from that of 1620. In the first place the chroniclers tell us that the ship of 1629 had 14 guns. Ordnance was supplied to ships only upon an order made by the Lord High Admiral; most of these orders are extant, and there is no record of guns having been supplied to Christopher Jones's ship. There is, however, a record of 14 guns having been supplied to a "Mayflower" "of London" in 1626; and this ship was not Christopher Jones's "Mayflower." In the second place it is not likely that Christopher Jones's ship, which was of some age and weak in 1620, would have been fit to carry 14 guns nine years later, in 1629. Thirdly, the "Mayflower" of 1629 was chartered by a wealthy body, the Massachusetts Bay Company, who would not have been likely to employ "a leaky, unwholesome" ship upon an arduous voyage, for which she had proved herself to be hardly fit nine years before. As to the ship of 1630, it is probable that she was the same ship as that which made the voyage of 1629. The subsequent history of this ship can be traced in the records with tolerable certainty and fulness. There is evidence to show that she was afterwards a "Mayflower" "of Yarmouth," owned in and after 1627 by Thomas Hoarth of Yarmouth, and that she also became a whaler.

Since this account was written it has been brought to the notice of the writer by the kindness of Mr. Henry F. Thompson, of Baltimore, that there was on board the Pilgrim Fathers' ship a Christopher Jones. It is known that he was not one of the colonists; he must, therefore, have been one of the ship's company. Modern research has discovered at Somerset House the will of William Mullins,* who died on board the "Mayflower" at Plymouth, in 1621. A copy of the will is certified by John Carver, the governor of the Plymouth colony, Giles Heale, who, there is reason to think, was the doctor of the "Mayflower," and "Christopher Joanes." It is submitted that, if further evidence were necessary, the discovery of Mullins's will leaves little doubt that the third witness to that will was Bradford's "Mr." Jones, the master of the "Mayflower;" that he was the Christopher Jones of the records, and that the ship whose career we have followed from 1609 to 1624 or 1626 was the Pilgrim Fathers' ship.

Note

The following references, except where otherwise stated to the records of the High Court of Admiralty, are the principal authorities for the statements in the text: —

Captain Thomas Jones, in the "Lyon:" "Acts" 29, 19 & 27 April 1619, ff. 335, 355; "Libels" 79, no. 60; in the "Falcon," "Lib." 77, no. 177; "Lib." 80, *ad med.*; "Examinations" 43, April to June 1621; "Exam." 109, 10 July 1621; "Warrant Books" 13, 20 April, 26 Oct. 1621; "Miscellanea" 1127.

Christopher Jones, in the "Josan:" "Lib." 75, no. 250; "Acts" 28, March 1610, April 1611; "War. Bks." 12, 6 March 1610; prohibition in Jones *c.* Campbell, "Common Roll East." 9 Jac. I, rot. 1506; party to Admiralty suits, "War. Bks." 13, 22 June 1614, 5 & 12 May 1618; "Acts" 29, ff. 249, 251; Jones *c.* Cawkin, "Lib." 79, no. 120; "Acts" 29, f. 253.

"Mayflower," voyage to Drontheim and suits of Rex *c.* Nottingham, Rex. *c.* Pawlin, Jones *c.* Pawlin: "Acts" 27 & 28, *passim*; "Lib." 73, nos. 27, 37, 69; "Lib." 74, no. 125; "Lib." 75, no. 143; "Exam." 40, 41, & 42, *passim*; "War. Bks." 12, 7 & 10 Dec.; in the "Thames," "Lib." 74, no. 60; "K. R. Customs" $\frac{91}{8}$; appraisement, "Acts" 30, f. 227; "Lib." 82, no. 167.

New "Mayflower," built at Aldeburgh, *S. P. Dom.* Chas. I, xvi. no. 25; voyage to Spain in 1630 and suit of Totten *c.* Bowyer: "Lib." 91, nos. 17, 121, 176; "Exam." 112, 27 Jan. 1633; "Exam." 113, 21 & 26 June 1634; "Exam." 50, 4 March 1633, 24 April 1634; "War. Bks." 19, 27 Sept. 1633, 22 July 1634; "Monitions" 5, no. 72; "Miscellanea" 949; "Miscellanea" 1423, f. 20 b.

"Mayflower" whaler and the Hull whaling fleet: "Exam." 45, Jan. & Feb. 1626; "Exam." 46, 19 April 1627; "Exam." 50, 12 & 14 Nov. & 8 Feb. 1633; "Exam." 51, 15 & 24 Nov. 1634; "Exam." 112, 30 Oct. 1633; "Lib." 82, no. 5; "Exam." 148; "Interrogatories" 7, *ad med.*; "Miscell." 1141; *S. P. Dom.* Chas. I, xvi. no. 30.

Miles White, "Exam." 43, 30 May 1621; "Exam." 114, 1 Dec. 1635; "War. Bks." 15, 17 Feb. 1624.

* The Somerset House reference is 68 Dale, ff. 68, 69.

THE WILLS OF JOHN[1] BROWN, SENIOR AND JOHN[2] BROWN, JUNIOR

TRANSCRIBED BY THE EDITOR

THE wills and inventories of John Brown, Sr., and his son, John Brown, Jr., both of Rehoboth, Mass., are found in the Plymouth Colony Wills and Inventories, at Plymouth, Mass. They are here printed in full, at the expense of Mr. Winfield Martin Brown, a descendant of John Brown, Sr., through his son Lieutenant James, whose will was printed in our last issue.*

John Brown, Jr., made his will on 31 March, 1662; and John Brown, Sr., made his will just one week later, on 7 April, 1662. Both wills were probated on 3 October, 1662, at Plymouth; and both inventories were taken on 19 April, 1662. The two wills, and the inventories, were recorded together, in the second part of the second book, pages 77a, et seq.

[THE WILL OF JOHN BROWN, JR.]

[2 : 2 : 77a] The last Will and Testament of m^r John Browne Juni^r of Rehoboth; exhibited before the Court held att Plymouth the third Day of october 1662 on the oath of John Allin of Rehoboth

Know all men that I John Browne of Wannamoisett in the Jurisdiction of Plymouth being sicke but in pfect memory Doe leave this as my last Will and Testament in maner and forme as followeth; wheras my fatherinlaw Willam Buckland standeth engaged unto mee in the sume of three score pounds which was to bee for the portion hee was to give mee in marriage with my wife and was to bee payed mee in the yeare 1660 : this sume which is now in my fatherinlaw his hand I Doe give unto my wife for her better preferment Desiring that my fatherinlaw would bee Carfull to pay it; and morover I Doe give unto my wife; the like sume of threescore pounds to bee payed unto her by my Exequitor out of my estate and I Doe give unto my eldest son John Browne my little mare that is now great with foale as alsoe yearling Coult shee brought forth the last yeare; and one yeoke of oxen; and such Iron or Iron takeling as is ptable betwixt my brother James and my selfe I Doe give my pte unto my son John Browne; and Conserning all my five Children I Doe wholly leave them all to the ordering and Dis-

* Mayflower Descendant, XVII : 193.

poseing of my owne father Mr John Browne for him to bring them up not once questioning but that his love and Care for them wilbee as it hath bine for my selfe ; and for all the rest of my estate I Doe wholly leave unto him to Dispose amongst them as in his Descretion hee shall see meet ; and I Doe leave my said father mr John Browne sole exequitor of this my last Will ; In Witnes wherof I have sett to my hand and seale this last Day of march in the yeare 1662

Signed Sealed and Delivered
in the prsence of
Thomas Willett
John Allin ;

John Browne
and a seale

[fol. 78] Aprill 19 : 1662

An Inventory of the estate of mr John Browne Junr lately Deceased exhibited to the Court held att Plymouth the third Day of October 1662 att which Court mr James Browne Deposed soe farr to it as Concerning all such pteable goods as were between his brother John Browne aforsaid and himselfe ;

	£	s	d
Impr eight yards of teicking vallued att	01	12	00
Item a featherbed and bolster and pillow 2 ruggs and six blanketts att	10	05	00
Item two paire of sheets vallued att	00	18	00
Item a paire of sheets vallued att	00	10	00
Item 2 paire of pillowbeers att	00	11	00
Item 2 Napkins vallued att	00	04	00
Item 5 bands vallued	00	09	00
Item 4 handkerchifes 2 Capps one neckcloth	00	04	00
Item a smale truncke vallued att	00	02	06
Item one remnant of stuffe vallued att	00	09	00
Item a remnant of Cotton Cloth att	00	04	04
Item an old table vallued att	00	08	00
Item one hogshead vallued att	00	04	00
Item 4 Chaires vallued att	00	05	00
Item 3 paire of Crookes vallued att	00	09	00
Item 2 Chaires vallued att	00	18	00
Item 4 axes vallued att	00	13	00
Item 2 hoes vallued att	00	05	00
Item a Crow of Iron and a barr of Iron att	00	10	00
Item 2 wedges att	00	05	06
Item a little Sledg and an hammer att	00	04	00
Item a fier pan and tonggs vallued att	00	06	00
Item a gridiron and frying pan	00	04	06
Item a paire of bellows	00	02	03

Item for Cart and wheeles and Irons about them	01	12	06
being ptable between the brothers his pte att	00	18	06
Item a Cloake and briches att	01	10	00
Item a paire of gray briches and troopers Coate	02	10	00
Item one gray Cloake	02	05	00
Item a Cloth Doublet vallued att	00	15	00
Item a serge suite vallued att	01	10	00
Item a serge Doublett and Cloth briches att	01	10	00
Item a troopers Coate vallued att	01	00	00
Item a hatt vallued att	00	14	00
Item 10 yards of serge vallued att	02	16	00
Item 6 yards and an halfe of stuffe	00	16	03
Item a yard and three quarters of kersy	00	10	06
Item a paire of boothose topps att	00	03	00
Item 4 yards of Tammy vallued att	00	10	00
Item 2 knives one botkin	00	02	00
Item a smale remnant of serge att	00	04	00
Item 4 paire of stockings vallued att	00	12	00
Item a paire of holland stocking att	00	03	00
Item gloves and hatbands and other smale thinges		04	00
Item a bed and bolster fild with woole	01	17	00
Item an old hatt att	00	02	00
Item a Chist and a box vallued att	00	06	00
Item 2 bedsteeds and a Case	00	16	00
Item a pcell of porke with a barrell	00	18	00
Item a pcell of beefe with a barrell	01	00	00
Item a paire of holland sheets att	01	15	00
Item 42 yards of Osenbrigg att	03	03	00
Item an old holland shirt att	00	06	00
Item 6 smale peeces of lynnine att	00	05	00
Item 2 old shirts vallued att	00	05	00
Item a brasse kettle vallued att	01	17	00
Item an Iron kettle vallued att	00	17	00
Item an Iron skillett vallued att	00	04	00
Item a warming pan vallued att	00	08	00
Item 4 pewter Dishes and a bason att	01	04	00
Item a pcell of smale pewter vallued att	00	13	08
Item eleven alcomy spoones att	00	04	06
Item a pcell of earthen ware and a grator	00	06	00
Item 2 bookes vallued att	00	06	00
Item a paire of snuffers a paile and a little tray	00	02	00
Item a paire of Cobirons att	00	14	00
Item halfe a bushell of salt and a firkin	00	03	06
Item 2 paire of old boots and an old paire of shooes and a new paire	00	18	00
Item a pcell of earthen ware	00	12	00
Item a pcell of New lether	00	09	00
Item a pcell of sope att	00	06	00

[fol. 79a] Item a pcell of tallow att	00	08	00
Item six trayes and a bottle att	00	06	00
Item 22 pound of woolen yarne att	01	13	00
Item a pcell of woole att	00	04	00
Item 3 old sickles ptable att	00	04	00
Item a pcell of butter att	00	05	00
Item 2 paire of lether briches and other old thinges	01	10	00
Item a pannell vallued att	00	06	08
Item 22 bushell and an halfe of wheat	05	10	03
Item 54 bushells and an halfe of Indian Corne	08	02	00
Item 2 sackes vallued att	00	02	06
Item one saddle 2 bridles & girts att	00	16	00
Item a yard and three quarters of Cotten and woolen Clothe	00	07	00
Item six bushells of pease att	01	01	00
Item 2 seives vallued att	00	02	00
Item 3 old pailes att	00	03	00
Item in bacon eleven fliches amounting to	07	09	05
Item in silver	02	02	07½
Item in swine	04	05	00
Item in pitchforkes	00	02	06
Item in Dryed beefe 69[ll] vallued att	01	03	00
Item a brasse skillett vallued att	00	04	00
Item on Cake of sope att	00	03	00
Item 3 new sickles vallued att	00	04	06
Item 2 sickles	00	02	00
Item halfe a harrow vallued att	00	05	00
Item six oxen vallued att	46	00	00
Item 3 oxen 4 yeares old and 2 steers two yeares old	36	00	00
Item five Cowes vallued att	23	10	00
Item 2 heiffers and one bull of 2 yeares old	10	00	00
Item eleven Cowes vallued att	50	00	00
Item six Calves vallued att	05	00	00
Item one Cow more vallued att	04	10	00
Item one bull more vallued att	04	00	00
Item 9 yearlings vallued att	22	10	00
Item 18 sheep being ewes weathers lambes and one rame	08	12	00
Item 3 Cowes more and pte of 2 Calves and pte of one yearling	17	00	0
Item one mare and Coult and a yearling mare Coult att	23	00	0
Item five hydes vallued att	02	13	00
Item Due to him one pound more	01	00	00
summa	350	00	11

Stephen Paine
Thomas Cooper
Peter Hunt

[The Will of John Brown, Sr.]

[fol. 79b] The Last Will and Testament of Mr John Browne seni^r^: exhibited to the Court held att Plymouth the third of octo-ber 1662 on the oath of John Allin

Aprill the seaventh 1662

Know all men to whom this shall Come that I John Browne of Rehoboth in the Jurisdiction of Plymouth being weake in body but my understanding feirme and stable as in any pte of my life heertofore Doe appoint this for my last Will and Testament as followeth first I Doe give unto Mary my Daughter the wife of Thomas Willett the sume of twelve pence to bee payed att the end of every yeare During her life for a memoriall unto her; and it shalbee in full of all filliall portion which shee or any in her behalfe shall Claime; I Doe give unto my grandchild Martha Saffin the wife of John Saffin twenty pounds; I Doe give unto John Browne my grandchild the house that his father Died in with six acrees of land adjoyning to it; to make an orchyard and other Conveniencyes; and I Doe give him halfe the lott that Thomas Willett bought of Experience Michell for mee; and I Doe give him seaven hundred acrees of land lying in the Narragansett Countrey three hundred and fifty of it lyeth in the great necke; and the other three hundred and fifty is to bee Chosen where they shall thinke fitt; and I Doe give unto my grandchild Josepth Browne and Nathaniel each of them five hundred acrees of land lying in the Narragansett Countrey where my lot shall fall; and I Doe give unto my grandchild Lydia Browne and Hannah each of them five hundred acrees of land in the Narrangansett Countrey; and theire Unkell James to Dispose of it for them to raise them portions for all the rest of my lands and whole estate not yett Disposed of I Doe give unto my wife and my son James Browne whom I Doe make Joynt exequitors of this my last Will and Testament; my full Intent is that my two exequitors shall have the ordering of the Children as full as my selfe

Signed Sealed and Delivered in the p^r^sence of us
John Allin
Richard Bullocke
Sampson Mason;

John Browne
And a (seale)

Wee Testify that m^r^ Browne in his full understanding Did add those two lines Concerning the Children with his owne hand;

Roger Williams John Allin;

This followeing ordered to bee endorsed on the Will of m^r^ John Browne seni^r^:

Least any thinge mencioned in this will in reference to mistris Mary Willett the wife of Capt: Thomas Willett might bee by any mis Construed to the prejudice of of the said mistris Willett; wee thinke it meet to Declare that out of the longe experience of her Dutifull and tender respect to her said father from time to time expresed there hath never appeered to us the least ground of any such thinge to this p^r^sent

The Courts mind Declared;

Attested p me Nathaniell Morton
Clark:

[fol. 80] Aprill the 19th 1662

An Inventory of the estate of m^r^ John Browne seni^r^: Deceased; exhibited to the Court held att Plymouth the third Day of october 1662 on the oath of mistris Dorathy Browne; and on the oath of m^r^ James Browne in respect unto soe much as was in ptenorship betwixt his father viz m^r^ John Browne abovesaid and him;

	£	s	d
Imprimis one black suit with Cloake troopers Coate and wastcoate	09	00	00
Item one Coullered suite and Cloake and troopers Coate and hat	10	00	00
Item one Cloake more	02	00	00
Item one kersy suite with troopers coate	04	00	00
Item one long Coate and 2 wastcoates and one hatt	02	08	00
Item 2 paire of old briches one Doublit and three Coates and one old wastcoate and three paire of lether Drawers	04	00	00
Item seaven paire of stockens	01	00	00
It 2 Capps and one paire of gloves	00	07	00
It 2 paire of shooes one paire of boots and one paire of spurrs	00	15	00
Item one Case of knives with a single one	00	04	00
Item five shirts	02	10	00
Item seaven Capps	01	01	00
Item 4 Capps	00	08	00
Item 4 paire of boot hose topps	01	00	00
Item one Dozen of bands and 4 paire of Cuffes	01	05	00
Item 6 handkerchifes	00	05	00
Item five yards and an halfe of rid Broadcloth	02	15	00
Item four yards and an halfe of fine karsye	02	10	00
Item six yards and an halfe of Carsye	02	12	00

Item six yards and an halfe of kersy more	02	10	00
Item ten yards and an halfe of gray Carsy	02	18	10
Item 2 yards and a halfe of Doubble shagg		12	06
Item one bed in the Parlour with rid Curtaines and vallence with a rid wosted rugg and Coverlid and blankett with pillowes	24	10	00
[*Item one Coverlid more* *	*01*	*00*	*00*]
Item 3 ruggs with an old one	03	00	00
Item one featherbed and boulster with 4 Downe pillowes one rid stagg rugg one old Coverlid and blankett with Curtaines and vallence with a flockbed under it	13	00	00
Item one Coverlid more	01	00	00
Item one featherbed and bolster with a green rugg Coverlid and blankett	06	00	00
Item 2 old Curtaines and one old vallence	00	10	00
Item one featherbed and bolster with a green rugg and blankett	06	00	00
Item one flockbed with boulster & blankett	01	15	00
Item one pillow	00	10	00
Item one buffe coat	01	15	00
Item about 30[lb] pound of woolen yarne	03	00	00
Item a paire of sheets of hom made Cloth	1	13	00
Item 2 paire of sheets vallued att	02	10	00
Item 10 yards of lockerum	01	00	00
Item 6 yards of Dowlis	00	18	00
Item one Dozen of Napkins	01	00	00
Item one Dozen of Diaper Napkins	01	06	00
Item one Diaper Tablecloth	01	05	00
Item one Diaper Cobberdcloth	00	15	00
Item a holland Table Cloth and 2 pillowebeers	00	15	00
Item one Cubberd cloth	00	10	00
Item one old Table cloth	00	04	00
Item 2 paire of holland pillow beers		14	00
Item one Diaper towell and 3 other towells		07	00
Item 4 peeces of old linnine	00	10	00
Item 3 ould peeces of linnine more	00	10	00
Item 2 pillowbeers vallued att	00	06	08
Item 6 Diaper napkins vallued att		06	00
Item 3 East india Table Clothes	01	04	00
Item five pound of yarne	00	06	03
Item a looking glace	00	02	06
Item six napkins	00	08	00
[fol. 81] Item a great Wickcar Chaire	00	07	00
Item a wickcar Baskitt	00	02	00
Item an empty Case with bottles	00	05	00
Item 3 Chistes on trunke a box and a baskett	2	10	00

* This item was crossed out, in the same ink. See the third item following.

Item 3 yards of Cotten and woolen Cloth	00	10	00
Item one bedsted vallued att	01	10	00
Item one old bedsted att	00	07	00
Item a pcell of powder vallued att	02	05	00
Item one Chist vallued att	00	12	00
Item six rid lether Chaires	03	00	00
Item four great wooden Chaires	01	10	00
Item halfe a Dozen of Cushens	01	00	00
Item a pcell of bookes vallued att	04	12	00
Item 2 Carpetts vallued att	00	12	00
Item a looking glasse vallued att	00	05	00
Item 2 yards and an halfe of Cotten	00	06	03
Item 2 walking staves	00	05	00
Item a paire of bellowes	00	02	00
Item one Case of liquors and three empty Cases	01	15	00
Item in shott to the vallue of	02	00	00
Item a leaden bullett vallued att	00	02	00
A horn cup	00	02	00
Item a tinder box and a spice box	00	02	00
Item a silver bowle vallued att	04	10	00
Item 3 pewter bowles	00	04	00
Item a great fflaggon vallued att	00	08	00
Item a three pint pot	00	05	00
Item a pint pot	00	02	06
Item eleven pewter Dishes and a pewter plate	04	00	00
Item 9 peeces of pewter	01	12	00
Item 13 peeces of pewter	00	15	00
Item 3 pewter Candlestickes and one brasse one salt and pint pot and 2 vingers and one quart pot three 3 porringers a wine Cup a little Dram Cup 2 tinnin Candlestickes and a paire of snuffers all vallued att	01	17	00
Item 9 spoones vallued att	00	03	00
Item one brasse skimer and two brasse ladles att	00	04	06
Item one belmettle morter & pestell	00	07	06
Item an apple roster & a Cullender	00	03	00
Item one old Iron pott	00	10	00
Item 3 brasse potts & three brase skillits	02	05	00
Item 9 peeces of brasse vallued att	03	08	00
Item one Iron kettle vallued att	00	05	00
Item 3 spitts vallued att	00	10	00
Item 2 Choping knives and 2 smothing Irons	00	06	00
Item 1 Driping pan & a frying pan	00	06	00
Item 3 Dozen of trenchers	00	02	06
Item 2 Chamber potts	00	07	06
Item 3 Iron hakes 2 paire of pot hangers one trevit one paire of tonggs & one rosting Iron one Chaffing Dish & one tinnin Cover for a pott and an Iron to set before the fier all vallued att	01	03	00

Item one great fowling peece and a smale one with a barrell and a locke of a birding peece and a match locke muskett vallued att	03	05	00
Item in Nailes to the vallue of	00	15	00
Item 2 kettles & a frying pan	03	00	00
Item five Chaines vallued att	02	10	00
Item 3 Iron frowes 3 Augers one adds one Drawing knife 3 wedges and a paire of pincers 1 hand saw 3 Chissells 2 Cart Copses one Iron square; all vallued att	02	00	00
Item an Iron grate with fier shovel and tonggs forke and appurtenances therunto belonging with a hatchell all vallued att	02	15	00
Item a side saddle a hackney saddle with 2 briddles	02	10	00
Item 2 old sawes vallued att	00	10	00
Item 2 old Coulters and shares with a pcell of old Iron vallued att	01	00	00
Item one old hoe and an old locke and an old axe	00	05	00
Item a pcell of wooden vessells	01	12	00
[fol. 82] Item 2 fliches of bacon 91^{lb}	02	00	00
Item a pcell of earthen ware vallued att	00	10	00
Item 25^{lb} of hung beefe vallued att	00	08	04
Item 4 Iron hoopes for naves of wheeles	00	10	00
Item 20 bushells of wheat	04	10	00
Item 55 bushells of Indian Corne	08	05	00
Item in silver	00	06	00
Item 2 spining wheeles & powdering tubb	00	10	00
Item an earthen porrenger & a Drinking Cupp		00	08
Item 6 oxen vallued att	48	00	00
Item 3 bulls vallued att	16	10	00
Item 4 steers & one bull of 2 yeares old	24	00	00
Item 4 2 yeare old heiffers vallued att	14	00	00
Item 4 Cowes	19	00	00
Item 14 Cowes vallued att	70	00	00
Item 10 Calves	10	00	00
Item 10 yearlings	25	00	00
Item 18 ewes and lambes weathers and one ram	08	12	00
Item 11 swine att	10	06	00
Item 1 mare and a yearling mare Coult	21	00	00
It one mare and a horse Coult	17	00	00
Item one black ston horse vallued att	11	00	00
Item 2 horses	24	00	00
Item one mare vallued att	17	00	00
Item one younge mare of 2 year old	10	00	00
Item six bushells of pease vallued att	01	01	00
summa	655	01	02

Stephen Paine
Thomas Cooper
Peter Hunt;

UNRECORDED BARNSTABLE COUNTY, MASS., DEEDS

ABSTRACTS BY THE EDITOR

(*Continued from Vol. XVII, page 213*)

THE abstracts presented in this issue were made by the Editor, in August, 1908, from two original deeds owned by George T. Spicer, M.D., of Providence, R. I.

Both deeds were recorded at Barnstable; but they had not been re-recorded after the fire, in 1827, which destroyed nearly all of the records in the Barnstable County Registry of Deeds.

[JACOB TAYLOR TO ROWLAND TAYLOR]

"Jacob Taylor of ye Town of Barnstable . . . . in New England Yeoman For" £15 "Currant money old Tenour" sold to "Rouland Taylor of ye Town of Yarmouth . . . . Yeoman . . . . a certain parcel or track of Cedar Swamp & Scirt of upland thereto adjoyning Scituate lying and being in ye Town Ship of Yarmouth abovesd about three acres be ye Same moor or less butted & bounded begining att a white Oake Sapling in ye North Side of ye way y^t^ leads from ye Said Taylors to Capt John Baxters and y^n^ northerly upon a Straight line to ye Swamp by marked young Cedar Saplings untill you come to a Geat Cedar Stump with a Stone by it and then bounded by a pond and Creek untill you come to Barnstable line and Southerly untill you Come to line of ye aforesd Jacob Taylors Swamp and Southerly by his line untill you Come to a Great Dead pine tree and thence Southerly in the Same Range untill you come to a Stone & Stake within Six foot of ye way & So bounded Southerly within Six foot of ye way as it Leads Easterly untill it Comes to ye first mentioned bounds with all proffits privilledges & appurtences to ye Same belonging or in anywise appertaining —

The deed was dated 26 July, 1743, and was acknowledged 27 July, 1743, before Judah Thacher, Justice of the Peace. The witnesses were Richard Baxter and John Miller. It was recorded 16 January, 1749, in Barnstable County Deeds, Book 23, folio 3, by Solomon Otis, Register, and was not re-recorded, after the fire.

[Jacob, Benjamin and Roland Taylor — Partition]

"This Indenture made this 20th Day of march ann 1750/1 Petwen Jacob taylor of ye town of Plymouth . . . . mariner on ye one part and Benjaman taylor of ye town of yarmouth . . . . Husbandman on ye other part and Roland taylor of ye town of Barnstable . . . . Husbandman on ye other part . . . . Wittneseth yt ye Said Jacob Taylor Benjaman Taylor and Roland taylor are and Do Stand Now Sezed In yr own Right as of fee in Common and undevided of two farmes several Houses and Barns and Sundery Perseles or tracts of Lands meddows and Seder Swamps Lyining at a place Coleed South Sea Now to ye Intent yt a perpetual pertion and Devision Shall be had and made between ye sd parties of ye farmes housing and Sundery tracts of Land meddowes and Seder Swamps aforesd it is Covenanted Concluded and agreed betwen the Sd perties to these presents manner and forme following first the sd Jacob taylor & Benjaman taylor for themselves there heirs and assigns Doth Covenant and agree that ye said Roland taylor his heirs and assigns Shall have . . . . In Severalty . . . . for Ever . . . . the third part of all the above Sd farmes houseing Lands meddowes and Seder Swamps with the appurtenances yt is to Say the farme yt ye sd Roland taylor Now Lives upon with all ye buldings thereon Standing bounded as followes Southerly by ye sea or ocan westerly by George Gorhames Land as ye fence Now Stands Northerly by Capt John Bares* Land & Easterly by ye sd George Gorhames Land and so In to ye sea or ocan Reserveing to us Jacob taylor and benjaman taylor our heirs &c a Convenant way from ye old Gate thro Gates & bars to ye point yt formerly belonged to Shobal Gorham Now Dceased and also a peace of wood Land Laid out to our farther mr Jacob Taylor Dceased in the scond Devision of ye Commons of yarmouth bounded as followes on ye west side by John Baxters Land Sets from his : N : E : Corner Stake : N : as trees are marked about 72 Rods to a Stake marked I T Sets thence west as trees are marked about : 76 : Rods to a stake marked I T standing half a Rod to ye North west of the No tree of ye 125 Lot which Lot bounds it on ye west side Sd taylors a way two Rod wide alalong these by to Baxters Land and also a peace more of wood Land and Seder Swamp which is the westerly part of ye peace of Land yt was Laid out to our farther mr Jacob taylor Late of yarmouth Decased in ye first Division of ye Commons of yarmouth bounded as followes begining Neare ye midle of sd peace of

* This probably should have been "Baxters". — *Editor.*

Land on ye North Side at a marke oake tree Sets thence westerly as trees are marked to an old pine tree marked and so unto ye Swamp then Sets S : W : and by South to ye Swamp untill it meeteth with the Seder Swamp Brook then by Sd Brook to a Stake and a Stone thence North Easterly as trees are marked to the first mentioned bounds and in is further a Greed by ye perties to these presents y^t^ ye sd Roland taylor his heirs and assigns Shall have allowed to them all Convenant ways y^t^ Is or may hereafter be Needfull thro Gates or bars to any part of ye above mentioned Lands meddowes or Seder Swamps &c and that ye sd Roland taylor Nor his heirs Nor assigns Shall Not from hence forth Clam or Demand any Right title uese or possion in or to ye Same or any Part thereof but y^t^ ye sd Roland taylor his heirs and assigns Shall at all time and times here after from all actions Rights titles and Demands there of and there unto be utterly Excluded and for Ever Debarred by these presents —

Scondly the sd Jacob taylor and Roland taylor . . . . Doth Covenant and agree y^t^ ye sd Benjaman taylor . . . . Shall have hold and peacably Enjoy In Severalty . . . . for Ever . . . . the third part of all ye abovesd farmes houseing Lands and meddowes and Seder Swamps with the appurtanances that Is to Say the Easterly part of ye farme at ye old house in yarmouth bounded as followes Begining at : N : W : Corner of Capt John Baxters Land by ye way that Leads thro the Nabourhood thence southerly as ye fence Now Stands untill it Comes to a seder swamp to two oake trees marked thence in the same Range thro the swamp untill it Comes to Leweses bounds and so bounded by Leweses Range westerly untill it Comes to ye upland to a stake and a stone Still Ranging westerly untill it Comes to a mapole tree and a Stone thence Northerly to a stake and stone Standing at a place Called the Lower parsture thence Runing Easterly to another stake and stone standing by a fence in ye Lower parsture thence Northerly to another stake and Stone Standing in ye midlefield thence North westerly on a Strat Line thro the orchard a Letle to ye westward of ye old house to a Stake and Stone Stand on ye South Side of ye way thence Easterly by ye sd way as ye fence Now stands to the first mentioned bounds and also apeace more of upland and seder Swamp bounded as followes begining at a Stake and a Stone on ye North Side of ye way thence on a Strate Line to a seder tree and a Stone from thence on a Strat Line to Roland taylors bounds thence Easterly to ye way to a stake and Stone thence as the fence Now Stands to ye first mentioned bounds and also the westerly moitie or half part of ye 32nd Lot in 3rd Division of Commons of yarmouth bounded begining at a tree in Seth Hallets Range Sets then Easterly one halfe of sd Lot thençe on a Strat Line thro ye midle of sd Lot to the North End of Sd Lot thence westerly as trees are marked into a pond and then sets southerly as trees are marked untill it Comes to the first mentioned bounds and also the value of one halfe part of ye Seder Swamp Lying within ye bounderyes of ye sd 32nd Lot and also the Souther most moitie or half part of ye Land and meddow Lying at ye place Shelleys Cove and also one peace more of wood Land and Cleard Land and a smal peace of seder Swamp bounded as followes begining at a stake and Stone Neare ye mill River Stes * thence Northerly on a Strate Line to a Small oake tree and stone thence westerly as are marked to a black oake tree marked on three sides thence south westerly to a stake and stone & so in to ye Mill Brook and so by ye sd Brook to ye first mentioned bounds and one half part of all ye buldings on ye upper farme in ye town ship of yarmouth togather with One half of ye pew in yarmouth meeting house and that ye sd Benjaman taylor nor his heirs Nor assigns shall not from hence forth Clame or Demand any Right title uese or possesion in or to the same or any part there of but y^t ye sd Benjaman taylor his heirs and assigns shall at all times hereafter from all actions Rights titles and Demands thereof and there unto be utterly Excluded and for Ever Debarred by these presents and further agreed by ye parties to these presents that ye sd Jacob Taylor and Roland taylor there heirs and assigns shall have allowed to them all Convenant ways that is or may be Needfull thro Gates or bars to any part of ye above mentioned Land or meddow or seder swamp —

thirdly the sd Benjaman taylor and Roland taylor . . . . Doth Covenant and agree y^t ye sd Jacob taylor . . . . shall have hold and peacably Enjoy in severalty . . . . for Ever . . . . the third part of all ye abovesd farmes housing Lands meddows and seder swamps with ye appurtanances that is to say ye westerly part of ye farme at ye old house which Lyeth partly in yarmouth and partly in Barnstable bounded as followes begining at a stake and a stone in ye old orchard thence seting Easterly to a Stake and stone in ye midle feild thence seting southerly to a stake and a stone in ye same feild thence westerly to a stake and stone in ye Lower parsture thence Southerly to a mapole tree to a stake and stone In Leweses Range thence westerly in Leweses Range untill it Comes to a Stake and Stone thence Northerly untill it Comes to a Stake and Stone at Leweses Corner thençe westerly

* Sets.

to a Nother Stake and Stone at Seth Hallets Bounds thence Northerly in ye old Range untill it Comes to a ye way thence as ye way Goes Easterly to ye first mentioned bounds and also another peace of Land and Seder Swamp Lying on ye North Side of ye way begining at y^e^ : N : W : Corner thereof at a Stake and Stone Sets thence Easterly untill it Comes to yarmouth Line thence Northerly In ye same Line untill it Comes to Roland taylors Bounds thence South Easterly by ye sd Roland taylor untill it Comes to Benjaman taylor bounds thence South westerly untill it Comes to ye way to a Stake and Stone by ye fence thence as ye fence Now Stands Runing to a tree marked and thence as ye fence Now Stands to the first mentioned bounds and also the Easterly half part of ye 32nd Lot in ye 3rd Division of ye Commons of ye town of yarmouth bounded begining at a Stake and a Stone at ye North East Corner of sd Lot Sets thence : S : S : W : as trees are marked until it Comes to a Grate N° 32 : 33 by ye Edge of ye Swamp thence westerly by ye Edge of ye Swampe untill it Comes to ye South End of sd Lot thence still westerly untill it Comes to ye midle of ye sd Lot thence Northerly thro ye midle of sd Lot to ye North End of ye same thence Easterly to ye first mentioned bounds and also ye value of one halfe part of ye seder swamp Lying within ye Bounderyes of ye above sd 32nd Lot & also another peace of wood Land Laid out to our farther m^r^ Jacob taylor Late of yarmouth Decased in ye first Division begining at ye North East Corner at a stake and Stone Sets thence westerly to an oake tree at Roland taylers bounds thence as trees are marked Runing Southerly on ye west Side of ye old way untill it Comes to a grate Black oake tree marked on three sides thence Easterly as trees are marked untill it Comes Baxter Range thence as ye old Runs untill it Comes to ye first mentioned bounds and also ye Norther most half part of ye Land and meddow Lying at a place Colled Shelleys Cove and also one moitie or one halfe part of all ye buldings on ye upper farme in ye town ship of yarmouth to Gather with one halfe part of the pew in yarmouth meeting house and y^t^ ye sd Jacob taylor Nor his heirs Nor assigns Shall not from hence forth Clame or Demand any Right title uese or possesion in or to the same or any part there of but y^t^ ye sd Jacob Taylor his heirs and assigns Shall at all times hereafter from all actions Rights and titles and Demands thereof and thereunto be utterly Excluded and for Ever Debared by these presents . and it is further agreed by ye perties to these presents y^t^ ye sd Benjaman taylor and Roland taylor there heirs and assigns. Shall have allowed to them all Convenant ways y^t^ is or may be Needfull thro Gates or bars to any part of ye above mentioned Lands meddowes or Swamps In wittness whereof the perties to these presents have hereunto Enterchangably set there hands and seals the Day and yeare above written"

This document was signed by Jacob Taylor and Benjamin Taylor, and was acknowledged by both, in Barnstable County, on 22 March, 1750, before Solomon Otis, Justice of the Peace. The witnesses were Richard Baxter and Isaac Baxter. It was recorded the same day, in Barnstable County Deeds, Book 23, folio 80, by Solomon Otis, Register, and was not re-recorded, after the fire.

(*To be continued*)

PLYMOUTH, MASS., VITAL RECORDS

TRANSCRIBED BY THE EDITOR

(*Continued from Vol. XVII, p. 138*)

[p. 246] A Purpose of Marriage between m^r^ Thomas Murdoch & m^rs^ Elizabeth Doggett both of Plymouth March 19th 1736/7

A Purpose of marriage between m^r^ Thomas Gardner of Plymouth and m^rs^ Hannah Baker of Boston March 19th 1736/7

A Purpose of Marriage between m^r^ Francis Adams & Keziah Atwood both of Plymouth March 19th 1736/7

A Purpose of Marriage between m^r^ James Cushman & m^rs^ Hannah Cobb both of Plymouth March 19th 1736/7.

A Purpose of Marriage between Josiah Connet & Mima B[*]ant Indians both of Plymouth March 19th 1736/7.

A Purpose of Marriage between m^r^ Abner Holmes & m^rs^ Bathsheba Nelson both of Plymouth April 16th 1737.

A Purpose of Marriage between m^r^ Benejah Pratt & m^rs^ Elizabeth Winslow both of Plymouth April 22th 1737.

A Purpose of Marriage between Jo titus Ned and Esther Lawrance Ned Indians both of Plymouth April 30th 1737

A Purpose of Marriage between Jabez Twiney and Mary Simons Indians both of Plymouth Sepr 10th 1737.

A Purpose of Marriage between m^r^ Joseph Holmes son of Nathaniel Holmes of Plymouth deceased and m^rs^ Lydia Bradford of Brantry September 24th 1737.

A Purpose of Marriage between m^r^ Joseph Smith and m^rs^ Lydia Barnes both of Plymouth October 15th 1737.

A Purpose of Marriage between Joseph Gifford of Agawam in the Township of Plymouth and Content Irish of Litle copton October 22th 1737

* A hole in the paper has destroyed about two letters here.

A Purpose of Marriage between John Deerskins and Kate Shanks Indians both of Plymouth October 22th 1737

A Purpose of Marriage between m^{r} Lemuel Cobb and m^{rs} Fear Holmes both of Plymouth November 5th 1737.

A Purpose of Marriage between m^{r} Timothy Morton and m^{rs} Marcy Wilson both of Plymouth November 12th 1737

A Purpose of Marriage betwen m^{r} Ebenezer Brigs of Rochester and m^{rs} Betty Gibs of Agawam in the Township of Plymouth Novr 22th 1737

A Purpose of Marriage between m^{r} Timothy Heley and m^{rs} Alce Chubbuck of Agawam both in the Township of Plymouth Novr 26. 1737

A Purpose of Marriage between Mathew Unquit and Sarah Acquit Indians both of Plymouth December 10th 1737

A Purpose of Marriage between m^{r} Benjamin Harlow and m^{rs} Elizabeth Stevens both of Plymouth December 24 : 1737.

A Purpose of Marriage between m^{r} Job Bourn of Sandwich & m^{rs} Lydia Swift of Plymouth December 27th 1737 to send ye certificate to John Blackwell

A Purpose of Marriage between m^{r} Return Waite & m^{rs} Martha Tupper both of Plymouth January 14th 1737/8

A Purpose of Marriage between m^{r} Josiah Swift of Sandwich & m^{rs} Mary Mory of Plymouth January 17th 1737/8 not paid

[p. 247] A Purpose of Marriage between Richard Tommas and Marcy Cunnet Indians both of Plymouth January 21th 1737/8 not paid

A Purpose of Marriage between m^{r} Simeon Totman and m^{rs} Sarah LittleJohn both of Plymouth January 21th 1737/8.

A Purpose of Marriage between m^{r} John Staff and m^{rs} Rebecah Stermy both of Plymouth february . 4th 1737/8

A Purpose of Marriage between m^{r} Josiah Cunnet of Midleberough and m^{rs} Sarah Norris of Agawam in the Township of Plymouth february 14th 1737/8

A Purpose of Marriage between m^{r} Isaac Hamblen of Rochester and m^{rs} Marcy Gibs of Agawam in the Township of Plymouth february 20th 1737/8.

A Purpose of Marriage between m^{r} Thomas Wethrell jun^{r} of Plymouth and m^{rs} Elizabeth Lothrop of Barnstable . May 13th 1738.

A Purpose of Marriage between William Harlow and Hannah Bartlett both of Plymouth May 26 . 1738 . not paid

A Purpose of Marriage between m^{r} Nathaniel Freeman and m^{rs} Martha Donham both of Plymouth May 27th 1738

A Purpose of Marriage between Ebenezer Besse and Deborah Sanders both of Agawam in the Township of Plymouth June 3^{d} 1738.

A Purpose of Marriage between m^{r} William Clarke & m^{rs} Experience Doty both of Plymouth June 10th 1738

A Purpose of Marriage between m^{r} Stephen Churchell jun^{r} and m^{rs} Hannah Barnes both of Plymouth June 10th 1738

A Purpose of Marriage between m^{r} Benjamin Warren jun^{r} and m^{rs} Rebecah Doty both of Plymouth June 18th 1738

A Purpose of Marriage between m^{r} Edward Doty and m^{rs} Phebe Finney both of Plymouth July 8th 1738

A Purpose of Marriage between m^{r} Uriah Savory of Plymouth and m^{rs} Deborah Bump of Rochester . August 5th 1738. p^{d}

A Purpose of Marriage between m^{r} Joseph Holmes and m^{rs} Hannah Donham both of Plymouth august 26th 1738

A Purpose of Marrage between Mr Thomas Wright and Abijah Roger both of Plymouth August 1st 1738

A Purpose of Marraige between Mr Joseph Morton Junr and m^{rs} Annah Bulluck of Rehoboth August 2^{d} . 1738

A Purpose of Marriage between m^{r} Miles Standish jun^{r} of Duxberough and m^{rs} Mehetibel Robins of Plymouth Sepr 20 1738

A purpose of marriage between m^{r} Eleazer Churchell jun^{r} and m^{rs} Sarah * Harlow both of Plymouth

[p. 248] A Purpose of Marriage between m^{r} Joseph Rider Junr of Plymouth and m^{rs} Elizabeth Crosman of Taunton Novr 11th 1738.

A Purpose of Marriage between m^{r} Nathaniel Shurtleff and m^{rs} Lydia Branch both of Plymouth November 22th 1738

A Purpose of Marriage between the Reverend Jonathan Ellis of Plymouth and m^{rs} Patience Blackwell of Sandwich Novr 29 . 1738.

A Purpose of Marriage between m^{r} Isaac Tinckcom of Plymouth and m^{rs} Keziah Wormall of Duxberough Decr 15th 1738. p^{d}

A Purpose of Marriage between m^{r} Zephaniah Holmes and m^{rs} Sarah Bradford both of Plymouth Decr 15 : 1738

A Purpose of Marriage between m^{r} Joshua Swift of Sandwich and m^{rs} Jean Faunce of Plymouth January 13th 1738/9.

A Purpose of Marriage between m^{r} John Barnes Senr of Plymouth and m^{rs} Ann Bonum of Plimton february 9th 1738/9.

A Purpose of Marriage between Jack a Negro man belonging to m^{r} Thomas Holmes of Plymouth and Patience a Molatto woman belonging to m^{r} Barnabas Churchell of s^{d} Plymouth March 17th 1738/9.

A Purpose of Marriage between m^{r} John Finny of Plymouth and m^{rs} Susanna Prat of Plimton March 31 . 1739.

A Purpose of marriage between m^{r} David Morton and m^{rs} Rebecah Finny both of Plymouth March 31 . 1739

Plymouth April 2^{d} 1739. Joannah Tupper came to my House and forbid the Banes of John Finnys marrying with Susanna Prat in as much as the s^{d} Finny had promised her marryage & that no thing but death should part & that he had asked her father & mothers consent.

A Purpose of Marriage between Ebenezer Burge jun^{r} of Plymouth and m^{rs} Zerviah Ney of Sandwich May 14th 1739

* "Hannah" was first written, but was crossed out and "Sarah" interlined, in the same hand and ink.

A Purpose of Marriage between m^{r} Charles Samson of Plymouth & m^{rs} Mary Church of Scituate May 26 . 1739

A Purpose of Marriage between m^{r} William Bowdoin of Boston and m^{rs} Phebe Murdoch of Plymouth June 2^{d} 1739.

A purpose of Marriage between m^{r} Ebenezer Harlow and Mrs Moriah Mory both of Plymouth . June 9 . 1739

A purpose of marriage between m^{r} Elisha Holmes Junr of Plymouth and m^{rs} Mary Ellis of Sandwich July 7th 1739.

A Purpose of Marriage between m^{r} Ebenezer * Samson & m^{rs} Hannah Harlow both of Plymouth July 14th 1739.

A Purpose of Marriage between m^{r} Seth Luce of Wareham & m^{rs} Hannah Morton of Plymouth August 11 . 1739

[p. 249] A Purpose of Marriage between m^{r} Joseph Abbet & m^{rs} Marcy Kempton both of Plymouth Sepr 1 . 1739

A Purpose of Marriage between m^{r} Nathaniel Morton and m^{rs} Mary Ellis both of Plymouth Sepr 29 . 1739

A Purpose of Marriage between Moses Nummuck and Sarah Deerskins Indians both of Plymouth Octob^{r} 11 . 1739

A purpose of Marriage between m^{r} Thomas Davie and m^{rs} Marcy Bartlett both of Plymouth Novr 11th 1739

A Purpose of Marriage between m^{r} Robert Toxe and m^{rs} Hannah Clarke both of Plymouth Novr 17 . 1739.

A Purpose of Marriage between m^{r} Thomas Shurtleff and m^{rs} Marcy Warren both of Plymouth Decr 8th 1739

A Purpose of Marriage between m^{r} Jonathan Tobe of Sandwich and m^{rs} Deborah Swift of Plymouth Decr 27 . 1739.

A Purpose of marriage between m^{r} Thomas Mayhew & m^{rs} Mary Wethrell both of Plymouth february 8th 1739/40

A purpose of marriage between William Cunnet Junr of Plymouth & Moll Wicket of Sandwich both Indians in the County of Plymouth & Sandwich february 23 1739/40

A Purpose of Marriage between m^{r} Abiel Shurtleff & m^{rs} Luce Clarke both of Plymouth february 23 . 1739/40

The Intention of Mariage betwen m^{r} Elkanah Cushman & m^{rs} Lydia Bradford both of Plymouth March 8 . 1739/40

A Purpose of Mariage between Lemuel Harlow of Plymoth and Joanna Paddock of Middleborough April 26 . 1740.

A Purpose of Marige between James Celler & Jane Crandon both of Plymouth May 10 . 1740.

A purpose of Mariage between Noah Peniss & Abigail Chumuck both of this Town Indians. July 19 . 1740.

A purpose of Mariage betwen John Jones and Sarah Barnes both of Plymouth July 26 . 1740.

A Purpose of Mariage between David Sepitt & Joanna Scoke Indians both of Plymoth Septr 21 . 1740

* "Benjamin" was first written, but was crossed out and "Ebenezer" interlined, in the same hand and ink.

A Purpose of Mariage between Isaac Wood & Lydiah Wait both of Plymouth August 7 . 1740:

[250] A Purpose of Mariage between Levi Stephens of Boston & Mary Marshall of Plymoth Sept[r] 27 . 1740.

A purpose of Mariage between Joshua Newcomb of Truro & Widdow Hannah Holmes of Plymoth Sept[r] 27 . 1740

A purpose of Mariage between Asa Hatch and Mary Waite both of Plymouth Oct[o] 18 . 1740.

A purpose of Mariage between Joseph Abbot & Mercy Kempton both of Plymouth November 22 . 1740

A purpose of mariage between Edward Sparrow and Jerusha Bradford both of Plymouth November 29 . 1740.

A purpose of Mariage between Thomas Tobey of Sandwich and Elizabeth Swift of Plymouth Dec[r] [*illegible*] 1740.

A purpose of mariage between John Torrey & Deborah Reed both of Plymouth Janr[y] 17 . 1740

A purpose of Mariage between Silv[a] Holmes, & Mary Harlow Janr[y] 17 . 1740 . both of Plymouth

A purpose of Mariage between Amos Ryder & Ruth Faunce, both of Plymouth March . 14 . 1740.

A purpose of Mariage betwen Charles Rider of Plym[o] & Rebecca Bartlet of Duxborough March 14 . 1740.

A purpose of mariage between Amos Dunham of Plym[o] & Abigal Hill of Plymouth March 14 . 1740.

A purpose of Mariage between Edward Winslow & Hannah Dyre both of Plymouth . March 21 . 1740.

A purpose of Mariage between William Holmes & Ruth Morton both of Plymouth March 21 . 1740.

N. B. The publication between William Holmes & Ruth Morton was taken down y[e] Same Week it was Set up, (by whom I do not know.)

A purpose of Mariage between George Holmes jun[r] & Lydia West both of Plymouth March 28 . 1741.

A purpose of mariage between William Holmes & Ruth Morton both of Plymouth April 4 . 1741

A purpose of Mariage between Benj[a] Bartlett & Abigail Morton both of Plymouth April 17 . 1741

A purpose of mariage between Joseph Bates of Plym[o] and Betty Gibbs of Sandwitch — May 16 1741

(*To be continued*)

PLYMOUTH COLONY DEEDS

TRANSCRIBED BY THE EDITOR

(Continued from Vol. XVII, p. 247)

[WHITE — KEMPTON — MORTON]

[p. 114]1662 Prence Govr

A Deed appointed to bee Recorded

To all people to whome these p^{r}sents shall Come Peregrine White of Marshfeild in the Gov^{r}ment of Plymouth in New England in America; Gen^{t}: sendeth greet &c

Know yea that I the said Peregrine White for and Consideration of the sume of thirty and five pounds sterling to bee payed by Mannasses Kempton of Plymouth aforsaid Plantor wherwith the said Peregrine White Doth acknowlidge himselfe fully satisfyed and paied; hath freely and absolutely bargained and sold graunted enfeofed and Confeirmed and by these p^{r}sents Doth bargaine sell graunt enfeofe and Confeirme unto the said Mannasses Kempton his heires and assignes for ever; all those his uplands and meddowes lying att the Eelriver in Plymouth Towneship aforsaid lately assigned and Confeirmed unto the said Peregrine by Mr Edward Winslow in the publick Court held att Plymouth the twenty eight of September Ann^{o} Dom: 1642; and all his Right title and Interest of and into the said p^{r}mises; and every pte and pcell therof; with all and singulare the appurtenances therunto belonging; To have and to hold; all the said uplands and meddowes with all and singulare the appurtenances therunto belonging; every pte and pcell therof unto the said Mannasses Kempton his heires and assignes forever; unto the onely proper use and behoofe of him the said Mannasses Kempton his heires and assignes for ever; To bee holden of our Sov^{r}: Lord the Kinge; as of his mannor of East Greenwich in the Countey of Kent in the Realme of England in free and Comon Scoccage; and not in Capite nor by Knights service; by the rents and services Due and of right accustomed; and with warrantice against all people whatsoever from by or under him or by his right or title Caiming any right title or Interest of and into the said p^{r}mises or any pte or pcell therof; And the said Peregrine White Doth alsoe Covenant promise and graunt by these p^{r}sents that it shall and may bee lawfull; to and for the said Mannasses Kempton; either by himselfe or his Attorney to record or enrowle these p^{r}sents or Cause them to bee recorded and enrowled; in his Maties Court att Plymouth before before the Govr: for the time being according to the usuall mannor & order of enrowling evidences in such Case provided [p. 115] provided; in Witnes wherof the said Peregrine White hath heerunto sett his hand and seale the twenty third Day of October in the nineteenth yeare of the Raigne of our Sovr: Lord Charles by the grace of God Kinge of England Scotland France and Ireland Defender of the faith &c Anno Dom 1643

Sealed and Delivered — Peregrine White
in the prsence of us — and a (seale)
Nathaniel Souther
Willam Collyare
Myles Standish
Resolved White;

To all people to whome these prsents shall Come; Know yea that I the said Mannasses Kempton of Plymouth yeoman Doe by these prsents make over the abovesaid Deed unto Ephraim Morton my soninlaw from mee and my heires to him and his heires for ever; and Doe by these prsents; Interest him and his heires as fully in all the pticulares therof; as I my selfe had by vertue of the Deed; onely I reserveing to my selfe During my life and my wifes life; that pte of the meddow which I Constantly make use of; att the Eelriver; alsoe as further Condition of the Surrender of the above said Deed I Doe reserve to my selfe for my owne proper right and use halfe of the meddow ground att Sagaquas which I formerly bought of Edward Banges; and the said halfe of marsh or meddow ground to bee equally Devided; In Witnes heerof I have sett to my hand this 14th of February one thousand six hundred fifty and nine; 1659

In the prsence of us — Mannasses Kempton
Thomas Southworth — his Marke
John Morton;

[Samuel Eddy to sons Zachariah and Obadiah]

[p. 116] 1662 Prence Govr:
The twenty fourth of March 1662

Memorand: That Samuell Eedey senir: of the Towne of Plymouth in the Jurisdiction of Plymouth in New England in America Tayler Doth acknowlidge that hee hath and Doth freely by these prsents give graunt allianate and make over unto his two sonns viz: Zacariah Eedey and Obadiah Eedey all that his share lott and portion of land which hee hath in the land graunted and Confeirmed by the Court in June last past before the Date heerof; unto sundry psons; lying neare unto Namassakett bounded as in the Indian Deeds of the said lands is att large expressed; To have and to hold all the said Samuell Eedey his lott Share and portion of the aforsaid Tract of land both upland and meddow with all and singulare the appurtenances therunto belonging; unto the said Zacariah Eedey and Obadiah Eedey to them and each of them theire and each of theire heires and assignes for ever to bee equally Devided betwixt them the said Zacariah Eedey and Obadiah Eedey in equall proportions; Provided and excepting that hee the said Samuell Eedey Doth by these p^r^sents reserve unto his owne use six acrees of the upland of the said lott of land viz: out of his whole Intire said share of land to bee for his use whiles hee liveth; to bee taken out of the whole said Share of land in any pte therof where hee shall thinke meet; before it is Devided betwixt his said sons; and incase hee shall see meet for the time of his life to place any other to Improve the said six acrees of land in his behalfe; it shalbee with theire likeing and approbation; and att the Decease of the said Samuell Eedey the said six acrees of land to returne unto the onely proper use and behoofe of the said Zacariah and Obadiah Eedey to them and theire heires and assignes forever; morover the said Samuell Eedey Doth Condition with his said sonnes that they shall winter for him yearely three Cowes; (if hee have soe many) or shall see Cause to Desire it of them; the said provisoes reservations and Conditions observed The said p^r^mises with all and singulare the woods waters and all other the appurtenances belonging therunto or to any pte or pcell therof with all the said Samuell Eedey his right title and Interest of and into the same; to belong unto the onely proper use and behoofe of them the said Zacariah and Obadiah Eedey to them and theire heires and assignes for ever To them the said Zacariah and Obadiah Eedey to them and each of them; theire and and each of theire heires and Assignes forever;

It was mutually agreed before the rattification of the premises by and between the said Samuell Eedey and Zachariah Eedey that incase Caleb Eedey shall Desire a quarter p^r^te of the above said land hee shall have it

The 26 of February 1672, Samuell Eedey abovesaid Came before the Govr: and Mr Hinckley and owned and acknowlidge the abovesaid Conveyanc of land to be his acte and Deed, and Doeth heerby fully rattify and Confeirme the same according to the tearmes and Conditions abovesaid

[Quachattasett to John Alden]

[p. 117] 1663 Prence Govr:

A Deed Appointed to bee Recorded

Know all men that I Quachattasett for the sume of six pounds to mee in hand payed have bargained sould and allianated from mee and mine for ever unto John Aldin a Tract or pcell of upland lying next adjoyning unto the land Purchased by Thomas Burge of Captaine Myles Standish runing for breadth unto a rockey Point neare unto a little beach which Comes to an Iland & for length into the woods one mile above the path with all the appurtenances belonging therunto as alsoe all such pcells of meddow marsh or upland lying about the said lands unto a brooke Called Abasatucksett allis * white brooke with free range for his Cattle as alsoe free use of the sea for fish of any kind for his use; In witnes wherof I have sett to my hand this 27th of the fift month 1661

Witnes Quachattasett
Sepitt his marke his marke
Scippauge his marke

This land above expressed was bought for the proper use and Inheritance of James Sciffe and his heires ffor ever pte of it being Due to him for his service

℣ me John Aldin

[John Cooper's Lands]

[p. 118] 1663 Prence Govr:

A Coppy of the record of the lands of John Cooper taken out of the towne booke of Barnstable being such lands as were ptely bought by him; and ptely given him by the Towne and lying together were recorded as one pcell in the yeare 1653 as followeth

viz: twenty four acrees of upland bee it more or lesse by his house buting northerly upon the marsh runing southerly into the woods bounded easterly by m^{r} Groomes his land and westerly by goodman Robinsons land with a pcell of mersh lying all the breadth of the said upland runing Northerly to the great creeke; bounded easterly by m^{r} Groomes; westerly by the said Robinsons mersh

This 27th of Aprill 1663 ℣ me Thomas Hinckley

* Alias.

[Obadiah Eddy to Zachariah Eddy]

The 29th of Aprill 1663

Memorand: That Obadiah Eedey Shoomaker Doth acknowli[dge] that for and in consideration of the sume of six pounds to him alreddy payed by Zacariah Eedey of the Towne of Plymouth in the Jurisdiction of Plymouth in New England plantor; hee hath by these p^r^sen[ts] Barganed allianated and sold enfeofed and confeirmed; and by these Dot[h] bargane sell enfeofe and Confeirme unto the said Zacariah Eedey his brother all that his pte portion and share of land lying neare unto Namaskett; viz: the one halfe of theire father Samuell Eedey his shar[e] of land there; the which whole share of land the said Samuell Eedey gave unto his two sonnes afornamed; as appeers by a Deed or conveyanc[e] of the said land upon record bearing date the 24th of March 1662; To have and to hold the said Obadiah Eedey his halfe pte of the said land according as in the aforsaid Deed is expressed with all and singu[lare] the appurtenances privilidges and emunities belonging therunto; unt[o] the said Zacariah Eedey to him and his heires and assignes for ever the said halfe share of land both upland and meddow with all and sing[ulare] the appurtenances belonging therunto or to any pte or pcell therof w[ith] all the said Obadiah Eedey his right title and Interest of and into th[e] same to belonge and appertaine to the onely proper use and behoof of [the] said Zacariah Eedey to him and heires and assignes for ever unto [the] onely proper use and behoofe of him the said Zacariah Eedey to him and his heires and assignes for ever;

Att the Court held att Plymouth; the 7th of July 1674 the said Obadiah Eedey and Zacariah Eedey Came into the Court, and Did before the Court Nullify and make void this Bargaine by a Joynt, and mutuall Consent of both prties *

[John Dunham, Sr., to His Son John]

[p. 119] 1663 Prence Govr:

The 28th of May 1663

Memorandum That John Dunham seni^r^: of the Towne of Plymouth in the Jurisdiction of Plymouth in New England in America weaver Doth acknowlidge that hee hath and Doth by these p^r^sents fully freely and absolutely give graunt allianate make over and confeirme unto his son John Dunham the one halfe of all that his share lot and portion of meddow att Winnatuxett in the Township of Plymouth as alsoe all his whole

* This paragraph is on the inner margin of the page.

portion of upland att the place fore named; on Condition that the said John Dunham the son of the said John Dunham seni^{r}: shall rest contented with it as his pte of the lands of his said father which hee might expect Demaund or require of him; or any after him; by filliall right; and alsoe that hee Doe not molest or trouble any that shall or may enjoy any other the houses or lands of the said John Dunham seni^{r}: either before or after his Decease; To have and to hold the said whole lott p^{r}te or portion of upland belonging to the said John Dunham seni^{r}: lying att a Place called Winnatuxett in the Towneship of Plymouth aforsaid with the one halfe of all his meddow there bee it more or lesse with all and singulare the p^{r}mises and appurtenances belonging to the said upland and meddow unto the said John Dunham the son of the said John Dunham seni^{r}: to him and his heires and assignes for ever; The said p^{r}mises with all the said John Dunham seni^{r}: his right title and Interest of and into the same; or any pte or pcell therof; on the Conditions above expressed to belong unto the onely proper use and behoof of him the said John Dunham the son of the said John Dunham seni^{r}: to him and his heires and assignes for ever;

[James Shaw to Samuel Hullme]

[p. 120] 1663 Prence Govr:
The 11th of June 1663

Memorand: that James Shaw of Acushena in the Jurisdiction of Plymouth in New England in america plantor Doth acknowlidge that for and in consideration of a valluable sume to him alreddy satisfyed and fully payed by Samuell Hullme somtimes of Road Iland, now resident att acushena aforsaid; hee hath freely and absolutely barganed allianated and sold enfeofed and confeirmed; and by these p^{r}sents Doth bargaine sell allianate enfeofe and Confeirme unto the said Samuell Hullme one quarter pte or one pte of foure of one whole share of land which was the land of John Shaw seni^{r}: lying and being att Acushena Coaksett and places adjacent; both upland and meddow with all other the appurtenances, to the said quarter pte or one pte of foure of the said lands belonging; excepting that the said Samuell Hullme is not to hav[e] or challenge any right or title to any pte of the house lott or homestead on which the said James Shaw now liveth att Acushena aforsaid which containeth forty acrees; but in liew of that which might bee the said Samuell Hullme his quarter pte therof; hee is to have ten acrees of the said James Shaw his land in the next Devision of the lands of Acushena

Coaksett and places adjacent; To have and to hold the said quarter pte or one pte of foure of the land aforsaid att the place or places aforsaid comonly called and knowne by the names of Acushena Coaksett and places adjacent bo[th] upland and meddow with all and singulare the woods waters and a[ll] other appurtenances privilidges and emunities belonging therunto o[r] to any pte or pcell therof; unto the said Samuell Hullme to him and his heires and assignes for ever; the said quarter pte or one pte of four of the land aforsaid both upland and meddow; except that which is above excepted, to belong unto the onely proper us[e] and behoofe of him the said Samuell Hullme; hee his heires and assignes for ever;

[JONATHAN PRATT TO JOHN RASHALL]

[p. 121] 1663 Prence Gov[r]:
The 20th of June 1663

Memorand That Jonathan Prat of the Towne of Plymouth in the Jurisdiction of Plymouth in New England plantor Doth acknowlidge that for and in consideration of a valluable sume to him alreddy payed by John Rashall of Acushena in the Jurisdiction aforsaid plantor; hee hath bargained allianated and sold enfeofed and confeirmed and by these p[r]sents Doth bargaine allianate sell enfeof and confeirme unto the said John Rashall one halfe of a whole share lot or portion of land lying or being att Acushena Coaksett and places adjacent excepting that which is after excepted in this Conveyance; and wheras fifty acrees of the said halfe share of land is layed out; twenty five acrees of the said fifty is to belong and now sold unto the said John Rashall; which said twenty five acrees of land is soe much of the said fifty or that twenty five of the said fifty as lyeth on the southerly side therof; the said whole fifty acrees lying and being on the west side of Acushena maine river; excepting alsoe twenty acrees of the said halfe share belonging to Willam Spooner; and two acrees of meddow belonging to the said halfe share of land appertaining to Thomas Pope To have and to hold the said halfe share of land lying and being att Acushena Coaksett and places adjacent both upland and meddow and all other appurtenances belonging therunto excepting that which is alreddy excepted; viz twenty five acrees of land being the one halfe of the fifty acrees of land above mencioned which said twenty five belongeth to Thomas Pope and the said two acrees of meddow belonging to the said Thomas Pope and the said twenty acrees of upland belonging to the said Willam Spooner; all the remainder of the said halfe share of land unto the said John Rashall hee his heires and assignes for ever; the said p^r^mises with all and singulare the appurtenances belonging therunto excepting those pticulares alreddy excepted to appertaine unto the onely proper use and behoofe of him the said John Rashall to him and his heires and assignes for ever

this was pte of the [l]and the said [J]onathan bought of Edward Gray *

(*To be continued*)

JOHN[1] CHURCHILL'S WILL AND INVENTORY

TRANSCRIBED BY THE EDITOR

THE will and inventory of John[1] Churchill, of Plymouth, recorded in the Plymouth Colony Wills and Inventories, Book II, Part II, folios 82 and 83, are here printed in full, at the expense of Mr. John W. Churchill, of Plymouth, a descendant of John[1] Churchill, through his son Eleazer[2] Churchill.

What purports to be a literal copy of this will and inventory was printed in "The Churchill Family of America", pages three, four and five; but that "copy" is not exact, as will be evident on comparison with the copy here presented.

[THE WILL OF JOHN CHURCHILL, SR.]

[On folio 82] The Will Nuncupative of John Churchill seni^r^: late Deceased exhibited before the Court held att Plymouth the 3 of March 1662 Attested upon oath as followeth

Abigaill Clarke aged twenty yeares [*and* †] or theraboutes being Deposed saith; That on Tusday the 24th of December last past before the Date heerof; her kinsman viz John Churchill seni^r^: being ill att ease but of pfect memory Did expresse him selfe in manor as followeth that his mind and will was that his son Josepth Churchill and his son Eliezer Churchill shall have and enjoy all his lands both uplands and meddowes within the Township of Plymouth excepting onely fifty acrees of land graunted to him by the Towne lying att Mannomett ponds; which hee gave then unto John Churchill his son; morover that his will was that his son William shall have his purchase land att Punckateesett viz: his share of the townes land there; further

* This paragraph is on the outer margin of the page.

† The word "and" was crossed out, in the same ink.

that hee Did expresse him selfe that his son Josepth shall have his New house att his wifes Death and for the use of all the lands aforsaid that they shalbee for the use and Improvement of his wife as long as shee lives; and that hee alsoe said that incase Josepth should marry or bee for him selfe that then hee should have the use of the old Dwelling house and some land to make use of; and as for his estate remaining hee said, that hee knew not whether there would bee any thing left when his Children were brought up or noe; but if his wife Could spare it then that Josepth should have a yeake of oxen and Eliezer a yeake of oxen and Hannah a Cow if not two and incase any thinge should bee left att his wifes Decease that then such of his Children as have had nothinge in p^r^ticulare as above given them should have what is left in equall proportions to equallice what is given to them forenamed as farr as it will goe

The oath of Abigaill Clarke taken in the Court held att Plymouth the third Day of March 1662

Attested p me Nathaniel Morton; Clarke:

Att the Court of his Matie held att Plymouth in New England the 2^cond^ Day of March ann^o^ Dom 1668 Joseph Churchill Came before the said Court and alowed approved Rattifyed and Confeirmed the will of his father John Churchill Deceased above expressed in all and every the p^r^ticulars therof; the said Will and Testament to stand remaine and Continew unalterable and Inviolable for ever

[fol. 83] An Inventory of the goods and Chattles of John Churchill late Deceased apprised by those underwritten on the 11th of ffebruary 1662 and exhibited to the Court held att Plymouth the third of March one thousand six hundred sixty two as followeth:

	£	s	d
Imp^r^: 4 oxen	16	00	00
Item 2 Cowes	06	00	00
Item 2 heiffers supposed to bee with Calfe	05	00	00
Item 2 steers of 2 yeares old and an heiffer of 2 yeares old	07	00	00
Item a yearling steer	01	00	00
Item 2 steer Calves	01	10	00
Item 2 sowes and three piggs	01	10	00
Item 2 featherbed teekes not full	03	10	00
Item 4 blanketts	01	10	00
Item 3 pair of sheets	02	00	00
Item 2 pillowes and 4 pillow beers	01	00	00

Item 5 napkins and a Table Cloth	00	06	00
Item his wearing Clothes	06	00	00
Item stokens and shooes and an home made coate	01	00	00
Item a hatt	00	08	00
Item 3 shirts	00	12	00
Item bands and handkerchifes	00	08	00
Item a great brasse kettle	01	00	00
Item a belmettle skillett	00	02	06
Item 2 great Iron potts	01	10	00
Item an old kettle & an Iron skillett	00	05	00
Item pot hookes and pot hangers & an old Iron ladle	00	04	00
Item a paire of tonges & a fier shovell	00	02	00
Item 4 pewter platters	00	12	00
Item 2 pewter basons one Drinking pott and seaven Alcomy spoones	00	05	00
Item in earthen ware	00	08	00
Item 2 treyes 7 trenchers & some other wooden vessell	00	04	00
Item 2 hogsheds 4 barrells	00	10	00
Item 2 beer barrells and a Chern & a washing tubb	00	08	00
Item a trundell bedsteed 2 Cheirs & 2 old tables	00	10	00
Item 2 axes a morticeing axe and 2 hatchetts	00	08	00
Item 2 pickaxes 3 hoes	00	06	00
Item 2 augers & some other smale iron tooles	00	03	00
Item 5 wedges & a beetle ringe	00	05	00
Item 2 guns	05	10	00
Item a sword & shott pouch 2 pound of powder and 4 pound of shott	00	12	00
Item 2 spining wheels and three paire of Cards	00	10	00
Item meale baggs and sackes & a sifting trough	00	10	00
Item one fan 2 Corn seives and 2 meale seives	00	10	00
Item 2 Cow bells	00	01	00
Item a Cart and wheeles	01	00	00
Item 2 Chaines a bolt and shakle	00	08	00
Item one wainhead yeake the ring and staple 2 sting yeake with hookes & staples	00	10	00
Item one plough share & Coulter	00	08	00
Item 3 sythes & 3 sickles	00	10	00
Item in bookes	00	06	00
Item in old lumber	00	05	00
suma	74	14	06

by us Nathaniell Morton
Ephraim Morton

Debts Due from the estate	£	s	d
Item to Robert finney	06	00	00
Item in other smale Debts	01	00	00

UNRECORDED PLYMOUTH COUNTY DEEDS

ABSTRACTS BY THE EDITOR

(*Continued from Vol. XVII, p. 123*)

IN this article we present exhaustive abstracts of four original, and unrecorded, deeds forming part of the collection of Barrows Papers, presented to the Massachusetts Society of Mayflower Descendants, in 1915, by Mrs. Mary F. Dexter.

[JOHN BARROWS TO SAMUEL BARROWS]

"John Barrow of Plimouth . . . . in New England sendeth Greeting &c: Whereas my Grandfather Georg Bonum of Plimouth afores^{d} did By deed under his hand & seale bareing Date" 21 February, 1679, "give grant Infeof & confirm unto my father & mother Robert & Ruth Barrow of Plimouth afores^{d} all that his one parsell of Lands be it more or less that he had lying & being at a place Commonly Called the newfield in Plimouth afores^{d} bounded on the north East End thereof with the Lands of Mr John Rainor & on the southwest end thereof with the lands of Andrew Ring & six acres of land of the s^{d} Georg Bonum & on the southeast side thereof with the lands of Sarah Attwood widdow & on the northwest side by the s^{d} Town-Common & a fence; Also the s^{d} Georg Bonum did give unto the s^{d} Robert & Ruth all that his one parsell of meadows containing four acres more or Less that he had Lying & being upon a brook whereon Southers marsh lyeth in s^{d} town with all & singuler the appurtenances & previleges thereunto belonging To Have & to hold . . . . Now Know yea that I the s^{d} John Barrow" for £8 "in Currant money of new England" sold to "my Brother Samuel Barrow of Plimouth afores^{d} . . . . all my right title Interest & demand whatsoever that I have hereafter may have or of right ought to have in all & every part & parsell of the aboves^{d} lands & meadows"

The deed was dated 26 February, 1696/7, and was signed by a mark. The witnesses were "Samauell Waterman" and Nathaniel Thomas, Jr. The deed was not acknowledged, and has not been recorded.

[James Barnaby to Samuel Barrows]

"James Barnabee . . . . of plimouth . . . . Cordwainer" for £38 "Currant Money of New England" sold to "Samuell Barrow of the town . . . . Aforesd yeoman . . . . All that my Dwelling house & all that my Litle platt of Land whereon my sd house now Standeth which sd house Standeth & Land Lieth in the town of plimouth aforesd & is Bounded as ffolloweth Viz[d]: On the East with the Street goeing to the Mill: On the South with the Lands of John wood Deceased: On the west with the Lands of Sd James Barnabee & on the North with the Land & house of Elieazar Roggers : Sd platt of Land Containg in Lenght : from the mill Street westward : one hundred & Seventeen foot : to Sd James Barnabees Bounds & Along Sd Bounds Northerly forty Eight foott to the Land of Eliezar Roggers aforesd : & Along Sd Land of Sd Roggers Easterly forty two foot to a bound Stone Neere the west End of Sd Rogers his house: & then Southerly from Sd bound Stone Nine foott towards Sd Samuell Barrows house to Another Bound Stone & from thence Easterly to a boud Stone att Side of mill Streett Aforesd : & all my Estate Right title & Intrest in or unto the Same :"

The deed was dated 20 April, 1699, and signed by "James barneby". The witnesses were "Nath[ll] Clarke" and "Le Baron"

The deed was not acknowledged, and has not been recorded.

[Isaac Howland, Sr., and John Bennet, Sr., Agents, to Samuel Barrows]

"we Isaac Howland Senior: and John Bennet Senior both of the town of middleborough . . . . being chosen and Impowered by the proprietors of the purchase of land called the Sixteen Shilling purchase in middleborough afore Said: as their agents: in their behalf : to give Deeds of confirmation for all the lands which the Said proprietors Sold by outcry at their meeting november the 29th 1715 : unto the Respective persons who bought the same : upon their producing a receit of their payment of the money for the Same under the hand of Capt Jacob Tomson : who is appointed to Receive Said money : and whereas at the aforesaid proprietors meeting the Said proprietors by outcry Sold unto Samuel Barrows of the town of middleboro aforesaid : the first lot in number in the last allotment in said purchase containing twenty five acres be it more or less the bounds of Said lot may appear upon the record of Said purchase : in consideration of Eleven pounds and five Shillings : and the Said

Samuel Barrows having produced a receit of the payment of Said money under the hand of the Said Jacob Tomson: Wherefore in consideration thereof : we the : agents : aforesaid : by Virtue of the power committed unto us: as is before mentioned . . . . by these presents do bargain Sell alienate Enfeofe and confirm : from us the Said Isaac Howland and John Bennet : as agents as aforesaid in behalf of Said proprietors : and from all : and Every of the proprietors aforesaid unto him the Said Samuel Barrows and his heirs Executors administraters and assigns for Ever : All the aforesaid lot of land containing twenty five acres be it more or less being in number the first lot in the last allotment in Said purchase: the bounds of Said lot may appear upon the Record of Said purchase . . . . And do by these presents warrant the Sale of the Same against all persons whatsover that in by or under : us : or any of the Said proprietors : or any other way Shall lay any legal claim title or Intrest of or Into the Same:"

The deed was dated 22 February, 1715/16, and signed by "Isaac Howland Sen[r]" and "John Bennet Seen[r]". The witnesses were Peter Thacher and Samuel Pratt. The deed was acknowledged, on 22 February, 1715/16, by both grantors, before Samuel Prince, Justice of the Peace; but there is no endorsement to indicate that it was recorded.

[EBENEZER AND ROBERT BARROWS TO COOMBS BARROWS]

"We Ebenezer Barrows and Robert Barrows both of Middleboro . . . . sons of Deacon Samuel Barrows of said Middleborough : for Divers Good & Valuable Considerations And Speciall Caus[es] us theirunto Moving & perticulerly that we have Receiv[ed] Considerable of our said father towards Our portions And being Minded to Strengthen and Confirm a Deed Indented & Dated Even with these presents wherein our said ffather for the Considerations therein Mentioned has Granted & Conveyd Unto Our Brother Coombs Barrows of Middleborough aforesaid Cordwainer all his Homestead in said Middleborough the Dwelling house, shop and half the Grissmill thereon Standing And two Lots of Land More in the Little Lot mens purchase in Said Middleborough all which premisses are More perticulerly Described in said Indented Deed Refference there to being had Wherefore for the Considerations Aforesaid we the Said Ebenezer Barrow[s] And Robert Barrows . . . . Release . . . . Unto him the Said Coombs Barrows his heirs And Assigns for Ever all our Right Title Intrest and Demand which we have or ought to have or by Any Means we might have Claim or Demand of and into the Premisses by the Said Deed Granted and Conveyed by our Said ffather unto him the Said Coombs Barrows"

The deed was dated 3 July, 1734, and signed by both grantors. The witnesses were "Beniaman barden" and Elkanah Leonard. The deed was not acknowledged, and has not been recorded..

ROGERS NOTES

BY THE EDITOR

(*Continued from Vol. XV, p. 167*)

IN this issue we present a copy of an agreement, dated 1 May, 1739, between heirs of John[4] Rogers (*John*[3], *Joseph*[2], *Thomas*[1]) of Harwich, Mass. The original document is now owned by Mr. Arthur E. Linnell, a member of this Society.

[AGREEMENT OF HEIRS]

Know all Men by these presents that we Ebenezer Rogers John Rogers Joseph Rogers & Reuben Nickerson & Sarah Rogers all of Harwich in the County of Barnstable & Jonathan Rogers of yarmoth in the County a fore Sd & Benjamin Rogers of Kings town in the County of plymoth Do agree as followeth viz that we the S^d Ebenezer Rogers John Rogers Benjamin Rogers Jonathan Rogers Ruben Nickerson & Sarah Rogers Do agree & Engage to alow & pay to Joseph Rogers above S^d the Sum of one hundred & fifty pounds for the Service done for our Honnoured father & Husband John Rogers Deseased for Labour done for him Since September ye 20th 1729 the Sum above written to be paid out of the Estate of our S^d father Desesed and Likewise I the Said Joseph Rogers do for my Self take up Satisfied with the above S^d one Hundred & fifty pounds & do for my Self My heirs Executors & asigns for Ever by these presents do aquit & Discharge the above S^d Ebenezer Rogers John Rogers Jonathan Rogers Benjamin Rogers Ruben Nickerson & Sarah Rogers theirs heirs or asigns for Ever from any further demands on the Estate of My Deseased father for the above Said Labour done done for my S^d father for the performance of the above S^d articles we the above Named Ebenezer Rogers John Rogers Jonathan Rogers Benjamin Rogers Joseph Rogers & Ruben Nickerson and Sarah Rogers have Set our hands & Seals this first day of May in the year of our Lord one thousand Seven hundred & Thirty Nine & in the twelf year of our Soveraign Lord George the Second by the Grace of God of Great Brittain France & Ireland King Defender of the faith &c

Signed Sealled & delivered	Ebenezer Rogers (seal)
in presence of	John Rogers (seal)
Jonathan Paine	Jona. Rogers (seal)
Thos freeman	Benj Rogers (seal)
mark	Joseph Rogers (seal)
marcy Paine	her
har	Sarah Rogers (seal)
	mark
	Reuben nickerson (seal)

Barnstable ss on ye 29th day of august 1739, Psonally appearing The above named Ebenezer John Sarah Jonathan & Joseph Rogers and Ruben Nickerson and acknowledged severally ye above writen Instrument to be their act and Deed

Coram M Bourn Justice Peace

[On the back of the deed] To all People to whome these Presents shall com Greeting Know ye that I Priscilla Nickerson wife of the within named Ruben Nickerson Daughter of the within Named John Rogers Deceased for the consideration within mentioned do freely Comply with & consent unto all & singuler the premises within writen as fully & absolutely to all Intents & purposes as if my name had been in the within writen & had signed thereunto as witnes my hand & seall this twentyeight day of August 1739.

Signed Sealled & delivered	her
in presence of	Priscilla Nickerson (seal)
Joseph Doane	mark
her	
Desire Doane	
mark	

Barnstable Ss at Eastham the day & year above writen the above named Priscilla Nickerson acknoleged the above writen to be her act & Deed

Coram me Joseph Doane Justice Peace

TRURO, MASS., CHURCH RECORDS

TRANSCRIBED BY GEORGE ERNEST BOWMAN

(*Continued from Vol. XVII, p. 239*)

[CHURCH PROCEEDINGS, THROUGH 1750]

[p. 2, *cont'd*]

Mr Humphery Purington desired a Dismission from the office of a Deacon and his desire was granted by a vote of the Church Novr 23 1746.

At a church meeting August 22 1750 Mr Joshua Freeman, was chosen by the written Votes of the Church to serve in the office of a Deacon.

[COVENANT OWNERS, THROUGH 1750]

[p. 29, *cont'd*]

1743/4	Fe	6	Ann Hatch
1745	July	7	Mary Newcomb
			Sarah wife to Stephen Atwood of Province Town
			John Stevens and Betty his wife
	Dec	8	Joseph Collins and Phebe his wife
1745/6	Feb	16	Jesse Newcomb
	March	2	Solomon Dyer and Sarah Dyer his wife
1746	July	13	George Lewis and Dinah Lewis his wife
1747	July	5	Silvanus Rich and mary his wife
		12	Elijah Dyer and Deliverance his wife
	Aug.	2	Joanna Savage
	oct	4	Isaiah Atkins and Ruth his wife
		18	Ebenezer Dyer Junr and Hannah his wife
	Dec	13	Robert Newcomb.
1748	April	3	Ephraim Lombard and his wife Joanna.
	June	12	Thos Kilburn of Province Town.
	July	3	Lot Hardin and Tamsin his wife
	Sept	10	Joshua Atkins Junr and Martha his wife
1748/9	Jary	29	Simon Lombard and Anna his wife
	Feb.	12	John Hatch Junr and Bette his wife
1749	March	28	Benjamin Lombard and Elisabeth his wife
	July	23	Daniel Lombard and Mary his wife
1750	Aug	12	Jonah Gross and Dorcas his wife
	Sept	23	Rachel Newhall
			John Smaley and Sarah his wife

[Baptisms, through 1750]

[p. 70, *cont'd*]

44	March	25	Hannah Dat[r] of David Dyer
	April	1	John Son of Micah Gross
			Jane Dat of Sam Smaley
			Lydia Dat[r] of Sam[ll] Elredg Junr
			Jamaes son of Francis Smaley 3[d]
			Susanna Dat[r] of Joseph Rich
		15	Benjamin Son of Benj[n] Hatch Jun[r] of Boston
		29	Susanna Dat[r] of Stephen Atwood of Province Town
	May	13	Elisabeth Dat[r] of Tho[s] Ridley Jun[r].
			Micah son of Richard Stevens.
			Ruth Dat[r] of Zacheus Rich.
			Joshua son of Benjamin Lewis
			Mary Dat[r] of Sam[ll] Treat
		27	Israel and Samuel sons of Israel Gross
	July	8	Mary Dat[r] of Tho[s] Newcomb of provincetown
		15	Isaac son of Isaac Smith
		22	Ephraim son of James Lombard
	Aug	5	Jonathan son of Jonathan Paine Jun[r]
		12	Jesse son of Jesse Newcomb
		19	Thankfull Dyer Adult
	Sept[r]	2	Elisabeth Dat[r] of Tho[s] Smith Jun[r]
			Mary Dat[r] of Joshua Atkins
		23	Isaac son of Sam[ll] Hatch
			Abner son of Abner Paine
		30	Issabel Dat[r] of George Bowoey *
	Oct[r]	7	Mary Dat[r] of Ambross Dyer
			Gamaliel son of Gamaliel Smith
			Anthony son of Will[m] Dyer
		28	Ruth Dat[r] of Jedidiah Lombard
			Hugh son of Hugh Paine
			Hannah Dat[r] of Sam[ll] Bickford
	Dec[r]	2	Martha Dat[r] of Lemuel Rich
1744/5	Jary	20	Mary Dat[r] of Joshua Snow
	Feb	17	Rachel Dat[r] of Sam[ll] Rich
	March	24	Samuel son of Sam[ll] Cash
1745	April	7	Joshua son of Nath[ll] Atwood
			Anthony son of Anthony Snow
		14	Mary Dat[r] of James Cobb
		21	Joseph son of Barnabas Paine
			Oliver and Samuel sons of Joshua meyrick of Boston

* Incorrectly printed as "Bowery" in Treat's "Truro Baptisms", page 18.

[p. 71]			
1745	May	12	Jaazaniah Son of Israel Gross
		26	Zacheus son of Isaiah Atkins
	June	2	Ebenezer son of Mr Solomon Lombard
			Ruth Datr of Job Avery
			Sarah Datr of Timothy Eldredg
		9	Benjamin son of Benjamin Collins Junr
			Martha Datr of Jonathan Hardin
			Thankfull Datr of Tayler Smaley
		23	Josiah son of Uriah Rich
		30	Hezekiah son of Nathll Hardin
	July	7	Richard son of John Stevens
	Aug	4	James son of James Ridley
			Ruth Datr of Obadiah Rich
		25	Samuel son of Samll Treat
	Sptr	1	Ruth Datr of David Dyer
		29	Jane Datr of George Bowoey *
	oct	6	Barzillai son of Barzillai Smith
		17	Barnabas son of Barnabas Higgins
	Dec	1	Joanna Datr of Thos Paine
			Ambrose son of Amasa Snow
		8	Paul son of Joseph Collins
		29	Mary Datr of Thos Hopkins
1745/6	Jary	19	John Son of Thos Cobb Junr
	Feb	9	Mary Datr of Joshua Atkins
	March	2	Solomon Son of Solomon Dyer
			Anna Datr of Abner Paine
1746	April	20	Israel son of Thos Lombard
			Joshua son of Benj Lewis
			Jonathan son of Joseph Rich
		27	Hannah Datr of Robert Rich
	May	4	Mary Datr of Keziah Conant
		11	Thos son of John Savage
		18	Lewis son of Lewis Lombard
			Sarah Datr of Danll Paine
	June	22	Thomas Son of Thos Ridley Junr
			Joseph son of Joseph Collins
		29	Isaac son of Ruben Higgins
	July	20	Elisabeth Dauth of George Lewis
[p. 72]			
1746	Aug	30	Tayler son of Tayler Smaley
	Sept	21	Elisabeth Datr of Samll Hatch
			Samuel son of Samll Smaley
	Novr	23	Hezekiah son of Mr Sol: Lombard
		30	Apollos son of Samll Rich.
			Unice Datr of Constant Freman

* Incorrectly printed as "Bowery" in Treat's "Truro Baptisms", page 19.

1746/7	Feb	8	Hannah Dat^r of Barnabas Paine
			Sarah Dat^r of Anthony Snow
			Zepheniah Son of Lemuel Rich
		22	Jesse son of Jedidiah Lombard
			Mary Dat^r of Richard Stevens
	March	1	Elisabeth Dat^r of Job Avery
		8	Isaac son of Joshua Snow
			Thankfull Dat^r of Hugh Paine
			Phebe Dat^r of Uriah Rich.
		15	Daniel son of Sam^ll Cash
			Samuel son of Sam^ll Airy
		22	Thomas Son of John Stevens
1747	[March]	29	Epraim son of Zacheus Rich
	April	12	Jonathan son of Jonathan Harding
			Paul son of Solomon Dyer
		26	Joanna Dat^r of Benjamin Collins Junr
	May	3	Nehemiah Son of Nath^ll Hardin
			Micah son of David Dyer
		10	Lot son of Gershom Rider of Province Town
		17	Sarah Dat^r of Jesse Newcomb
		31	Matthias son of Sam^ll Rider
	June	7	Hector Negro Servant to Mr Benjn Collins
		28	Constant son of Constant Hopkins
	July	12	Phanny Dat^r of Cate negro servant to Mr Jonath Paine
		26	Rebeckah Dat^r of Elijah Dyer
	Aug	9	Jerusha Dat^r of Ambrose Dyer
		16	Hannah Dat^r of John Lombard
			Hannah Dat^r of Jonathan Paine Junr
			George son of George Bowoey *
		23	Elisabeth Dat^r of Joanna Savage
	Sept	20	Sarah Dat^r of Isaac Cole Junr
	Oct	4	Sarah Dat^r of George Lewis
			Deliverance Dat^r of Isaiah Atkins Junr

[p. 73]

1747	oct	11	Isaiah son of Silvanus Rich and Huldah his Dat^r
		18	Mercy Dat^r of Thos Cobb Junr
			Hannah Dat^r of Eben^r Dyer Junr
		25	Rebeckah Dat^r of Lewis Lombard
	Nov	2	Barzillai son of Barzillai Smith
		15	Amasai son of Amasai Snow
		29	David son of Robert Newcomb
1747/8	Jan	31	Elisha son of Barnibas Higgins

* Incorrectly printed as "Bowery" in Treat's "Truro Baptisms", page 20.

1748	April	3	Sebaram * Dat^{r} of James Cobb
			Sarah Dat^{r} of Thos Hopkins
			Nathaniel Son of Sam^{ll} Treat.
		10	Hannah Dat^{r} of Jonathan Collins Junr
			Apphiah Dat^{r} of Joshua Freeman
		17	Ambrose son of James Ridley
	may	1	Hannah Dat^{r} of Eph^{m} Lombard
			Elisha son of Elkanah Paine Junr
		8	Shebna son of Sam^{ll} Dyer
		29	Eleazer son of Benjn Lewis
			Elisabeth Dat^{r} of Israel Gross
	June	5	Stephen son of Sam^{ll} Cash
			Levi son of Richard Stevens Junr
			Elisabeth Dat^{r} of Sam Hatch
		12	Betty Dat^{r} of Thos Kilburn
	July	3	Calvin son of Mr Sol. Lombard
			Easther Dat^{r} of Lot† Hardin.
		10	Elkanah son of Sam^{ll} Eldridg Junr
		17	Joshua son of Tim. Eldridg
		31	Richard son of Joseph Rich
			Daniel son of Daniel Paine
	Sept	10	Thos son of Joshua Atkins Junr
		25	Abigal Dat^{r} of Andrew Collins
	Oct	2	Joseph son of Tayler Smaley
		9	Huldah Dat^{r} of Sam^{ll} Rider
		16	Joseph son of Nat Atwood
			Mary Dat^{r} of Thos Ridley
		29	Elkanah son of Elkanah Paine Junr
	Nov	20	Richard son of Phebe Collins
			Nathaniel son of Gamaliel Smith
	Dec^{r}	11	Jonathan son of Sam^{ll} Aery
		18	Sam^{ll} son of Joshua Atkins
		25	Mary Dat^{r} of Eph Lombard
1748/9	Jary	15	Isaac son of Isaac Cole Junr
			Joshua son of Elijah Dyer
	Feb	12	Job son of Job Avery
			Joshua son of Sam^{ll} Smaley
[p. 74]			
1748/9	Feb	19	Lettice and Joanna twin Dat^{rs} of John Stevens
			Shubaal son of Isaiah Atkins Junr
		26	Sarah Dat^{r} of Simon Lombard
			Nailor Son of John Hatch Jun
	March	19	Jonathan son of Constant Hopkins

* Incorrectly printed "Lebanon son of James Cobb" in Treat's "Truro Baptisms", page 20, thus making an error in both name and sex.

"Sabra cobb the daughter of James and hannah Cobb was born in Truro october 8th 1747:" according to Truro town records.

† Incorrectly printed "Nathaniel" in Treat's "Truro Baptisms", page 20.

1749	March	26	Mary Dat^r of Benjamin Lombard
	April	2	Samuel son of Jerusha Paine
			James son of Lemuel Rich
			Treat son of Benjamin Collins Junr
			Experience Dat of Phillip Tilton *
		16	Elisabeth Dat^r of Anthony Snow
		23	Obadiah son of Obadiah Rich
	May	7	Anna Dat^r of Uriah Rich
		14	Alexander the son of Mary Bowoey †
		21	Rachel Dat^r of James Lombard
	June	4	Nehemiah son of John Savage
			Joanna Dat^r of Thos Smith
	July	9	Dorcas Dat^r of Sol. Dyer
		23	Thos son of Dan^{ll} Lombard
			David son of David Dyer
	Aug	6	Andrew son of Jesse Newcomb
	Sep^r	3	John Son of Jonathan Paine
	Oct	1	Asa son of Thos Cobb Junr
		15	Barnabas Son of Ambros Snow
		29	Abigal Dat^r of Robert Newcomb
	Nov^r	5	John son of Sam^{ll} Rich
			Sarah Dat^r of Joshua Atkins Junr
		12	Elisabeth Dat of Francis Smaley 3^d
	Dec^r	17	John Son of Jonathan Collins Junr
1749/10‡	Feb	11	Atkins Son of Barzillai Smith
1750	April	1	Joseph Son of Amasa Snow
			Rebecca Dat^r of Joshua Freman
	May	2[§]	John son of George Lewis
			Mary Dat^r of Timothy Eldridge
			Mary Dat^r of Israel Gross
			Lettice Dat^r of John Stevens
			Tamsin Dat^r of Lot Hardin
	June	3	Cornelius Son of Simon Lombard
			Jenny Dat of Thos Newcomb Province Town
		10	Sarah Dat^r of Sam^{ll} Treat
			David son of James Ridley
			Thomas son of Sam^{ll} Dyer
	July	15	Hannah Dat^r of Gamaliel Smith
			James son of Joseph Rich
		29	Margery Dat^r of Andrew Collins

[p. 75]

1750	Aug	19	Elisabeth Dat^r of Abner Paine
			Micah son of Jonah Gross

* Incorrectly printed as "Pilton", in Treat's "Truro Baptisms", page 21.

† Incorrectly printed as "Bowery", in Treat's "Truro Baptisms", page 21.

‡ Sic.

§ The second figure is illegible.

26 Thos son of Thos Kilburn
Sarah Dat of Sam^{ll} Cash
Sep^{t} 23 Jeremiah son of Thos Hopkins
Bette Daugh^{r} of Benjamin Lewis
Joseph son of John Smaley
Octr 21 Dinah Dat^{r} of John Savage
Novr 11 Charles son of Isaac Cole Junr
Decr 16 Rhuben Son of Jonathan Harding
30 Huldah Dat^{r} of Daniel Paine

[ADMISSIONS THROUGH 1750]

[p. 305, *cont'd*]
1743/4 Feb 19 David Dyer and Ruth his wife
1744 May 20 Elisabeth wife of Israel Gross
Hannah Cobb by Dismission from Barnstable
July 8 Mary wife of Willm Lombard
Aug 12 Constant Hopkins Phebe his wife
Hannah wife of Tim Eldredge
Mary wife of George Bowoey
19 Thankfull wife of Ambros Dyer
Barnabas Higgins mary his wife
Lydia Dat^{r} Deacon Moses Paine
Ezra Negro *Dismist to Boston Feb 3 1750/1* *
[*Ezra Negro again dismist to Chh in Brattle Street Boston under Care of Revd Saml Cooper*, *1756. April 25* †]
Decr 16 Thomas Gains and Bathsheba his wife Dismist from Hull
1744/5 Jany 27 Sarah Smith
1745 Nov 17 Richard Stevens Ju^{r}
1745/6 Feb 2^{d} Ambros Dyer
1746 Novr 23 John Hatch *dismist to boston may 29th 1755* *
[p. 306]
1746 May 4 John Lewis
Mercy Newcomb
July 20 Bathshua Smaley
Mary Newcomb
1747 May 17 Sam^{ll} Rider and Hannah his wife
Aug 16 Margery wife of Andrew Collins
1747/8 Jany 31 Anna Freeman *1768. Jan: 17. dismist to first Chh in Eastham* ‡
March 13 Hezekiah Purington

* The words printed in italics are later additions to the record.

† This entry is a marginal note in the hand of Rev. Caleb Upham.

‡ The words in italics were added in a different hand.

1748	April	10	Elkanah Paine Junr and Mary his wife
	May	29	Betty wife of John Stevens
	July	17	Mary wife to the Revd John Avery formerly of the Chh of Provincetown
	Nov^r	13	Jonathan Collins Junr
	Dec^r	18	Priscilla Hatch Sam Hatchs wife
1748/9	Jary	29	Joseph Collins and Deborah Collins Sam^ll Smith of Province Town
	April	2	Anna wife of Uriah Rich Desire wife of Phillip Tilton
1749	April	23	Dan^ll Paine Mercy wife of Thos Newcomb of Province Town
	June	25	Joseph Atkins Sarah Hardin Hannah Atkins
	July	23	Mehitable Kilburn wife to Thos Kilburn Hannah Conant Junr both of Province Town
	Aug	13	Susanna Walker of Province Town
1750	June	3	Mehittabel wife of Benjamin Rider Province Town

(*To be continued*)

PLYMOUTH COLONY VITAL RECORDS

TRANSCRIBED BY THE EDITOR

(*Continued from Vol. XVII, p. 203*)

[p. 35] The Regester of Eastham

William the son of William Merecke was borne the 15th of September 1643

Stephen the son of William Mericke was borne the 12th of May 1646

Rebeckah the Daughter of William Merricke was borne the 28 of July 1648

Mary the Daughter of William Merricke was born the 4th of November 1650

Ruth the Daughter of William Merricke was borne the 15th of May 1652

Sarah the Daughter of William Merricke was borne the first of August 1654

John the son of William Merricke was born the fifteenth of January 1656

Isacke the son of Henery Atkins was borne the 14th of June 1657

Annah the Daughter of Marke Snow was borne the 7th of July 1656

Mehetabell the Daughter of Richard Knowles was borne the 20th of May 1653

Barbery the Daughter of Richard Knowles was borne the 28th of Septem: 1656

Anna the Daughter of Josias Cooke and wife of Marke Snow Died the 24th of July 1656

Taunton Regester

Thomas Auger married to Elizabeth Packer the 14th of November 1665

Thomas Linkoln seni'r: married to Elizabeth Street widdow the 10th of December 1665

Patience the Daughter of John Bundey Died the 27th of March 1665

Johanna the Daughter of Nathaniel: Thayer was borne the 13th of December 1665

Taunton the 28th of ffebruary 1665 Shadrach Wilbore Towne Clarke

Plymouth Regester

John Bryant Married to Abigaill Bryant the 23 of November 1665

John Waterman married to Ann Sturtivant the 7th of December 1665

Edward Gray married unto Dorithy Lettice the 12th of December 1665

John Robins married to Jehosabath Jourdaine the 14th of December 1665

Isacke Barker married to mistris Judith Prence the 28th of December 1665

Jonathan Barnes married to Elizabeth Hedge the 4th of January 1665

Ephraim Tilson married to Elizabeth hoskins the 7th of July 1666

Isacke the son of Ephraim Tinkham was borne the 11th of April 1666

Samuell the son of John Waterman was borne the 16th of october 1666

John the son of Sacariah Eedey was borne the 10th of october 1666

Hannah the Daughter of William Harlow was borne the 28 of october 1666

Jacob Michell married to Sussanna Pope the 7th of November 1666

Benjamine Bosworth married to Hannah Morton the 27th of November 1666

Robert Barrow married to Ruth Bonum the 28th of November 1666

Nathaniel the son of Nathaniel Morton Died the 17th of ffebruary 1666

Marcye the wife of Joseph Dunham Died the 19th of ffebruary 1666

John Phillips Married to ffaith Dotey the 14th of March 1666

John Cole married to Elizabeth Ryder the 21 of November 1667

John Nelson married to Sarah Wood the Daughter of Henery Wood the 28th of November 1667

John Doged of Martins Vinyard married to Bathshebath Prat widdow the 29th of August 1667

Joseph Williams married to Elizabeth Watson the 28th of November 1667

Nathaniel Holmes Married to Marcye ffaunce the 29th of December 1667

Edward the son of Edward Gray born the 31 of January 1666

Rowland the son of m^r John Cotton was borne the 27th of December 1667

Joseph The son of Samuell Sturtivant was born the 16th of July 1666

Gabriel ffallowell aged fourscore and three yeares Died the twenty eight of December 1667 and was buryed the 31 of the same month with great respect and honor and much lamented in respect of the loss of him whoe was a good old man and a faithfull servant of the lord

John ffallowell married to Sarah the Daughter of John Wood the 13th of ffebruary 1667

Bathshua the Daughter of William Harlow was borne the one and twentyeth of Aprill 1667

[p. 36] Abigaill the Daughter of Jonathan Pratt was born the sixteenth of June 1665

Bathshebah the Daughter of Jonathan Pratt was borne the 20th of ffebruary 1666

Ruth the Daughter of Jacob Cooke was borne the seaventeenth of January 1665

John Ivey of Boston was married to Marcye Bartlett the 25th of December 1668

Susanna the Daughter of Edward Gray was borne the 15th of October 1668

Jonathan the son of Jonathan Pratt was Borne the 20th of March 1668

John Doten the son of John Doten was borne the 24th Day of August 1668

Edward the son of John Doten was borne the 28th of June 1671

Jacob the son of John Dotey was born the 24th of May 1673

Elizabeth the Daughter of John Waterman was born the fifteenth of January 1668

John Dunham seni^r: of Plymouth aged about fourscore yeares Died the 2^cond of March 1668 hee was an approved servant of God; and a usefull man in his place being a Deacon of the Church of Christ att Plymouth;

Gyles Rickard seni^r: was Married to Hannah Churchill seni^r: the 25th of June Ann^o Dom 1669

Joseph Dunham was marryed to Hester Wormall the 20th of August 1669

Jacob Cooke seni^r: was marryed to Elizabeth Shirtliffe widdow the 18th of November 1669

on the eight Day of December Anno: Dom 1669 The honored Capt: Thomas Southworth Changed this life for a better; being then about the age of fifty three yeares; whoe was a majestrate of this Jurisdiction and otherwise a good benifactor to both Church and Comonwealth and that which is more then all hath bine named hee was a very godly man and soe lived and Died full of faith and Comfort being much lamented by all of all sorts sects and Conditions of people within our Jurisdiction of New Plymouth

Eliezer the son of Robert Barrow was borne on the fifteenth Day of September 1669 and Died on the thirteenth Day of December 1669:

Eliezer Jackson the son of Abraham Jackson was borne [*] of October 1669

Hannah the Daughter of Benjamine Bosworth was borne the one and twenty Day of December 1669

Joanna the Daughter of Willam Harlow was born the 24th of March 1669

(*To be continued*)

ABSTRACTS OF BARNSTABLE COUNTY, MASS., PROBATE RECORDS

By George Ernest Bowman

(*Continued from Vol. XVI, p. 61*)

[William Crocker's Will]

[p. 71] The will of "Deacon William Crocker of Barnestable" was made 6 September, 1692. Bequests were as follows:

To "Patience my Loving wife besids ye Liberty to dispose of all ye estate which she brought with her or had at ye time of our Intermarriage and besids ye forty pounds I then promised to give her in case she should survive me I give unto her my best bedd and bedstead with all ye ffurniture there to belonging"

To "my eldest Son John Crocker my now dwelling house and Lands both uplands and ffresh meadows Adjoyning and belonging thereunto now and of Late under my occupation and Improvement .... to him his heirs and assignes for ever he or they paying to ye sd Patience my wife Twenty pounds of ye foresd forty pounds she is to Receive and I do also here by confirm to him .... all those parcels of Land I here to fore gave unto him and are well knowen to have been in his quiatt possession for Sundry years: I further also give .... my Son John my two oxen which he hath had in his possession som years"

To "my Son Job Crocker besids ye Land I here to fore gave him and knowen to be in his possession, Twenty acres of that fifty acres at ye ponds which I purchised of John Coggin .... to him my Son Job .... and that he Chuse it on which side of sd Land he please"

* Space was left for the day; but it was not filled in.

To "my Sons Josiah and Eliazer Crocker besids those Lands I here to fore gave to each of them and are in their perticuler knowne possession all my upland at the marsh together with all ye marsh Adjoyning there unto (Except Such perticuler parcel or parcels there of as I have here to fore given and is possest of Late by any other or is in these presents here after mentioned) to be equally divided between them .... each of them ye sd Josiah and Eliazer paying" £7, 10s., "apeice to ye sd Patience in part of ye forty pounds above mentioned : And I further will .... to my sd Sons Josiah and Eliazer to each of them one Cow"

To "my son Joseph Crocker, besids ye two parcels of upland and one parcel of marsh which I here to fore gave him and is knowen to be in his possession, ye house and Land which he hiered of me and now Lives on, that is to say So much of my sd Land as he hath now fenced in: togeather with that parcel of marsh wich he hath from year to year of Late hiered of me .... to him ye sd Joseph his heirs and assignes .... he or they paying five pounds to ye sd Patience to make up ye full of sd forty pounds I promised to her as abovesd"

"I give .... all ye Rest of my Lands att ye ponds to my Grand Sons viz to Nathaniel ye Son of John Crocker Samuel ye son of Job Crocker and Thomas ye Son of Josiah Crocker to be Equally divided between them"

"Son Job Crocker to be my Sole Executor .... with whome I Leave all ye Residue of my Estate .... to be Equally distributed amongst all my children unless I shall signifie my minde to have such part or parts there of to be disposed to any in perticuler .... on my further Consideration I signifie my mind before ye Ensealing here of .... that m^r^ Russell shall have my two steers which are att Isaac Howlands And that m^r^ Thomas Hinckely shall have my Negro boy if he please he paying fourteen pounds to my Executor for him"

The witnesses were "Samuel Chepman" and "Mercy Chepman", both of whom made oath to the will on 19 October, 1692. It was recorded on 22 October, 1692, by Joseph Lothrop, Recorder.

[p. 72] An inventory of the personal property "of Deacon William Crocker" was taken "att his house in Barnestable" 20 September, 1692, by John Otis and Joseph Lothrop. The "Negro Boy" was valued at £20. The total amount was £327, 18s., 5d. "Deacon Job Crocker made oath" to the inventory 19 October, 1692, and it was recorded 22 October, 1692, by Joseph Lothrop, Recorder.

[Robert Shelley's Will]

[p. 73] "Robirt Shelley of Barnestable" made his will 11 March, 1688/9. Bequests were as follows:

"And as for that Small Estate I am possesed of I Leave it wholy to my wife after my decease for her support and them that I Leave with her: And for ye preventing of further Trouble I thought good to Inseart in this my Last will that ye two Acres of Land that I exchanged with Henry Taylor for ye Land that my house now standeth on that my Son John Shelley freely gave it to me"

The will was signed by a mark. The witnesses were Henry Taylor and Jabez Lumburt, both of whom made oath to the will, but the clerk failed to enter the date. It was recorded 22 October, 1692, by Joseph Lothrop, Clerk.

"An Invintory of ye Estate of Robirt Shelley of Barnestable deceased ye Sixt day of September 1692 taken this third day of October 1692" by Shubael Dimack and Jabez Lumburt. The only real estate was "his house and Land" £20. The total amount was £41, 18s. "Susanna Shelley vid Relict of Robirt Shelley" made oath to the inventory 19 October, 1692, and it was recorded 22 October, 1692, by Joseph Lothrop, Recorder.

[Estate of Samuel Smith, Jr.]

[p. 74] "The Invintory of ye Estate of Samuel Smith Ju^r^ of Eastham deceased September ye 22: 1692" was taken by Joshua Bangs and Constant Freeman on 29 March, 1693. No real estate is mentioned. Three interesting items are: "halfe a whale Boate" £2, 10s.; "halfe a whale Boate" £3, 10s.; "the Income of half a Boate" £15.

"Bathsua Smith vid Relict of Samuel Smith Late of Eastham deceased made oath to" the inventory "Before Barnabas Lothrop Esqr Judg of the prerogative Court" 31 March, 1693, and it was recorded the same day, by Joseph Lothrop, Register.

[p. 75] "April ye first 1693 By Barnabas Lothrop of Barnestable Esqr Judge of ye prerogative Court .... Letters of Administration was Comitted unto Bathsua Smith vid Relict of Samuel Smith Ju^r^ Late of Eastham .... deceased .... And then the Estate of said deceased was Setled by Said Judg as followeth: viz to Samuel Smith Eldest Son of said deceased to have for his part and portione of sd Estate fifteen pounds in money: and to Joseph Smith youngest Son of sd deceased to have for his part and portion out of ye Estate of sd deceased ye Sum of ten pounds in money: And ye sd Bathsua Smith Relict of sd deceased to have ye Remainder and Residue of ye Estate of said deceased for her Supporte and Bringing up ye Childern of sd deceased

"Attest Joseph Lothrop : Regester"

[Estate of Thomas Gibbs]

"An Invintory of ye Estate of Thomas Gibbs Late of Sandwich deceased" was taken 27 March, 1692/3, by Thomas Tupper and Jacob Burge, the latter signing by a mark. The only real estate mentioned was "Land both upland and meadow" £30. "John Gibbs made oath" to the inventory, at Barnstable, 14 April, 1693, before Barnabas Lothrop, Esq., Judge of the Prerogative Court, and it was recorded 15 April, 1693, by Joseph Lothrop, Register.

[p. 76] On 14 April, 1693, Barnabas Lothrop, Esq., of Barnstable, Judge of Probate, appointed as administrator "John Gibbs of Sandwich .... Eldest Son of Thomas Gibbs Late of Sandwich aforesd deceased .... And at ye same time by vertue of an agreement under the hands of John Gibbs Thomas Gibbs and Samuel Gibbs all Sons of sd deceased ye estate of sd deceased was settled and the Agreement is as followeth"

"wee John Gibbs and Thomas Gibbs and Samuel Gibbs All of Sandwich .... yeomen have made a divission of ye Estate Left by our Deare ffather Thomas Gibbs deceased: and to ye end that our mother may be Comfortably maintained ye time of her Life wee have to that end ordered all ye moveables to be Improved for her Comfort and if God Lengthen her dayes so Long as to spend the same wee Joyntly Agree to mainetaine her out of our owne estates and also that percel of Land that was given In up on ye Invintory Lately exhibeted to ye Court wee joyntly Agree that said Land Shall according to our ffathers desire be and Remaine to be to ye only proper use and behoof of ye said John Gibbs .... And that Thomas Gibbs and Samuel Gibbs above Named do by these presents quitt Claime to any part or parcel of ye before mentioned Land And desire that sd Land may be setled up on him ye said John Gibbs for his owne proper Inheritance And because wee All desire peace and union amongst us wee have so don And do all Intreate that what we have don may be accepted"

The agreement was dated 11 April, 1693, and signed by John Gibbs, Thomas Gibbs and Samuel Gibbs. The witnesses were Mathias Ellis and Thomas Tupper. It was approved by the court, and was recorded 15 April, 1693, by Joseph Lothrop, Register.

(*To be continued*)

MEMBERSHIP REQUIREMENTS OF THE MASSACHUSETTS SOCIETY OF MAYFLOWER DESCENDANTS

Eligibility

Every living descendant of a Mayflower Passenger, as far as known, is descended from one of the twenty-two Passengers named in the following list, and applications for membership must show descent from one of these men.

John Alden	Edward Doty	Henry Samson
Isaac Allerton	Francis Eaton	George Soule
John Billington	Edward Fuller	Myles Standish
William Bradford	Dr. Samuel Fuller	Richard Warren
William Brewster	Stephen Hopkins	William White
Peter Brown	John Howland	Edward Winslow
James Chilton	Degory Priest	
Francis Cooke	Thomas Rogers	

Applications for Membership

Applicants, of either sex, must be at least eighteen years of age.

Preliminary Application blanks, which may be obtained from the Secretary, must be endorsed by two members of the Society.

The sum of ten dollars ($10.00), to cover the Entrance Fee and the Annual Dues for the current fiscal year, must accompany the Preliminary Application, when it is filed with the Secretary.

After the Preliminary Application has been approved by the Membership Committee, the Pedigree Blanks are sent to the applicant, to be filled out in duplicate and returned to the Secretary within six months. After the line of descent is approved by the Historian, the application is voted upon by the Board of Assistants.

Entrance Fee—Annual Dues—Life Membership

The Entrance Fee is five dollars.

The Annual Dues of members elected after 28 March, 1912, are five dollars, payable when the application is filed, and on the first day of each succeeding March; and all such members, after they have paid their dues for the current fiscal year, receive, without additional charge, the Society's two magazines, "The Mayflower Descendant," which is issued quarterly, and "Pilgrim Notes and Queries," which is issued eight months in the year, omitting June to September.

Members elected in December, January and February are not required to pay annual dues again on the first day of March.

The Life Membership Fee is one hundred dollars. Life Members receive both of the Society's magazines free.

PLYMOUTH COLONY WILLS AND INVENTORIES

ABSTRACTS BY THE EDITOR

(*Continued from Vol. XVII, page 218*)

[ON folios 77a to 83 are recorded the wills and inventories of John Brown, Sr., and John Brown, Jr., both of Rehoboth, and of John[1] Churchill of Plymouth. They are printed in full in two separate articles, in this issue. — EDITOR.]

[THOMAS BURMAN'S WILL]

[On fol. 83] The will of "Thomas Burman of Barnstable late Deceased exhibited before the generall Court held att Plymouth the 4th of June 1663 on the oathes of John Smith and John Chipman of Barnstable aforsaid;" The will was dated 9 May, 1663, and bequests were as follows:

"I Doe make my wife sole exequitor of what estate I have"

To "my son Thomas forty acrees of land att Namassakett;"

To "my wife threescore acrees of land att Namassakett the one halfe to bee att her Dispose;"

"I Doe give twenty five acrees that is to bee layed out to bee equally Devided between my Daughter Hannah and my son Trustrum; of the said lands to bee layed out att Namassakett; in Plymouth Collonie; and the meddowes and privilidges to bee equally Devided according to the quantities of that land;"

To "my sonne Thomas and my son Samuell my great lott in this Towne of Barnstable; and alsoe the privilidges of the comons that I have in this Towne;"

To "my son Thomas my young mare and Tristrum my son shall have the first Colt that shee bringes"

To "my son Samuell the Coult of the white faced mare"

To "my Daughter Hannah two Cowes"

To "my Daughters Desire Mary and Mehetabell each of them one Cow apeece;"

The will was signed by a mark. The witnesses were John Smith and John Chipman.

[fol. 84] The inventory was taken by William Crocker, John Howland and Moses Rowley. No real estate was mentioned.

"Hannah the late wife of the said Thomas Burman was Deposed to the truth of this Inventory before mee Thomas Hinckley Assistant July 6 : 63"

[Receipt of James Phillips]

1664 Prence Govr:

A receipt appointed to bee recorded as followeth

Memorand: this written is to Testify that James Phillipes of liveing in the Collonie of New Plymouth husbandman Testifyeth that I have received the bed with its appurtenances and the halfe of a mare that was given to mee on will by my unkell Willam Parker aforsaid yeoman I say received of my Aunt Allis Paine of Rehoboth . . . . and I Doe by these p^{r}sents bind my selfe . . . . never to mollest nor trouble nor Challenge any thing more of my aunt or her heires . . . . and Doe owne my selfe fully satisfyed . . . . for that which was given to me on will by my unkell late Deceased"

The receipt was dated "the third Day of the seaventh month" 1662. [The seventh month was September.] The witnesses were James Wyatt and Peter Pitts.

(To be continued)

FORM FOR A BEQUEST

I give and bequeath to the Society of Mayflower Descendants, a corporation organized under the laws of the Commonwealth of Massachusetts, the sum of . . . . dollars.

THE MAYFLOWER APPROACHING THE LAND

We are much indebted to The John A. Lowell Bank Note Company, of Boston, for supplying, without charge, the half-tone plates, "The Mayflower Approaching the Land", used as the frontispiece of this issue.

The original painting, by Marshall Johnson, was presented to the Massachusetts Society of Mayflower Descendants, in 1904, by Messrs. John A. Lowell and Company (the predecessors of the present company), who had reproduced it in a handsome steel engraving, 22 × $18\frac{1}{2}$ inches in size.

Inquiries about copies of the engraving should be addressed to The John A. Lowell Bank Note Company, 147 Franklin St., Boston, Mass.

THE PILGRIM MEMORIAL MONUMENT AT PROVINCETOWN, MASS.

[See page 127]

THE MAYFLOWER DESCENDANT

Vol. XVIII APRIL, 1916 No. 2

ABSTRACT OF THE TWENTIETH ANNUAL REPORT OF GEORGE ERNEST BOWMAN, SECRETARY OF THE MASSACHUSETTS SOCIETY 1896—28 MARCH—1916

THE Massachusetts Society of Mayflower Descendants has elected 1,407 members in its first twenty years; but deaths, resignations, etc., make our present membership 780.

Every one of the 49 Mayflower Passengers from whom descent can be proved is represented in the Massachusetts Society; and the 1,407 members have filed 2,783 different lines of descent from these Passengers. One member has proved descent from 23 of the 49 possible ancestors. Another member has proved 35 different lines of descent, from 19 Passengers.

The first column of figures, in the following table, shows the number of members of the Massachusetts Society descended from each Mayflower Passenger. The second column shows the number of different lines of descent, from each Passenger, already filed by our members.

John Alden	327	405
Isaac Allerton	82	83
John Billington	20	23
William Bradford	188	210
William Brewster	311	376
Peter Brown	41	47
James Chilton	90	96
Francis Cooke	150	182
Edward Doty	47	51
Francis Eaton	35	35
Edward Fuller	32	32
Dr. Samuel Fuller	25	25
Stephen Hopkins	171	215
John Howland	223	294
Degory Priest	27	30
Thomas Rogers	79	87
Henry Samson	37	38
George Soule	66	74
Myles Standish	72	85
Richard Warren	285	367
William White	18	23
Edward Winslow	5	5

In 1898 we elected a lady on her 105th birthday, and she lived to the age of 106 years, 2 months, 18 days. She was only fifth in descent from Mary Chilton, and at the same time we had a member who was twelfth in descent from John Tilley, another Mayflower Passenger. In the same year we elected twin sisters, three days after their joint ninety-third birthday.

When I founded the Massachusetts Society of Mayflower Descendants, and began to study the claims of descent presented by applicants for membership, I soon found that much of the data in print about the genealogy of the Mayflower families was very unreliable; and it has been my exceedingly unpleasant duty to reject scores of incorrect claims of Mayflower descent.

I soon found that it would be necessary to rebuild the genealogies of the Mayflower families from their foundations; and the care exercised in this rebuilding is evidenced by the fact that less than one-twentieth ($\frac{1}{20}$) of one per cent. of the descents I have approved (including not only the lines filed by members of the Massachusetts Society, but also hundreds of others on which my judgment has been sought) were later found to be incorrect; and in these few cases the error was discovered by this Society.

Our quarterly magazine, "The Mayflower Descendant," begun in 1899, very soon became the recognized authority on Mayflower Genealogy; and our monthly magazine, "Pilgrim Notes and Queries," begun in 1913, is steadily adding to the invaluable material preserved and made accessible as a result of our researches.

At our fifth annual meeting, 21 November, 1900, on motion of your Secretary, it was voted to begin preparations for publishing, in commemoration of the Pilgrim Tercentenary in 1920, a series of memorial volumes of Pilgrim Genealogy and History. This series it was later decided to name "The Mayflower Genealogies," and we hope to include in it every descendant, in all male and female lines, of all the Mayflower Passengers.

This date, 21 November, 1900, is the earliest date known to the Society on which any organization of any kind passed a vote to begin preparations for the Pilgrim Tercentenary. A notice of this vote was printed in the January, 1901, issue of "The Mayflower Descendant."

We have also published a number of separate volumes of town records, etc., and our publications already amount to more than 6,000 pages. By the end of 1916 we expect to add another 1,000 pages.

The Society owns thousands of abstracts of wills, deeds, court records, vital records, etc., nowhere to be found in print.

Our library contains about 1,450 volumes of genealogical and historical works.

We own two books printed by Elder William Brewster, in 1618 and 1619, while in exile at Leyden, Holland.

We also own two original deeds of land, dated 1650 and 1651, each bearing the autograph of a Mayflower Passenger.

During the whole twenty years the Society has received but one gift as large as $500, and that was a bequest received two weeks ago, too late to have any effect on our twenty years' record. Less than half a dozen gifts of $200 each, and perhaps a score of $100 each, have been received. The average amount contributed for the Society's work during the twenty years has been less than $500 per year.

In spite of the very small amount of money available for research work, we have collected thousands of pages of manuscript data and prepared thousands of index cards.

As a result of our twenty years' researches, many new lines of Mayflower descent have been brought to light, and with our accumulated data, and especially with our system of arrangement, we are in a position to continue the work to far greater advantage, and at much less expense, than it could possibly be carried on under any other management.

Hundreds of persons throughout the country are looking to the Massachusetts Society of Mayflower Descendants to carry on and complete, in due time, "The Mayflower Genealogies"; but this Society should not be expected to do all the work and also bear all the expense.

It may become necessary, therefore, to notify the large numbers who are anxious to be included in "The Mayflower Genealogies," but are unwilling to contribute even a postage stamp towards the expense, that their names cannot be printed in these volumes.

FORM FOR A BEQUEST

I GIVE and bequeath to the Society of Mayflower Descendants, a corporation organized under the laws of the Commonwealth of Massachusetts, the sum of . . . . dollars.

PLYMOUTH COLONY VITAL RECORDS

(*Continued from page 58*)

[p. 37] on the 26 Day of March 1670 Mistris Allic[e] Bradford senir: Changed this life for a better haveing attained to fourscore yeares of age or therabouts shee wa[s] a godly Matron; and much loved while shee lived and lamente[d] tho; aged when shee Died and was honorabley enterred on the 29 Day of the month aforsaid; att New Plymouth;

on the 12th Day of December 1671 Mistris Allice Bradford Junir: Changed this life for a better, about the age of 44 yeeres Shee was a gracious Woman liveed much Desired Died much lamented and was buried on the 14th Day of the month aforesaid att Plymouth abovesaid;

Sarah the Daughter of Mr John Cotton was borne on the fift Day of Aprill 1670:

Maria the Daughter of mr John Cotton was borne on the 14th of January 1671

Hannah the Daughter of Jonathan Prate was Borne on the 28th of June 1671

Elizabeth the Daughter of Zacariah Eedey was borne the third Day of August 1670

Nathaniel: Bosworth Junir of Nantaskett allies Hull was married to Elizabeth Morton of Plymouth on the seaventh Day of December 1670

Joseph Prince of Nantaskett Alies Hull was married unto Joanna Morton of Plymouth on the 7th of December [*1670* *] one thousand six hundred and seaventy;

Richard Willis was married to Patience Bonum on the 28th of December 1670

Lydia Bumpas the Daughter of Joseph Bumpas was borne the 2cond of August 1669

Francis Curtice was Married to Hannah Smith on the 28th of December 1671

John Laythorpe was Marryed to Mary Cole Junir: on the third of January 1671

Nathaniel Southworth marryed to [*Mary* †] Desire Gray the tenth of January 1671

Joseph Churchill married to Sarah Hickes the third of June 1672

Thomas Faunce married to Jane Nelson the 13th of December 1672

* "1670" appears to have been crossed out when the original entry was made.

† "Mary" was first written; but it was crossed out in the same ink, and the entry completed as here printed.

[p. 38] Mercye the Daughter of Joseph Warren was borne the 23 of September 1653.

Abigaill the Daughter of Joseph Warren was borne the 15th of March 1655

Joseph the son of Joseph Warren was borne The 8th of January 1657

Patience the Daughter of Joseph Warren was borne the 15th of March 1660

Elizabeth the Daughter of Joseph Warren Was borne the 15th of August 1662

Benjamine the son of Joseph Warren was borne the 8th of January 1670

Lydia the Daughter of Joseph Bumpas was Borne the 2cond Day of August 1669

Wybra the Daughter of Joseph Bumpas was Borne the fifteenth of May 1672

[p. 39] Mehittabell the Daughter of Willam Harlow was borne the 4th of October 1672

The 23th of February 1672 Mr John Howland senir of the Towne of Plymouth Deceased; hee was a Godly man and an ancient professor in the wayes of Christ hee lived untill hee attained above eighty yeares in the world, hee was one of the first Comers into this land and proved a usefull Instrument of Good in his place & was the last man that was left of those that Came over in the shipp Called the May Flower, that lived in Plymouth hee was with honor Intered att the Towne of Plymouth on the [*fift**] 25 of February 1672

Thomas Prence Esquire Govr: of the Jurisdiction of New Plymouth Died the 29th of March 1673 and was Interred the 8th of Aprill following; after hee had served God in the office of Govr: sixteen yeares or neare therunto hee finished his Course in the 73 yeare of his life; hee was a worthy Gentleman very pious; and very able for his office and faithfull in the Discharge therof studious of peace a welwiller to all that feared God; and a terrour to the wicked, his; Death was much lamented, and his body honorably buryed att Plymouth the Day and yeare abovemensioned

Nathaniel Bosworth the son of Nathaniel Bosworth Junir of Nantaskett was borne the 22cond of March 1672 att Plymouth

Elizabeth Bosworth the wife of Nathaniel : Bosworth Junir of Nantaskett Died the sixt Day of Aprill 1673 being the lords Day, shee was a vertuous young woman; her Death was much bewaild by her husband and Relations and other frinds; shee was honorably buried att Plymouth the 8th Day of Aprill 1673 which was the same Day that Govr Prence was Interred, about two houres before him;

* "fift" was crossed out, and "25" interlined, in the same hand and ink.

Samuell the son of Zachariah Eedey was born the 4th Day of June 1673

John Eedey the son of Obadiah Eedey was borne the 22cond of March 1669

Hasadiah Eedey the Daughter of Obadiah Eedey was borne the 10th Day of Aprill 1672

Jabez Howland the son of Jabez Howland, was borne on the 15th Day of November Anno: 1669

Bethya Howland the Daughter of Jabez : Howland was borne on the third Day of June 1674

John Howland the son of Jabez Howland was borne about the 15th Day of January 1672 and soone after Deceased within the same month;

Mistris Lydia Morton the wife of Nathaniel : Morton senir Deceased on the 23 of September 1673 after shee had lived with her said husband neare the space of 38 yeares after much Dollorus paine and sicknes shee ended her life with much peace and Comfort shee was a good woman and lived much Desired and Died much Lamented especially by her poor sorrowfull husband; shee was honorablely buried on the 25th of the said monthe att Plymouth

Mistris Elizabeth Warren an aged widdow aged above 90 yeares Deceased on the second* of October 1673 whoe haveing lived a Godly life Cam to her Grave as a shoke of Corn fully ripe shee was honoralby buried on the 24th * of October aforsaid

John Morton senir: of Middleberry Died on the third of October 1673 hee was a Godly man and was much lamented by sundry of the Inhabitants of that place It pleased God notwithstanding to put a period to his life after a longe sicknes and somtimes som [*worn off, or trimmed off in binding*]

[p. 40] Jabez Pratt the son of Jonathan Pratt, was borne on the first of November 1673

Melletiah the Daughter of Jonathan Pratt was borne the eleventh of December 1676

Nathaniel : Morton of Plymouth was married to Anne Temp[lar] † of Charlstown the 29th Day of Aprill Anno : Dom 1674

Judith the Daughter of serj Willam Harlow was born the 2cond of August 1676

Mary the Daughter of John Rickard the son of Gyles Rickard ; was borne the 27th of October 1677 :

(*To be continued*)

* Sic. The date of death probably should read "twenty second" instead of "second". — *Editor*.

† Anne Templar, widow of Richard. See Plym. Col. Wills, 4 : 1 : 17. — *Editor*.

PLYMOUTH COLONY WILLS AND INVENTORIES

(*Continued from page 64*)

[A Railing Paper by Humphrey Norton, Quaker]

[fol. 85] A Railing paper sent from Humphrey Norton one of those Comonly Called Quakers unto the Govr:

Ordered by the Court to bee Recorded as followeth

Tho: Prence thow whoe has bent thy hart to worke wickednes and with thy Tongue hast sett forth Deceite; Thow Imaginest mischeife upon thy bed and hatchest thy hatred in thy Cecrett Chamber the strength of Darknes is over thee and a malliciouse mouth hast thow opened against God and his Anointed and with thy tongue and lipps hast thou uttered pverse thinges; thow hast Slaundered the Innocent by railing lying and falce accusations and with thy barbarouse hart hast thou Caused theire bloud to bee shed thow hast through all these thinges broken and Transgressed the lawes and waies of God; and equitie is not before thy eyes the Curse Causles Cannot come upon thee; nor the vengance of god unjustly Cannot fetch the up; thow makest thy selfe merry with thy Cecrett Mallice; and when thow actes or exequtest it; Its in Dirision and Scorn; the Deadly Drinke of the Cup of Indignation thou can not escape and the greife and Cause of Gravell will not bee greater then thyne; since first I saw thee and before; thy falce and lying tongue hath ben forged against mee; I shall not writ nor speake this without ground; as thou hast Done by mee; but plainely shall p^r^sent thy Doeings before thy face; as firstly thou may remember thy former warrant was forged upon a filthy lye; and therin thou titlest mee an extravigant pson; thy 2^cond^, thy healping hand in causing mee to bee recorded for severall Errors; and like a shamles man would neither it acknowlidg nor Deney; thy third that John Rouse and I were Inordinate fellowes; and never in the least made it appeer wherin; thy fourth that I Intended within two Daies after the time thow spake it; to make a preachment as thou in thy Derision called it therawaies; thy fift thy promise that I should have the law and afterwards went about to Deney it; soe that as from thee I never had it yett; Thy sixt popish and Jesuiticall names; withall thy lyeing Slaund[ers] and falce asperssions Cast upon us from thy Clamorouse tongue thy seaventh Acting

Contrary to law equitie and Justice and Judg[*] according to the Evill of thyne owne hart all these art thow guilty of besides the Deneying of my paper which was presented to thee Containing pte of my Grounds of my Coming; thy eight thy striven[g] to Dash my words backe upon mee and to hinder mee to speake in the peo[p]le['s] hearing striveing what thow Could to staine the truth of God with thy enviouse tongue all which thinges is Charged upon thy head and as a peal of haile stones will pealt upon thy hart thou hast pverted Justice and true Judgment and hast Defrauded the poor and needy thow hast Caused to Defraud the righteouse owner of his goods and is heaping it up as upon a hill wherwith thow wilt purchase to thy selfe and others a feild of blood wherin to bury youer Dead; John Alden is to thee like unto a Packhorse wherupon thow layes thy beastly bagg Cursed are all they that have a hand therin; the Cry of vengance will psue thee Day and Night for other mens goods hard speeches unrighteouse actions which thou hast Done and spoken against others and us without and Contrary to the righteouse law; soe shall rest upon thee as frontletts upon thy head and as wee have suffered without law soe shalt thow perish without law if thou repent; not; The Days of thy wailing wilbee like unto that of a woman that murthers the fruite of her wombe; the Anguish and paine that will enter upon thy reignes wilbee like knawing wormes lodging betwixt thy hart and liver; when these thinges Comes upon thee and thy backe bowed Downe with paine in that Day and houre thou shalt know to thy greife that prophetts of the Lord God wee are and the God of vengance is our God;

Humphrey Norton

I have sent thee heer Inclosed A reply to C: Winters Deposition alsoe I have sent alreddy a true relation of pte of thy proceedings towards London; with a Coppy of the fines layed on and levied of the people of God; with a Coppy of thy late lawes

And thuse was this paper Superscribed
For the Gov[r]: of Plymoth Pattent This with Care And Speed

[Another Railing Paper]

[fol. 86] A Raileing paper sent from Humphrey Norton one of those Comonly Called Quakers Directed to John Alden Majestrate and ordered by the Court to bee Recorded As followeth

* Probably "ing" has been worn off here.

John Alden I have weighed thy waies and thou art like one fallen from thy first love; a tendernes once I Did see in thee and moderation to Act like a Sober man; which through evill Councell and selfe love thou art Drawne aside from; if there bee in thee any expectation of mercy Doe thow follow the example of Timothy Hatherley; and withdraw thy body forever appeering att that beastley bench; where the law of God is Cast behind youer backes; and from whence God hath withdrawne himselfe untill hee have ovrturned it and settled such as shall acte according to his law and Contrary to the will of man; alsoe account thou must for that wicked acte in sending forth thy warrant to force away other mens goods for keeping the law of Christ; againe lett the Cursed purse bee Cast out of thy house wherin it held the goods of other men least through it a moth enter into thy house and a mildew upon thy estate for in keeping of it and acteing for it thow art noe other then packhorse to Thomas Prence; which if in the Councell of God thow stand his p^{r}sent flattery to thee wilbee turned into enmitie and wrath against thee and then would thow see that thow art sett in the midest of a Companie thats like a hedge of vipers the best of them is not worthy to hew wood in the house of our god receive my Instruction into thy hart as oyle and Depart from amongst them; and thow wilt see that it is beter to live of thyne own like a poor wise man and att peace with God and his people then like a selfe Conceited foole puffed up with the prid of his hart becaus[e] hee hath Gotten the Name of a Majestrate as some of them is; in love this is written to Disharten thee in time before the evill Day overtake thee lett it bee soe received from thy frind

Humphrey Norton

Consider how Coruptly thow Dealt Concerning the paper p^{r}sented to Tho: Prence and thee and others
Road Iland this 16th 4th mo: 58:

And Superscribed thuse For John Alden Called Majestrate in Plymouth Pattent these Deliver

[Christopher Winter's Deposition]

The Deposition of Christopher Winter heer ordered to bee Recorded as followeth

Christopher Winter being Deposed saith that Humphrey Norton and hee being Reasoning Concerning the use of the

Scriptures the aforsaid Humphrey Norton said they were not for the Inlightening of man att the first nor yett afterwards for hee said that hee had the true light in him and hee never had any from the Scriptures att the first neither had hee any now;

Further hee said that Christ Inlightened every man that came into the world and hee said that hee that obeied this light it would save him and if hee obeied not this light it would Condemne him

Further hee alsoe Deneyed that Christ Jesus was man for hee said if hee were man how could hee Come into his Desiples when the Dores were fast Shutt; and likewise if he were man how could he fast forty Daies

Further I asked him whether God the father were in heaven and his son Christ Jesus att his Right hand; and hee said I Doe believe it thou and I Doe agree

Then I asked him where this heaven was that I might pray in faith according to the Comand; and hee said knowest thou not that heaven is within you and that youer bodyes are the Temples of the Holy Ghost and hee Delighteth to walke in his Temple;

Further I asked him whether I must pray unto the father which is in that heaven that is in him and in such as hee was and hee said that I would not hold unto the Scriptures

Further hee Deneyed that the body of Christ assended up into heaven or that wee should expect his body to Come from thence for hee said that hee was Come alreddy

Further I brought him many places of Scriptures to prove his assending into heaven and likewise his Coming againe to Judgment; his answare was Concerning Christ his comeing in the cloudes that it was the true light that was in every man; and when a man Did obey this light then Christ broke up the Cloudes and this was his Coming in the Cloudes; For if thow has not seen Christ Coming in the Cloudes thow hast never seen him yett; and for the rest of the Scriptures that I brought hee said thow talkest of men that are Dead and gone Did they not Speake as if Christ should then Come Did they ever see him Come noe; nor thow shalt never see him Come Neither; farther hee said that hee had the originall of the Scriptures in him; and I asked him whether hee had bine brought up in the Scooles of learning to learne the Toungues and hee said hee had that sperit that spake forth the Scriptures which was the originall

Further hee said that hee that obeyed the light that was in him might know a Reprobate if they see him;

[Reply to Christopher Winter's Deposition]

[fol. 87] A Reply to Christopher Winters Depositions as followeth

The pjured pson being Deposed saith that I Humphrey Norton being Reasoning with him said that the Scriptures were not fore the Inlightening of man which words were never soe spoken by mee; therfore this is falce; but this I say that those that say the Scriptures giveth light or Doth Inlighten men are blind as touching the light for then might they see Christopher Winter and the Rest of the wicked whoe are full of the Scriptures to bee fild with light yea and the Divell himselfe whoe is th[ei]re father would not bee without it if the Scriptures Could or Did afford it whose Dwelling and himselfe is in utter Darknes, yett hee Can gitt as much of them as hee Can Carry; and lett the Deposed or the Deposers answare mee this in plaine words what pte of the Scriptures the Divill can not gitt and Carry (and if soe) wherin Christopher Winter and they whoe say that the Scriptures giveth light Differs from the Divill and in what; Againe C W: saith hee asked mee whether God the father were in heaven and his son Christ Jesus att his right hand; and hee Confesseth that I said I Did beleive it and that hee and I Did agree; Compare this with his following passage wherin hee saith that I Deneyed that the body of Christ assended up into heaven and soe if the Deposers; if not Ignorant or wilfully blind as well as the Deposed would have received in such a Deposition as this; not seeing it to bee filthy Confusion att the best that Could bee made of it; Could I acknowlidge it of a truth that hee was in heaven and att Gods Right hand, and Deney him to bee assended I say how then Came hee there if not assended; and how that Christopher Winter Caught mee not in this Confusion if soe I spake Another expresse lye heer is in this passage viz: that Christs body should not bee expected to Come from thence viz: from heaven for this I say unto you of a truth that such as are not witnesses of Christs body must both expect it and receive it from heaven if ever they Injoy it soe farr ame from the Deneying of it; therfore this is [a lye*] falce; againe that my answare was Concerning Christ his Coming in the Cloudes that it was a true light that was in every man; and when a man obeyed this light then Christ broke up these Cloudes &c which words was never soe spoken by mee take the last line of this passage along with it viz: Did they ever see him Come noe; nor thow shalt never see him Come

* These two words were crossed out, in the record.

neither; heer is two wicked and abominab[le] lyes for they Did see him Come viz: the Desiples and thow alsoe must see him either to salvation or Condemnation; Goe yea Cursed,

againe that I said that hee that obeyed the light that was in him might know a reprobate if they see him; Answare if they see him is a falce adition; but wee bei[ng] speaking of such a thinge hee spake words to that purpose that hee knew not a rep[ro]bate; and then I told him hee was not fitt to preach for this I say that hee that knowe[s] not the elect from the reprobate knowes not light from Darknes truth from Erro[r] nor the blessed from the Cursed and such an one is C W:

Againe I say that the Deposed gave it upon oath that all that is mencioned in the paper is falcehood or untruth and the Depossers received it upon the fa[lce] account hee hath given and they have received it upon oath which is both aga[ins]t G[od] and Christ and the Scriptures and they that received it from him are p[takers] with him of the same sin and must ptake of the same Plague with him; as for Instance take [the] 2[cond] passage where I said that Christ Inlightened every man that Comes into the w[orld] and said that hee that obeyed this light it would save him; and if hee obeyed not th[is] light it would Condemne him; this I acknowlidge to bee truth and would have all men and wemen to try it and Compare with these Scriptures John . 1 . 9 and 3[d] from the 16th verse to the 22[cond]: & 8 . 12 . 1 John 15.

Frinds if the late lawes sett forth in youer Collonie were stated upon Christopher Winter you may safely title them winters lawes or the lyers lawes and lett them bee recorded for an example of Shame against both the Deposed and the Deposers with theire Names att it; and this reply with it from him that is a Witnesse against you and all the workes of Iniquitie with my Name att it;

Frinds againe all into whose hands this Comes you may take notice of the Injustice I had and the Impudence of those shameles men youer majestrates whoe would not suffer mee publickly to speake and testify against these thinges; together with theire proceedings against us in the audience and hearing of youer Court and Countrey; but Caused mee to bee pulled Downe and forced away to prison with out mittimus bill of Charge Coppy of theire lawes or Justice in the least; all which was Demaunded of them by mee Humphrey Norton;

Hold not thy peace oh God of my praise for the mouth of the wicked and the mouth of the Deceightfull are oppened against mee they have spoken against mee with a lying tongue Psal: 10 . 9 : 1 : 2 :

I Rejoysed in the Lord in the behalfe of Timothy Hatherley or any other harmles man whoe shall withdraw his hand from meddling with them in theire wicked and malliciouse workes ; much more if the life of God in him or any other were Raised up to Testify against them ; whose workes and all they Doe must Come into Contempt

H Norton

The Court Duely Weying and Considering the p^r^mises viz: the horible Railing Contempt and pniciouse Wickednesse expressed by the said Norton Contained in these papers together with other like Carriages of this Incendiary of Mischeife ; att other times expressed both against foundation truthes of God against his holy word the lawes of the Collonie those in Authoritie and others ; Ordered that the aforsaid papers should bee Recorded ; And forthwith Issued out Warrants in his highnes Name to the Constables of the severall Townes of this Jurisdiction Respectively to Apprehend the body of the said Humphrey Norton that soe hee may bee Comitted to Ward and to Receive punishment according to his Demerritts

[END OF VOLUME II OF ORIGINAL RECORDS. — EDITOR.]

MIDDLEBOROUGH, MASS., VITAL RECORDS

TRANSCRIBED BY THE EDITOR

(*Continued from Vol. XVII, page 22*)

[p. 24] February : 6 : 1745/6 Then Josiah Richmond and Lydia Crocker both of the Town of Middleborough was married by me Benjamin Ruggles

February : 19 : 1745/6 Then Joseph Peirce of Middleborough and Phebe Smith of Taunton was Married by me Benjamin Ruggles

April : 17 : 1746 : Aaron Seekins and Hannah Wescoat Junr both of Middleborough was Married by me Benjamin Ruggles

May : 8 : 1746 Then Jacob Caswell of Middleboro & Deliverance Caswell of Taunton was Married by me Benjamin Ruggles

May : 29 : 1746 : Caleb Jenney of Dartmouth and Silence House of Middleborough was Married by me Benjamin Ruggles

June : 20 : 1746 : Samuel Allin Junr & Betty Willis both of Middleborough was Married by me Benjamin Ruggles·

September : 18 : 1746: Joseph Phinney of Middleborough & Phebe Cole of Berkley was married by me Benjamin Ruggles

September : 23 : 1746: Then Ithamar Hoskins of Middleborough and Mercy Fry Junr of Taunton was married by me Benjamin Ruggles

January : 27 : 1746/7: John Macumber & Elisabeth Phinney both of Middleborough was married by me Benjamin Ruggles

February : 12 : 1746/7: Thomas Richmond of Middleborough and Mary Dodson of Freetown was Married by me Benjamin Ruggles

March : 5 : 1746/7: John Richmond Junr & Hannah Paddake both of Middleborough was Married by me Benjamin Ruggles

Plymouth Sc: This may Certifye that Samuel Thacher & Deborah Bennet, both of Middleborough, were Joined in Marriage according to Law, on the 24th of September Instant, By me Peter Oliver Just: of Peace Middleborough September : 25th : 1747.

Plimouth Sc: This may Certifye that Prince, a negro man & Servant to Capt Ebenezer Morton of Middleborough, and Jenny, a negro woman & Servant to Capt Peter Bennet of Middleborough, both belonging to Middleborough, were Joined in Marriage according to Law on Thursday the first Day of october Instant, by me Peter Oliver Just. of Peace Middleborough October : 2 . 1747

[p. 25] Plimouth Sc: Middleborough January 22^d^ 1747. This may certifye that on the 26th Day of november last past, William Winslow & Patience Cob, both of Middleborough aforesaid, were Joined in Marriage according to Law by me the Subscriber: And that on the 21st Day of January instant, John Morton & Elizabeth Bennet, both of Said Middleborough, were also Joined in Marriage according to Law by me the Subscriber Peter Oliver Just. of Peace

June the 6th 1744 Then was Married at Middleborough Eben^r^ Vaughan and Rachel Soul Both of Middleborough by me Benj^a^ White Justice of Peace

August the 21st : 1744 Then was Married at Middleborough Joshua Sprague & Elizabeth Keen both of Abington In the County of Plimouth p^r^ me Benj. White Justice of Peace

Novemb^r^ 8th : 1744: Then was Married at Middleborough James Keith & Lydia Perkins both of Bridgewater By me Benj^a^ White Justice of Peace

Decemb^r^ 27th : 1744 Then was Married at Middleborough Jabez fuller & Hannah Pratt both of Middleborough by me Benj^a^ White Justice of Peace

January 14th : 1744 Then was Married at Middleborough Manassah Clap & Rebekah Cushman both of Middleborough by me Benj^a^ White Justice of Peace

January 24th : 1744: Then was Married at Middleborough Jeremiah Howland and Betty Vaughan both of Middleborough by me Benj^a^ White Justice of Peace

March 4th : 1744 Then was Married at Middleborough Noah Allden & Joanna Vaughan both of S^{d} Middleborough by me Benj^{a} White Justice of Peace

June 4th : 1745 Then was Married at Middleborough George White of Raynham & Hannah Bryant of Middleborough P^{r} me Benj^{a} White Justice of Peace

october 15th : 1745 Then was Married at Middleborough Benj^{a} White Junr & Betty Prat both of S^{d} Town by me Benj^{a} White Justice of Peace

october 17th : 1745 Then was Married at Middleborough Jabez Soul of Hallifax & Abigail Bennet of Middleborough by me Benj^{a} White Justice of Peace

January 23^{d} : 1745 Then was Married at Middleborough Benj^{a} Shelley Junr of Raynham & Lydia Wood Junr of Middleborough by me Benj^{a} White Justice of Peace

february 5th : 1745 Then was married at Middleborough Seth Simmons of Freetown and Priscilla Booth of Middleborough by me Benj^{a} White Justice of Peace

[p. 26] March 27th : 1746 Then was Married at Middleborough Joseph Leonard Junr & Ruth White both of Middleborough by me Benj^{a} White Justice of Peace

March 30th : 1746. Then was Married at Middleborough Sam^{ll} Rickard & Sarah Joslin both of Pembrook by me Benj^{a} White Justice of Peace

April 4th : 1746 Then was Married at Middleborough Elisha Vaughan & Esther Tinkham both of S^{d} Town by me Benj^{a} White Justice of Peace

June 17th : 1746 Then was Married at Middleborough Jacob Green & Sarah Jackson both of S^{d} Town by me Benj^{a} White Justice of Peace

August 21st : 1746 Then was Married at Middleborough Nathan Trewant of Middleborough and Leah Hoskins of Taunton by me Benj^{a} White Justice of Peace

Decem^{r} 12th : 1746 Then was Married at Middleborough Jedidiah Holmes and Ruth Barrows both of S^{d} Town by me Benj^{a} White Justice of Peace

Decemb^{r} 25th : 1746 Then was Married at Middleborough Uriah Samson & Ann White both of S^{d} Town by me Benj^{a} White Justice of Peace

December 26th : 1746 Then was Married at Middleborough Israel Felix an Indian man of S^{d} Town, and Deliverance Cowet of Barnstable, an Indian woman by me Benj^{a} White Justice of Peace

January 8th : 1746 Then was Married at Middleborough Zebulun Thayer of Brantrey & Sarah Bennet of Middleborough by me Benj^{a} White Justice of Peace

January 22nd : 1746 Then was Married at Middleborough Jonath^{n} Snow & Ruth Bennet both of S^{d} Town by me Benj^{a} White Justice of Peace

Novembr 12th : 1747. Then was Married at Middleborough Joshua White & Abthier Bryant both of Sd Town by me Benja White Justice of Peace

Novembr 26th 1747 Then was Married att Middleborough James Fance & Abigial Rickord Both of Sd Town by me Silvanus Conant

December 3d 1747 Then was married Thomas Paddock : and Hannah Thomas Both of Middleborough by Me Silvanus Conant

febr 4th : 1747 Then was Married at Middleborough James Leboron of Sd Town and Hannah Turner of Rochester by me Silvanus Conant

febr 4th 1747 Then was Married at Middleborough Thomas Reding and Sarah Smith both of sd Town by me Silvanus Conant

[p. 27] Joseph Waterman the Son of Joseph Waterman by Patience his wife Deceased November the : 19th : 1747 . In the Second year of his age

Elisabeth Tomson the Daughter of Jacob Tomson by Elisabeth his wife Deceased December : 4th : 1747 : In the Seventh year of her age

Samuel Lyon the Son of Jedidiah Lyon by Mary his wife Deceased January : 4th : 1747. Aged Three years, Three months & Three Days.

Solomon Severy the Son of Thomas Severy by Mary his wife Deceased December : 14th . 1747. In the Sixth year of his age.

Lydia Tinkham the Daughter of Samuel Tinkham Junr (Deceasd) by Mary his wife Deceased December the : 24th : 1747. In the Seventh year of her age

John Smith the Son of John Smith by Mary his Wife Deceasd December the : 13th 1748 : in the 46th year of his age

Mehetabel Barrows the Daughter of Silvanus Barrows by Ruth his Wife Deceasd December : 31st 1748 in the Eigheth year of her Age

Lydia Barrows the Daughter of Silvanus Barrows by Ruth his Wife Deceased January 7th 1748/9 in the Sixth year of her age

Miriam Cob the Wife of Garshom Cobb Jur Deceasd January ye 31st 1749.

Sarah Soul the Daughter of James Soul by Deborah his Wife Deceased December : 23rd 1747.

Lydia Alden the wife of John Alden Deceasd aprel the : 6th 1749.

Martha Wood the Daughter of Nathaniel wood by mary his wife Dceased Novm the 1st 1753. in in the Seventh year of her age

Elisabeth Wood the Daughter of Nathaniel Wood by mary his wife Deceased Novm the 9th in the third year of her age

Hannah Leonard the Daughter of Joseph Leonard by Ruth his wife Deceased December the 5th 1751.

Benajah Leonard the Son of Joseph Leonard by Ruth his wife Deceased December the 8th 1751.

Mercy morton Daughter of Ebenezer Morton By Sarah his Wife Deceased Febuary the 28th 1755

Thankfull Thomas Daughter of Ebenezer Thomas by Anna his wife Deceased february the 15th 1754

Seth Tinkham Deceased February the 9th 1751 & In the 47 year of his age

Manasseh Clap Deceased March the 17th 1757 and in The 32d year of her * age

mary Thacher Daughter of Samuel Thacher by Deborah his wife Deceased august [†] in the 2d year of her age 1749

[p. 28] April : 22 : 1747 Then Josiah Jones & Naomi Peirce Junr both of Middleborough was Marryed by me the Subscriber Benj. Ruggles

May : 22 : 1747 : Then Alexander Pegley of Dighton & Mary wascoat of Middleborough was Marryed by me Benj: Ruggles

July 30 : 1747 : Then Gershom Richmond & Phebe Richmond both of Middleborough was marryed by me Benj: Ruggles

June : 16 : 1747 Then John Parris of Middleborough & Lydia Samson of Taunton was Marryed by me Benj: Ruggles

December : 3d : 1747 Then Benjamin Hacket & mercy Richmond both of Middleborough was marryed by me Benj: Ruggles

December : 3d : 1747 Then Nathan Prat & Margaret Samson both of Middleborough was Marryed by me the Subscriber Benj: Ruggles

febr 18th 1747 Then Robert Mackfun and Jemeima Samson both of Middleborough was married by me Silvanus Conant

March 3d 1747 Joseph Barden Jur and Marcy Vaughan both of Middleborough was marryed by me Silvanus Conant

Plimouth Ss Middleborough april : 26 1748 Moses Sturtivant junr and Elisabeth Thomas Both of Said Middleborough were this Day Joined in Marriage according to Law by me Peter Oliver Just: of Peace

This May Certyfie that on the 11th Instant mr Abishai Washburn of Bridgwater and Mrs Hannah Morton of Middleborough were joined in Marriage according to Law by me Peter Oliver Just ad Peace Middleboro : August 15th 1748

December the 19th 1748 Ephraim Bryant of Plimpton and Abigail Samson of Middleborough : Were Married by me Silvanus Connat

To the Town Clerk of Middleborough

This Certifies that Nathanael Southworth Junr and Susanna Smith both of Middleborough where this Day Joined in Marriage According to Law pr me Peter Oliver Just: ad Pac : Middleborough February 16th 1748

febr 23/1748. John Labaron and Mary Raymond Both of Middleborough Where Married by Silvanus Connant

* Sic.

† Space was left for the day of the month.

febr 23 : 1748. SamBo (Servt to Madm Thacher) of Middleboro : and Martha Chummuch of Scituate Were marriad by Silvanus Connant

[p. 29] November : 24 : 1748 : Then David Shaw and Abigail Richmond both of Middleborough was Marryed by me Benjm Ruggles

febaruary : 21 : 1748:/9 Then Willam Macfall and Elizabeth Dugglass both of Middleborough was Married by the Subscriber Benjm Ruggles

March the 2nd 1748/9 : then Capt Josiah Winslow of Freetown and Mrs hannah booth of Middleborough was marryed by me Benjm Ruggles

June the 8th 1749 Ebenr Sproutt and Bathshabe Wood both of Middleborough where Married by Silvanus Connant

august 3rd 1749 Giddion Hacket and Betty Samson both of Middleborough Were Married by me Silvanus Connant

September 19th 1749 Nathan Fuller* of hallifax and Mary Parlow of Middleborough were Married by me Silvanus Conant

October 12th 1749 James Shaw and Lois Thomas Both of Middleborough were Married by me Silvanus Conant

Plimouth Ss: This May certifie that Ichabod Morton of Sandwich and Deborah Morton of Middleborough Ware joined in marriage according to Law on the Day of the Date hearof by me Peter Oliver Justs ad Pacs Middleborough October 26th 1749.

November 16th 1749 Joseph Bates Junr and Eunice Tinkham both of Middleborough Ware Married by me Silvanus Conant

December 7th 1749 Nelson finney and Martha Simmons both of Middleborough Ware Married by Silvanus Conant

Decemr 20th 1749 Jacob Lazell of Middleborough and Elizabeth Devenport of Bridgwater Ware Married by me Silvanus Conant

Christopher Thresher of Taunton and Thankfull Thomas of Middleborough Were Marryed May 14th 1747 by me Thomas Weld

Abraham Barden of Middleborough and Susanna Durfey of Taunton Were Marryed September : 22nd 1748 : by me Thomas Weld

Jedediah Thomas Junr of Middleborough and Keziah Churchell of Said Town were marryed December 28th 1749 by me Thomas Weld

May 22nd : 1749 : Then I Marryed Nathan Holloway Jur and and Sarah Booth both of the Town of Middleborough Benjm Ruggles

June 2nd 1749 : then I Marryed Accro Mr Mr Samuel Williams Negro Man of Taunton : and Pegg Capt Nathaniel Southworths woman of Middleborough Benjm Ruggles

[p. 30] September : 1st 1749 Then was marryed by me the Subsirber Elnathan Wood Junr and Susannah Horskins both both of the Town of Middleborough by Benjm Ruggles

September : 12th 1749 Then was marryed by me Joseph Allen and Hannah Willis both both of the Town of Middleborough Benjm Ruggles

* "Conant" was first written, evidently by mistake; but it was crossed out, and "Fuller" written after it, in the same hand and ink.

November : 13th 1749 Then Was Marryed by me George* Willimson and Deborah Clark both of the Town of Middleborough pr Benjm Ruggles

November : 16th 1749 : Then was marryed by me Beniamain Dean of Taunton and marcy Barrows of Middleborough Benjm Ruggles

December : 21st 1749 : Then Was marryed by me Mr William Southworth : and mrs Bathsheba Smith both of Middleboro : pr Benjm Ruggles

This May Certifie that on the 19th Day of April : 1750. Lemuel Thomas and Mehitable Weston both of Said Middleborough were joined in marriage at Said Place by me Peter Oliver Jst ad Pace

January 17 : 1749 . Benjamin Phillips of Easton and Hannah Cox of Middleborough were Married by Silvanus Conant

April ye 12 : 1750. John Soul and Mary Leach both of Middleborough were Married by Silvanus Conant

May 10 : 1750 Elkanah Elms & Sarah Lazell both of Middleboro were Married ℣ Silvanus Conant

May 23rd 1750. Samuel Thurber of the Town of Warren and Alice Wood of Middleborough Ware Married pr Silvanus Conant

These are to Inform you as Town Clerk of Middleborough that on the 31st of august 1749 : I did according to Law joyn in wedlock Seth Heskel of Rochester in ye County of Plimouth and Abia Nelson of Middleborough Aforsd which marriage was Consumated in that Part of Said Middleborough which lies in the parish of which I am the Minister From your freind and Humble Sert Thos West Darthmouth Novr 20th 1749 :

[p. 31] July : 12th 1750 John Alden and Rebeckah Weston both of Middleborough Were Married by Silvanus Conant

July : 26 : 1750 George Shaw Jur and Marcy Thomas both of Middleborough were marred by Silvanus Conant

August 30th 1750. Samuel Leach Jur of Bridgwater and Phebe Rickard of Middleborough were married by Silvanus Conant

November 22 : 1750. Joseph Eaton and Hannah Crosman both of Middleborough were marriad by Silvanus Conant

December 13 : 1750. Noah Benson of Middleborough and Abigail Turner of Rochester were marred by me Silvanus Conant

December 13. 1750 Consider Samson of Middleborough and Rachel Randol of Rochester were married by Silvanus Conant

December 28 : 1750 Nathanil Fry of Taunton and Lydia Caswell of Middleborough were married by Silvanus Conant

January 3th 1750. Joseph Cole of Plimton and Ruth Samson of Middleborough were married by Silvanus Conant

March : 13 : 1749/50 then was marryed by me Joshua Dean of Taunton and Keziah Paddock of Middleborough Benja Ruggles

* "Joseph" was first written, evidently by mistake ; but it was crossed out, and "George" written after it, in the same hand and ink.

July 4th 1750 then was Marryed by me George Smith and Hannah Hoar both of the Town of Middleborough Benja Ruggles

July 5th 1750 then was Marryed by me Giddion Brayley and Patince Mayo both of the Town of Middleborough Benja Ruggles

October 11th 1750 then Was Marryed by me Jonathan Reed and Joanna Tinkham both of the town of Middleborough. Benja Ruggles

October 25th 1750 then was Marryed by me Job Howland and Jamima Booth both of Middleborough Benja Ruggles

November 6th 1750 then was marryed by me Decon Edward Richmond of Taunton and mrs Elizabeth Samson of Middleborough Benja Ruggles

Novmr 15th 1750 then was marryed by me Christipher Richmond and and Susanna Barden both of Middleborough Benja Ruggles

January 1st 1750/51 : then was marryed by me the Subscriber : Israel Dean of Taunton Called the third : and Hannah Barrows of Middleborough Benja Ruggles

Plimouth Ss: Middleborough May 2 : 1751 To the Town Clerk of Middleborough This Certifyes that Obed Edson of Bridgwater and Martha Thomas of Middleborough both of Said County were joined in Marriage on the Day of the above Date by me Peter Oliver Just ad Pacs

March . 14th 1750 Seth Barrows of Plimton and Mary Lovell of Middleboro : were married by Silvanus Conant

[p. 32] April 11th 1751 William Cushman and Priscilla Cobb both of Middleborough were married by Silvanus Conant

April 29th 1751 Ichabod Cushman and Patience Mackfun both of middleborough were married by Silvanus Conant

March : 28th 1750/51 I marryed Daniel Thrasher and Abiah Richmond both of the Town of Middleborough Benj Ruggles

april 4th 1751 Then I marryed Jonathan Cobb Jur and Patince Benson both of the Town of middleborough Benja Ruggles

April 25th 1751 I marryed Peter Vaughan and Joanna Barrows both of Middleborough pr Benja Ruggles

May 3 1751 Then I marryed Robert Richmond of Taunton & Hannah Ramsden of middleborough pr Benja Ruggles

May 16th 1751 Then I marryed The Rvnd Nathan Stone of Southborough & mrs mary Thacher Jur of middleborough pr Benja Ruggles

May 23rd 1751 I marryed Jonathan Washburn Jur of Bridgwater and Judah Wood of middleborough Jr Benja Ruggles

March 22nd 1750/51. Jacob Bennet and Hope Nelson both of Middleborough were Married at Middleborough Aforsd according to Law ℘r Thomas West

Plimo Ss: Middleborough September : 26 . 1751 To the Town Clerk of Middleborough This Certifies that Mr Elkanah Leonard Junr and Mrs Deliverance Smith; both of Middleborough afforsd were joined in Marriage on the Day of the above Date by me Peter Oliver Justis ad Peas

Plimouth Ss: Middleborough Decm^{r} 12th 1751 This Certifies that Garshom Cob jun^{r} & Elisabeth Corbet both of Middleborough, were joined in Marriage on the Day of the above Date by me Peter Oliver Justis ad Pacs

Decem^{r} 12th 1754. Joseph Booth to Sarah Horskins both of Middleborough were marred by Thomas West

[p. 33] Easter Samson the Daughter of Obadiah Samson by Mary his Wife Was born November the 12th 1749.

Sarah Simmons the Daughter of David Simmons by Priscilla his Wife Was born April 12th 1749

Lydia Severy the Daughter of John Severy Ju^{r} by Mary his Wife was born february 27th 1747.

Hulday Samson the Daughter of Nathanil Samson by Martha his Wife was born January the 23rd 1749.

Mary Sproutt the Daughter of Eben^{r} Sproutt by Bathsheba his Wife Was born May the 1st 1750.

Samuel Southworth the Son of Samuel Southworth by Eisabeth his Wife was born July the: 9th 1750.

Hephzibah Samson the Daughter of Benjamin Samson by mary his Wife was born August y^{e}: 21st 1749.

John Soul the Son of James Soul by Deborah his Wife Was born December 23rd 1748.

Deborah Soul the Daughter of James Soul by Deborah his Wife was born: may: 27th 1750.

Lurayna Southworth the Daughter of Ebenezer Southworth by Elizabeth his Wife was born January the 8th 1749

Mary Southworth the Daughter of Nathaniel Southworth Ju^{r} by Susanna his Wife Was born June the: 6th 1749:

Gideon Southworth the Son of Gideon Southworth by Rebeckah his wife was born May the 16th 1750.

Thomas Severy the Son of thomas Severy by Mary his wife was born april the 6th 1751.

Ebenezer Sproutt the Son of Ebenezer Sproutt by Bathsheba his Wife was born february the: 9th 1752.

Priscilla Simmons the Daughter of David Simmons by Priscilla his wife was born December the 21st 1751.

(*To be continued*)

PLYMOUTH COLONY DEEDS

(*Continued from page 40*)

[THOMAS BURGE, SR., TO EZRA PERRY]

[p. 122] 1663 Prence Govr:

The 10th of July 1663

Memorand: That Thomas Burge sen^r of the Towne of Sandwich in in the Jurisdiction of Plymouth in New England plantor Doth acknowlidg that for and in Consideration of a valluable sume; to him alreddy payed by his son in law Named Esra Perrey of the Towne aforsaid in the Jurisdiction aforsaid plantor; hee hath bargained and sold enfeofed and Confeirmed and by these p^rsents Doth bargaine allianate sell enfeof and Confeirme unto the said Esra Perrey the one halfe of a Certaine tract of land lying and being att a place Called Mannomett in the Jurisdiction aforsaid; which said Tract of land was purchased by Captaine Standish by the appointment of the Court of Josias of Nausett an Indian Sachem; in the behalfe of the said Thomas Burge as appeers by a Deed bearing Date the third Day of march Ann^o Dom 1652 and is bounded to the southwards by the marked tree by the marsh and from that tree to a fresh brooke and from the said tree to another marked tree to the Nortwards; which said tree stands to the Eastward of the said Esra Perreys house; to have and to hold the one halfe of the whole said Tract of land both upland and meddow with all and singulare the appurtenances belonging therunto; unto the said Esra Perrey to him and his heires and assignes for ever; The said halfe of the said Tract of land; both upland and meddow: soe bounded as aforsaid with all the said Thomas Burge his right and Interest therin or belonging therunto or to any pte or pcell of the said halfe share; with all and singulare the appurtenances belonging therunto; to appertaine to the onely proper use and behoofe of the said Esra Perrey hee his heires and assignes for ever;

[QUACHATASETT — ALDEN — STANDISH]

A writing appointed to bee Recorded

Know all men that I Quachatasett have barganed and sold unto m^r John Aldin one tract of upland lying on that side of Mannomet River next unto Sandwich; the bounds of which is from the lands of Esra Perrey unto a little Creeke alongst the River and for breadth unto the topp of the hills which lye in a Ridge; with libertie for timber for building; alsoe with libertie for feed for Cattle; with libertie of basse or oysters for his use; alsoe a certaine tract of meddow lying on Mannomett side of the River; adjoyning to the meddow of Richard Bourne for the uper bound with all the mersh lying Round a little necke together with the said necke and soe unto a point; wheron stands some Dead burnt trees; for all which pcell of land and meddow above expressed the said John Aldin is to pay the sume of fourteen pounds in Cloth unto Quachatase[tt] in Convenient time before winter; unto which the said Quachatasett hath sett to his hand this 27th of the fift month 1661

Witnes Quachataset his marke
Sepitt his marke
Scippague his marke;

the above said tract of land was bought by m^{r} Aldin by order of Court for Josias Standish and is by the Court Confeirmed to him

[ARTHUR HOWLAND, SR., TO JOHN WALKER]

[p. 123] 1663 Prence Govr:

A Deed appointed to bee Recorded

Know all men by these p^{r}sents that I Arther Howland $seni^{r}$ of the towne of Marshfeild in the Jurisdiction of New Plymouth in New England; for and in Consideration of moneyes payed for my use in old England by my wife Margarett Howland to the sume of seaventeen pounds fourteen shillings and ten pence which said sume was given by the above said Margarett in the time of her widdowhood unto her son John Walker; for the satisfaction of which said sume of seaventeen pounds fourteen shillings and ten pence abovesaid; I the said Arther Howland Doe by these p^{r}sents graunt and sett over unto the said John Walker; his heires and exequitors for ever twenty acrees of upland bounded for breadth from the land of Willam Foard $seni^{r}$ to a Rocke and abuting on the south River and for length on on a Northwest line into the woods as alsoe the house and land which John Walker now lives in with the land Improved buting on the aforsaid River; also from the easterly Corner of the Improved land aforsaid on a straight line unto the Rocke above said; which includes a smale valley of low land; alsoe a pcell of marsh meddow lying alonge the south River Containing three or foure acrees bee it more or lesse; bounded by a brooke over which the old way went to Scittuate; and on the other end a creeke next the Improved meddow lands of the above said Arther Howland; all which pcells of upland and meddow with the house and Improved land with all and singulare the appurtenances and privilidges and emunities therunto belonging; I the said Arther Howland Doe sett over and allianate; from my selfe and heires for ever unto the above said John Walker and his heires and exequitors To have and to hold for ever In Witnes wherof I have sett to my hand and seale this nineteenth Day of May in the yeare of our Lord God 1663

Witnes ꝑ me Arther Howland

John Aldin and a (seale);

Willam Foard seni^r:

[THOMAS BURGE, SR., TO LT. JOSIAS STANDISH]

[p. 124] 1663 Prence Govr:

The 10th of July 1663

Memorand: That Thomas Burge seni^r: of Sandwich in the Jurisdiction of Plymouth in New England in America plantor Doth acknowlidge that for and in Consideration of a Considerable sume to him alreddy payed by Leiftenant Josias Standish of Sandwich aforsaid in the Jurisdic[tion] aforsaid hee hath freely and absolutely bargained and sold enfeofed and Confeirmed; and by these p^rsents Doth bargaine allianate sell enfeofe and Confeirme unto the said Leiftenant Standish one quarter pte or one pte of foure of a Certaine Tract of land lying and being att a place Called Mannomett in the Jurisdiction aforsaid which said Tract of land was purchased by Captaine Standish by the appointment of the Court of Josias of Nausett an Indian Sachem; in the behalfe of the said Thomas Burge; as appeers by a Deed bearing Date the third Day of March ann^o Dom: 1652 which said Tract is bounded to the Southward by the marked tree by the marsh; and from that tree to a ffresh brooke; and from the said tree to another marked tree Northward; which said tree stands to the eastward of Esra Perreys house; To have and to hold the one quarter pte or one pte of four of the said whole tract of land both upland and meddow with all and singulare the appurtenances belonging therunto unto the said Leift: Josias Standish to him and his heires and assignes for ever; The said quarter pte or one pte of foure of the said tract of land bounded as aforsaid both of the upland & meddow with all the said Thomas Burge his Right title and

Interst of and into the said quarter pte of the said tract of land; with all and singulare the appurtenances belonging therunto; To appertaine to the onely proper use and behoofe of the said Leift: Josias Standish to him and his heires and assignes for ever unto the onely proper use and behoof of him the said Leift: Josiah Standish to him and his heires and assignes for ever;

[On the lower part of this page the recording clerk began to enter a deed of gift from Thomas Burge, Sr., to his son Joseph Burge, dated 10 July, 1663; but he made an error in copying, and crossed off the incomplete record, starting anew at the top of page 125. — *Editor.*]

[Thomas Burge, Sr., to Son Joseph]

[p. 125] 1663 Prence Govr:
The 10th of July 1663
Memorand: That Thomas Burge seni^r^ of the Towne of Sandwich in the Jurisdiction of Plymouth in New England plantor Doth acknowlidge that hee hath & Doth by these p^r^sents fully freely and absolutely give graunt allianate make over enfeofe and Confeirme unto his son Josepth Burge one quarter pte or one pte of foure of all that whole tract of land which Captaine Standish bought for him, by the appointment of the Court; of Josias the Indian Sachem of Nausett which said tract is lying and being att Mannomett in the Jurisdiction aforsaid; and is bounded as in the Deed of the sale therof bearing Date the third Day of March 1652 is expressed; To have and to hold all the said Thomas Burge his Right and title of and into one quarter pte or one pte of four of the said land; unto the said Josepth Burge to him and his heires and assignes for ever; the said one quarter pte or one pte of four of the aforsaid whole tract of land both upland and meddow with all and singular the appurtenances belonging therunto; and to appertaine unto the onely proper use and behoofe of him the said Josepth Burge to him and his heires and assignes for ever;

[Edward Gray to Constant Southworth, Treasurer]

[p. 126] 1663 Prence Govr:
A Deed Appointed to bee Recorded
Know all men by these p^r^sents that I Edward Gray of the towne of Plymouth in the Jurisdiction of Plymouth in New England in America plantor Doe acknowlidge that for and in

Consideration of the sume of ninety and five pounds to mee in hand payed by m^r Constant Southworth Treasurer in the behalfe of the Collonie of Plymouth aforsaid; wherwith I Doe acknowlidge my selfe satisfyed Contented and fully payed; and therof and of every pte and pcell therof Doe exownarte acquite and Discharge; the said Constant Southworth his heires exequitors and adminnestrators feirmly by these p^rsents; have fully freely and absolutely bargained allianated and sold enfeofed and Confeirmed and by these p^rsents Doe bargaine allianate sell enfeofe and Confeirme unto the said Constant Southworth all that my house and land att a place comonly Called and knowne by the name of Plaindealing in the Township of Plymouth aforsaid; Containing three lotts or threescore acrees bee it more or lesse; viz: all that tract or pcell of land which I bought of my fatherinlaw m^r John Winslow of Boston; with all additions or Inlargments any way belonging therunto; with a pcell of meddow att Joanes River belonging to the aforsaid land; with a pcell of land I bought of Stephen Bryant; lying att blacke brooke next adjoyning to the aforsaid; viz: all the land I formerly bought of Stephen Bryant aforsaid; To have and to hold the aforsaid house and land outhouses ffences orchyards Barnes meddowes woods waters and all other appurtenances; bounded on the one side with the land of the aforsaid Stephen Bryant and on the other side with the land of Samuell Kinge with all the appurtenances and privilidges belonging therunto or unto any pte or pcell therof with all the additions or enlargements belonging to the aforsaid land and all and singulare the appurtenances belonging therunto; with all my Right title and Interest of and Into the same or any pte or pcell therof unto the said Constant Southworth in the behalfe of the Collonie of New Plymouth To his and theire heires and assignes for ever To bee holden as of his Maties his manor of East greenwich in the Countey of Kent in free and Comon Scoccage and not in Capite nor by Knights service nor by the Rents and services therof and therby Due and of Right with warrantice against all people what soever that by my Right might claime any Right or Interest therin whatsoever; in Witnes wherof I have Subscribed my hand and affixed my seale this seaventh Day of June Ann^o: Dom: 1662 one Thousand six hundred sixty and two;

Signed Sealed and Delivered in the p^rsence of
Josias Winslow Junr:
Thomas Southworth

The marke of
Edward Gray & (his seale)

Mary the wife of Edward Gray Consented to the sale of what her husband hath sold within this Deed expressed; before us this seaventh of the 4th month * 1662

William Collyar
John Aldin Assistants,

[Thomas Robinson to John Otis]

[p. 127] 1663 Prence Govr:

A Deed appointed to bee Recorded

To all people to whom these prsents shall come Thomas Robinson of Scittuate in the Jurisdiction of New Plymouth in New England in America yeoman sendeth greet; Know yea that I the aforsaid Thomas Robinson for and in Consideration of a sufficient sume of money in full satisfaction to mee in hand by John Ottees of Hingham in the goverment of the Massachusetts yeoman; wherwith I Doe acknowlidge my selfe sufficiently satisfyed Contented and payed; and therof and every pte and pcell therof Doe exownarate acquitt and Discharge the said John Ottees himselfe his heires exequitors adminnestrators and assignes for ever by these prsents; have freely and absolutely bargained and sold enfeofed and Confeirmed; and by these prsents Doe bargaine sell enfeofe and Confeirme from mee the aforsaid Thomas Robinson and my heires exequitors adminnestrators and assignes To him the said John Ottees and his heires exequitors adminnestrators and assignes for ever all that my now Dwelling house barne and all my out houses and buildinges together with twenty acrees of upland more or lesse and all my meddow therunto adjoyning; which hous and land are lying and being in Scittuate aforsaid; the upland aforsaid being bounded towards the southeast to the meddow land aforsaid towards the southwest to the aforsaid meddow in pte and pte of it to the meddow of Walter Woodward towards the Northwest to the upland of the said Walter Woodward towards the North east to the highway and pte of it to the meddow of Thomas Clapp; the meddow land aforsaid is all that tract or prcell of meddow lying between the meddow of Thomas Clapp aforsaid and Walter Woodward aforsaid and is bounded towards the Northeast to the meddow of Thomas Clapp aforsaid as now the ffence stands bounded towards the southeast and southwest to the first herring brooke; towards the Northwest to the meddow of Walter Woodward aforsaid; as the fence now stands between them att the end of the said meddow; and is bounded by the side of it towards the northwest

* The fourth month was June, in old style dating.

and northeast to the twenty acrees of upland aforsaid ; To have and to hold the aforsaid Dwelling house and other housing together with the said twenty acrees of upland and the aforsaid pcell of marsh with all the privilidges and appurtenances therunto belonging or any way appertaining either to all or any pte or pcell ; therof and all my Right title or Interest in the p^r^mises or any pte or pcell therof from mee the aforsaid Thomas Robinson and my heires exequitors Adminnestrators and assignes To him the said John Ottees and his heires exequitors adminnestrators and assignes for ever To bee holden according to the mannor of East greenwich in the Countey of Kent in free and comon Soccage and not in Capite nor by Knightes service nor by the Rents and services therof and therby Due and of Right accustomed and Warranting the sale therof against all people whatsoever from by or under mee the said Thomas Robinson or by my Right or title claiming any Right title or Interest in the p^r^mises or any pte or pcell therof And I the said Thomas Robinson Doe by these p^r^sents Covenant promise and graunt that Mary Robinson my wife shall surrender up her Right in the p^r^mises before a majestrate according to order and law in that Case provided And I the said Thomas Robinson Doe heerby further Covenant promise and graunt that it shall and may bee lawfull to and for the said John Ottes either by himselfe or his attorney to Record or enrowle these p^r^sents or to Cause them to bee Recorded and enrowled in the Court att New Plymouth before the Govr: for the time being or any other majestrate in that case provided provided according to the usuall manor of Recording and enrowling evidences in that Case provided ; In Witnes wherof I the aforsaid Thomas Robinson have heerunto sett my hand and seale the thirtieth Day of October in the yeare of our Lord one Thousand six hundred fifty and eight ; 1658,

Signed sealed and Delivered in the p^r^sence of
Thomas Clapp
James Torrey ;

Thomas Robinson
and a (seale)

[Thomas Robinson to John Otis]

[p. 128] 1663 Prence Govr:

A Deed appointed to bee Recorded

To all people to whom these p^r^sents shall Come Thomas Robinson of Scittuate in the Jurisdiction of New Plymouth in new England in America yeoman sendeth greet ; Know yea that I the afore said Thomas Robinson for and in Consideration of a sufficient sume of money in full satisfaction to mee in hand payed before the sealing and Delivery heerof by John Ottees of Hingham in the Jurisdiction of the Massachusetts in New England aforsaid wherwith I Doe acknowlidge my selfe sufficiently satisfyed Contented and fully payed and therof and of every pte & pcell therof Doe exownarate acquitt and Discharge the said John Ottees himselfe his heires exequitors adminnestrators and assignes for ever by these p^r^sents have freely and absolutely bargained and sold enfeofed and Confeirmed and by these p^r^sents Doe bargaine sell enfeofe and Confeirme from mee the said Thomas Robinson and my heires exequitors adminnestrators and assignes To him the said John Ottees and his exequitors Adminnestrators and assignes for ever a Certaine pcell of upland and meddow land lying and being in Scittuate aforsaid lying neare upon the north River att or neare the brooke Comonly Called by the name of the stony brooke; the upland is the one halfe of seaventeen acrees of land that is undevided; the other halfe therof being formerly sold by mee Thomas Robinson unto Thomas Chambers of Scittuate aforsaid; the whole being bounded towards the west to the land of Thomas Chambers aforsaid towards the east and north to the land of James Torrey towards the south to the meddow land aforsaid; which meddow is bounded towards the west and south to the brooke Comonly Called and knowne by the name of stony brooke towards the north to the upland aforsaid towards the east to the meddow land of of James Torrey aforsaid; and to a pcell of upland lying between the said meddow and the way; which upland is a pte of the aforsaid seaventeen acrees of upland to have and to hold the said meddow land and the one halfe of the aforsaid seaventeen acrees of upland; from mee the said Thomas Robinson and my heires to him the said John Ottees and his heires and assignes for ever; with all and singulare the privilidges and appurtenances therunto belonging or any way appertaining either to all or any pte or pcell therof; and all my Right title or Interest in the p^r^mises or any pte or pcell therof to bee holden of our Sov^r^: Lord the Kinge as of his manor of East greenwich in the Countey of Kent in free and Comon Scoccage and not in Capite nor by Knightes service nor by the Rentes and services therof and therby Due and of Right accustomed; warrenting the sale and title of the p^r^mises against all psons whatsoever from by or under mee the aforsaid Thomas Robinson or by my Right or title claiming any Right title or Interest in the p^r^mises or any pte or pcell therof And I the said Thomas Robinson Doe Covenant promise and graunt by these p^r^mises; that It shall and may bee lawfull to and for the said John Ottees either by himselfe or his attorney to Record and enrowle these these p[r]sents or to Cause them to bee Recorded in the Court att New Plymouth aforsaid; before the Gov[r]: for the time being or any other Majestrate according to the order of Court in that case provided; In Witnes wherof I the said Thomas Robinson have heerunto sett my hand and seale the twentyninth Day of September in the yeare of our Lord one Thousand six hundred and sixty 1660

Signed sealed and Delivered in the p[r]sence of
Willam Witherell
John Witherell;

Thomas Robinson
and a (seale)

(*To be continued*)

WIDOW DOROTHY BROWN'S WILL

TRANSCRIBED BY GEORGE ERNEST BOWMAN

JOHN BROWN, SR., of Rehoboth, by his will, dated 3 October, 1662, and printed in our last issue,* made his wife Dorothy and his son James residuary legatees.

The widow, Dorothy Brown, of Swansea, made her will on 17 December, 1668, and it was probated, at Plymouth, on 29 March, 1674. She had died at Swansea on the twenty-seventh of the preceding January.

Her will and inventory are found in the Plymouth Colony Wills and Inventories, Volume III, Part I, pages 97 and 98, and are here printed in full, at the expense of a descendant, Mr. Winfield Martin Brown.

[WIDOW DOROTHY BROWN'S WILL]

[3 : 1 : 97] In the Name of God Amen I Dorethy Browne of Swansey in the Jurisdiction of New Plymouth being of Great age, Doe make this for my Last Will and Testament in manor and forme following; That is first I Comend my soule to God my maker, and redeemer, and my body to be buried; and then after my funarall expences and Debts payed, which I owe either of Right or Consience; I Doe Give and bequeath unto my

* Mayflower Descendant, 18 : 18.

Daughter Mary Willett my best petticoat and a Cow for all her p^r^te and portion

Item I give to every one of my Daughter Maryes Willetts * Children that shalbe liveing att my Decease, six shillings and eight pence a peece;

Item I give unto Sarah Elliott Daughter of Sarah Elliott Deceased a Cow;

Item I Give and bequeath unto James Browne my son all my p^r^te of the house hee now Dwelleth in and alsoe my p^r^te of the New barne;

Item I give unto James Browne, my Grandchild, my p^r^te of the two hundred acrees of land, lying by m^r^ Blackstones;

Item I give and bequeath unto my Grandson John Browne all and every p^r^te of upland and meddow that I have or shall have, att my Decease; with all the appurtenances therunto belonging lying or being in any place or places, upon the Condition that John Browne shall make his two brothers Joseph and Nathaniel: equall with him in the land, of the Narragansetts; upon the p^r^formance of this Condition all the land and meddow; that I have or shall have; with the appurtenances I give to the said John Browne, except my pte of land att Quidnesse; which I give to Dorethy Browne my Grand Daughter;

Item I give to Lydia Browne my Daughter in Law a silke petticoate;

Item I give to my Daughter in law Dorethy Browne A silke Petticoate;

Item I Give to Lydia Browne and Anna Browne my Grand Children all the Rest of my wearing Clothes;

Item I Will that all the Rest of my estate; shalbe Devided into five equall p^r^tes, and Given unto my five Grandchildren, the Children of John Browne Deceased; but if any of these my Grandchildren should Dye before they be one and twenty yeares of age; or before they be Marryed, then theire p^r^tes shalbe Given to them that shall survive them;

Item it is my will that my son James Browne shall Give John Browne ten pound, upon the Condition the said James Browne haveing the house hee now Dwelleth in;

Item I make my son James Browne the sole executor of this my last Will and Testament;

Item I make and ordaine John Butterworth and Thomas Eastabrooke of Rehoboth, overseers of this my last Will and Testament;

* "Willetts" was interlined in the same hand and ink.

In Witnesse wherof I Doe heerunto put my hand and seale this 17th* Day of December; one Thousand six hundred sixty eight

Signed and sealled in the prsence of us witnesses
John Butterworth
Thomas Eastabrooke

The marke of
Dorethy Browne
And a (seale)

This Last Will and Testament of Dorethy Browne Deceased was Testifyed upon oath by the abovesaid witnesses the 29th of March 1674 Before mee Willam Bradford Assistant;

these prticulars appertaine to the following Inventory			
Item a Red broadcloth petticoate	03	15	00
Item 2 silke petticoates and a wascoate	01	10	00
Item 5 petticoates 2 wastoates	02	06	00
Item 1 serge Gowne	02	00	00
Item 2 Green say Aprons & a whitle	00	18	00
Item 2 hoods 2 scarffes a peece of blacke loue	01	05	00
Item 1 paire of Gloves and a muffe	00	10	00
Item 4 aprons 2 shifts 1 white wastcoate & smale linnin	03	10	00
	15	14	00

[p. 98] An Inventory of the estate In prtenorship betwixt mr James Browne and mistris Dorethy Browne Deceassed exhibited unto the Court held att Plymouth in March Anno: 1673 on the oath of mr James Browne aforsaid;

Imr: 1 bed in the parlor with Red Curtaines vallence and a wosted Rugg 1 Coverled and blanketts with pillowes and the bedsted	15	00	00
Item 1 bed 1 old Rugg 1 blankett bolster pillowes and bedsted	04	10	00
Item 1 bed 1 Rugg three blankets bolster pillowes and bedsteed	04	15	00
Item 1 bedteick 1 bolster 1 Rugg two blanketts 2 Curtaines and bedsteed	03	10	00
Item 1 bed 1 bolster 3 blanketts 1 Curtaine Chaire and lookeing glasse	04	15	00
Item 2 blanketts 1 pillow 2 paire of vallence 1 bedsted 1 Carpett	02	02	00
Item 1 fflocke bed 1 bolster 1 Coverlid 1 Rugg 1 blankett and bedsteed	03	10	00
Item 15 paire of sheets and 2 paire of sheets more	13	13	00

* "seaventh" was first written; but it was crossed out and "17th" interlined in the same ink.

Item 5 Table clothes 44 napkins 7 pillowbeares 10 towells		[*]	
Item 32 yards of Course linnin & one Cubbert Cloth	11	03	00
Item 3 Chestes 1 trunke 1 Case a linnine wheele 2 Cubbert Clothes	01	05	00
Item 6 Red lether Chaires 3 great wooden Chaires 1 twiggen Chaire a twiggen baskett and 6 Chaires more and a p^r^sell of bookes	07	12	00
Item 5 old Cushens 1 old Carpett 1 old window Curtaine	00	07	00
Item 1 Case of bottles 1 looking Glasse and smale thinges	00	10	00
Item 1 woolen wheele a hetchell 1 paire of two† Cards 70 pound of fflax and 5 bushells of seed fflax and hempseed	03	19	00
Item 10 pewter Dishes 1 plate 6 smale plates 3 kandle stickes 1 salt Celler	04	02	00
Item 9 peeces of pewter 3 sawsers 1 fflaggon 1 quart pott 1 pint pott 1 bowle 1 silver bowle 3 bottles 1 Chamber pott	06	12	06
Item 2 brasse potts 1 posnett 1 belmettle skillett and six peeces of brasse	02	17	00
Item 2 old Copper kettles 1 morter and pestle 10 alcomy spoones	01	04	oc
Item 3 Dozen of trenchers 1 earthen salt Celler 2 Juggs	000	03	06
Item 1 Driping pan 1 Candlesticke & other old tinn	000	06	00
Item 1 Iron pott 3 spitts 2 Choping knives 2 smoothing Irons and some brase, 2 hakes 2 paire of pothookes a Rosting Iron	02	00	00
Item 1 fier shovell tonggs and fier forke	00	07	00
Item 4 pailes 4 trayes 2 washing tubbs 2 keelers 1 Can 1 bruing tubb and 21 barrells and a p^r^sell of sugar	03	11	08
Item 6 old sythes 1 stubb sythe 2 axes 1 syde of lether	01	15	00
Item 5 Chaines 5 augers 2 sawes 1 handsaw 2 guns 1 sword	04	12	00
Item 4 Chissells 1 Drawing kniffe 1 adds 2 ffrowes 1 horsechaine	000	15	06
Item 1 Cart 2 Cart Ropes, Coller haines Coulter and share	003	09	00
Item 3 stubbing hoes 3 broad hoes a square and and a paire of Crookes	001	00	00
Item 2 barrells of beeffe 3 barrells of salt and an halfe	004	12	00

* The value was not entered. Possibly this item and the following should have been united.

† Sic.

Item 60 bushells of Indian Corne 4 bushells of Rye 30 bushells of oates 40 bushells of barly	008	00	00
Item 4 smale ffliches of Bacon and a smale psell of woole	02	04	00
Item 4 oxen 3 Cowes 6 steers 6 bulls	040	13	00
Item 8 Cowes: 10: 2 yeare olds: 5 yearlings 1 Calfe 1 bull	032	03	00
Item 22 swine	09	10	00
Item 4 mares 1 horse 2 Colts	06	15	00
Item 3 horses	04	10	00
Item 4 mares 2 yearlings 3 Colts	06	15	00
Item 3 mares 1 horse 1 Colt	05	00	00
Item horses and mares	04	00	00
Item 1 syde saddle	00	15	00
Item 1 buffe Coatę	00	15	00
	253	14	02

By us Hugh Cole
Samuell Luther

UNRECORDED BARNSTABLE COUNTY DEEDS

Abstracts by the Editor

(*Continued from page 28*)

The abstracts presented in this issue were made by the Editor, in 1906 and 1907, from original deeds then owned by Hon. John Kendrick, Mr. Charles E. Rogers and Mrs. Frank Gould, all of Orleans, Mass.

[Kenwrick to Kenwrick *]

"Sammuel Kenwrick of Harwich In the Countey of Barnstable .... phitisian" for £40, "Lawful Money" sold to "Thomas Kenwrick and Jonathan Kenwrick the Second borth of Harwich in the Countey of Barnstable yeomans .... all that my homested Hous orchard and Lands and my Barn and all my Lands to the Eastward of the Rod that Leads from Eastham to Chatham and all my part or parts of Seader Swamps in Harwich and also all my medo or Seeg grownd in Eastham"

The deed was dated 9 July, 1771, and acknowledged the same day, before John Freeman, Justice of the Peace. The

* Original owned by Hon. John Kendrick, in 1906.

witnesses were Joshua Hopkins and "Joseph Eldredg". The deed was recorded 16 October, 1771, in Barnstable County Deeds, Book 33, folio 221, by Solomon Otis, Register, and has not been re-recorded, since the fire in 1827.

[Yates to Kenwrick *]

"John Yeats of Eastham in the County of Barnstable .... yeoman" for £9, 6s., 8d., "Lawful Money" sold to "Samuel Kenwrick afore Sd Phisitian & Jonathan Kenwrick afore Sd maraner .... all that my Percel of medo & Seg ground Lying at a Place Called Namacoit Crik beginnig at the gutter as the Shore runs out to the mouth of Sd Crick together with anather Point of marsh to the westward of Sd Creek a Joining to Reuben Nickersons Landing With a Quarter of the Share Round Sd Namacoit together with a Quarter of a share of Seader swamp Called Namacoit Swamp ajoining to our Rang .... and the Sd Samuel Kenwrick & Jonathan Kenwrick are Equil Propriaters in Sd granted & Barganed Premises"

The deed was dated 3 May, 1774, and signed "John Yates". It was not acknowledged. The witnesses were Deborah Rogers and Molley Riordan. The deed was not recorded.

[Rogers, Nickerson and Rogers †]

"Articles of agrement made" 23 May, 1750, "Between Judah Rogers Ruben Nickerson and Ebenezer Rogers all of Harwich .... yeoman as followeth the said Judah Rogers for his part for and in Consideration that the said Ebenezer Rogers and Ruben Nickerson Doth by these presents Grant Liberty for him his heirs and assigns for Ever to pass and Repass Either by him self or famely and Drive Cretures as Needed in the way that Leads from the said Judah Rogurs fort hill pastor as the way now goes westerly by the south east end of the Ceder Swamp up to the said Judah Rogers other Land in Consideration of which the sd Judah Rogers Doth Quit Claim Challeng or Demand to a small parcel of Land at the south East End of the above said Ceder Swamp Bounded Begining at a stone set in the Ground Called petters Bound thence westerly two poles to a stone set in the Ground by the aforsaid way thence South‡ West Southerly as the fence Now stands Eight-

* Original owned by Hon. John Kendrick, in 1906.

† Original owned by Mr. Charles E. Rogers, in 1906.

‡ This word looks as though an attempt had been made to blot it out.

een poles to a stone set in the Ground which is the Corner Bound between the said Judah Rogers & Said Ruben Nickerson said Judah Rogers Doth Quit Claim Challeng or Demand to said Land to said Ruben Nickerson his heirs and assigns only Reserving Liberty for him self and Ebenezer Roger[s] to pass & Repass and Drive through said piece of Land as needed and the the said Ruben Nickerson for and in Consideration of the abovesaid small piece of Land Doth Grant Liberty for the above said Judah Rogers to pass and Repass and Drive Creaturs as Needed across the above said small piece of Land and so westerly as the Cart way now Runs through the said Ruben Nickersons Land also Doth Quit Claim Challeng or Demand to Ebenezer Rogers to a small piece of Land Lying by the said way adjoyning to the North East Corner of the Said Ebenezer Rogerses Land and now Enclosed with said Rogers Land and the said Ebenezer Rogers for and in Consideration of the abovesaid small piece of Land Doth Grant Liberty to the said Judah Rogers to pass and Repass in the way above said begining where said way Comes out of said Ruben Nickersons and so leads up on the Northerly side of the said Ebenezer Rogers Land to the North west Corner of said Land in Confirmation of the above articles of agreement we the above named Judah Rogers Ebenezer Rogers and Ruben Nickerson have herunto set our hands and seals the Day and year above written"

The witnesses were Sarah Rogers, by a mark, and Thomas Freeman.

The agreement was acknowledged by the three parties, at Eastham, 30 October, 1754, before Joseph Doane, Justice of the Peace.

It was recorded 28 February, 1755, in Barnstable County Deeds, Book 24, folio 97, by Solomon Otis, Register, and has not been re-recorded, since the fire in 1827.

[John Yates to Judah Rogers *]

"John Yates of Eastham .... yeoman" for £122, 10s., "Lawfull Money" sold to "Judah Rogers of Eastham .... a Peice of Land lying and being in Eastham aforesaid, containing Seven Acres, be it more or Less, Butted and Bounded as follows begining a little to the Westward of Hezekiah Rogers's House, Runing from the North East Corner of Said field with the Way that Leads to Namacoik and on the Southerly Side therof untill it comes to the Corner of Said Rogers's Land, on every other Side

* Original owned by Mr. Charles E. Rogers, in 1906.

bounded by Said Judah Rogers's Land 'till it comes to the first mentioned Bound which Land together with all the Priveledges and Appurtenances thereunto belonging, I the Said John Yates do hereby Sell, and Convey unto the Said Judah Rogers"

The deed was dated 21 June, 1779, and signed by John Yates and Abigail Yates. The witnesses were Rachel Myrick, Sarah Myrick, and "Lombardd".

The deed was acknowledged, in Barnstable County, on 3 January, 1781, by John Yates, before Thomas Paine, Justice of the Peace. It was recorded 21 November, 1781, in Barnstable County Deeds, Book 36, folio 131, by Edward Bacon, Register, and has not been re-recorded, since the fire in 1827.

[MARY STONE TO JUDAH ROGERS*]

"Mary Stone of Harwich . . . . Widow" for £5, sold to "Judah Rogers of Eastham . . . . yeoman . . . . a Certain peice of Wood Land lying in the South Westerly part of Eastham in the Tract of Land called the Eleven Share purchase bounded as may appear by the Eleven Share purchase Book of Reccords and is the lot of Land which Samuel Freeman Mortgaged to me which he bought of Benjamin Higgins and Contain[s] about Eight Acres be the same more or less"

The deed was dated 23 July, 1787, and witnessed by Silvanus Stone and Olive Stone. It was acknowledged 2 August, 1787, before Joseph Snow, Justice of the Peace. It was recorded 3 April, 1793, in Barnstable County Deeds, Book 45, folio 175, by Ebenezer Bacon, Register, and has not been re-recorded, since the fire in 1827.

[AMOS SIPSON TO JOSEPH ROGERS†]

"Amos Sipson of the Town of Sandwitch in the County of Barnstable . . . . grandson to John Sipson who was the principall proprietor of the Lands lying att or near a place Called potanomacut Indian Labourer" for £50, current money, sold to "Joseph Rogers of the Town of Eastham in the County afore said yeoman . . . . one parcell of upland & to his Heirs and Assigns for ever, laying in the Township of Harwich in said County of Barnstable att potanomacut aforesd Joyning on the south side of the Lands of Nathan[ll] gould Containing by Esteemation twenty one acres be itt more or less begining att the northeast Corner there of

* Original owned by Mr. Charles E. Rogers, in 1906.

† Original owned by Mrs. Frank Gould, in 1907.

att a great Rock from thence Runing westerly in Sipsons Range to the Comon Road that leads to chatham thence Runing by said Road south westerly to an other great Rock which is also the bounds of the lands of Nathan Young : from thence Runing south easterly to an olde pine tree & stone set In the ground by it : from thence Runing north easterly to the sault water pond so called to a white oak tree on the Bank by sd pond side from thence by the pond side Runing north westerly to the first specifyed Bound Comprehending all the Lands within the Compas of the afforesd Bounderies with all previledges there to belonging or In any ways appertaining"

The deed was dated 4 October, 1736, and signed by a mark. It was acknowledged the same day, at Eastham, before Nathaniel Freeman and Joseph Doane, two Justices of the Peace. The witnesses were Samuel "Bate" and Crisp Rogers. It was recorded, 20 October, 1736, in Barnstable County Deeds, Book 17, folio 21, by John Thacher, Register, and has not been re-recorded, since the fire in 1827.

[Josiah Sparrow to Joshua Gould*]

"Josiah Sparrow of the Town of Orleans County of Barnstable . . . . Yeoman" for $31.00, sold to "Joshua Gould of the Town of Orleans . . . . Yeoman . . . . a piece of Land Lying in the Town of Orleans on a neck of Land Called namacoit on the north part of said neck and bounded as follows viz — begining at the south west corner bound by the edge of a swamp thence runing northerly to a river Called Higgins river thence runing easterly to the said Goulds range thence runing southerly to the said swamp thence runing westerly by the edge of the said swamp untill it comes to the first mentioned bound — Containing five acres be it more or less — Together with all the previlidges and appurtenances there unto belonging"

"In Witness whereof, I the said Josiah Sparrow : Together with Marcy Cole Ephraim Cole and Elenar Cole have hereunto set our Hand and Seal this" 10 April, 1804.

The deed was signed by Josiah Sparrow, Marcy Cole (by a mark), Ephraim Cole and Eleanor Cole. The witnesses were Timothy Bascom and Rebecca Bascom. It was acknowledged, by Josiah Sparrow only, on 2 May, 1804, before Timothy Bascom, Justice of the Peace, and was not recorded.

* Original owned by Mrs. Frank Gould, in 1907.

[Town of Orleans to Joshua Gould*]

"We John Myrick Jabez Sparrow & Daniel Cumings Select men of the town of orleans in the County of Barnstable Yeomen" for $117.00, sold to "Joshua Gould of Orleans in said County yeoman .... in our capasity as select Men of s[d] Orleans a piece of cleard land situated in barly neck in a field known by the name of Peppers field all the part of said Land owned by the s[d] town of Orleans in common and undivided with Joshua Higgins & others about three acres more or less"

The deed was dated 2 December, 1816, and acknowledged the same day, by the three grantors, before Jonathan Bascom, Justice of the Peace. The witnesses were Jonathan Bascom and Israel Linnell. The deed was not recorded.

[Joanna Smith, Administratrix, to Nathaniel and Thomas Gould*]

"Joanna Smith of Orleans in County of Barnstable Administratrix upon the Estate of Seth Smith late of said Orleans deceased intestate, by an order of the Curent Court of Common pleas begun and holden at Barnstable .... on the third Teusday of April Last past was licensed and duly empowered to sell and pass deeds, to convey all the real estate of the said Seth Smith for the payment of his just debts and incidental charges.

"And whereas I, the said Joanna Smith having given thirty days public notice of the intended sale, at the dwelling house of Gideon S. Snow in S[d] Orleans; and having first given bonds, and taken the oath, by law in such cases required, did on the Sixteenth day of November Last past pursuant to the license and notice aforesaid, sell at public vendue the following tract of land, being a part of the real estate of said Seth Smith deceased to Nathaniel Gould & Thomas Gould of Orleans aforesaid yeomen for the sum of Eight dollars—They being the highest bidders therefor : one peice of wood land lying in Brewster in said County of Barnstable containing by estemation about one acre and half an acre bounded as follows on the South end by Arvin Kenrick's Land on the North End by William Myrick's of Eastham Land . on the west Side by Elisha Smith Land, on the east side by the road or Godfrey Sparrows Land, and is all the Land bought by the said Seth Smith of Joseph Myrick in that place (to the Said Nathaniel one half and his heirs and Assigns an[d] to the said Th[omas one] half and his heirs and Assigns)

* Original owned by Mrs. Frank Gould, in 1907.

"Therefore know ye, That I, the said Joanna Smith as aforesaid, by virtue of the power and authority in me vested as aforesaid, and in consideration of the aforesaid sum of Eight dollars to me paid by the said Nathaniel & Thomas Gould . . . . do hereby . . . . convey unto him the said Nathaniel & Thomas . . . . the tract of land herein above mentioned and described, or howsoever the same is reputed to be bounded or described."

The deed was dated 5 December, 1818, and acknowledged the same day, before Simeon Kingman, Justice of the Peace. The witnesses were Simeon Kingman and Thankful "Knoles". The deed was not recorded.

[OLIVER A. NICKERSON TO NATHANIEL GOULD*]

"Oliver A Nickerson of Chatham in the County of Barnstable Gentleman" for $200.00, sold to "Nathaniel Gould of Orleans in Said County yeoman . . . . a certain tract of Cleared land Swamps and Orchard lying in the Town of Orleans, Commonly Called the Commons — to the eastward of the Dwelling House of Thomas Gould, Joining the post road, on the west, the Road that leads from the Post road to Joseph Areys Dwelling house on the South, and lands of Thomas Gould, W^o Lucy Higgins and the old Orchard land on the east, Containing about five acres be the same more or less including the young Orchard included in said boundarys reserveing a road by gates or bars where the road now goes on the easterly side of said premises, also reserveing the Barn Standing on Said premises to be removed off, as soon as may be, together with all the priviliges and Appurtenances to said premises, belonging the barn is to be removed in the Space of six months"

"In Witness whereof, I the said Oliver A Nickerson & Betsey wife of said Oliver, and Polly Doane wife of Zeanus Doane in testimony of relinquishing our right in and to said premises have hereunto set our hands and seals this" 24 February, 1836.

The deed was signed by Oliver A. Nickerson, Betsey Nickerson and Polly Doane. The witnesses were John Kenrick, Sparrow M. Nickerson and Rebecca S. Kenrick. The deed was acknowledged 24 February, 1836, by Oliver A. Nickerson only, before John Kenrick, Justice of the Peace, and was not recorded.

(*To be continued*)

* Original owned by Mrs. Frank Gould, in 1907.

ALDEN — BASS — ADAMS — THAYER

By George Ernest Bowman

In the following pages we give exhaustive abstracts of all records, and original documents on file, in the Suffolk County Probate Records, in Boston, relating to the estates of two sons and two sons-in-law of John and Ruth (Alden) Bass of Braintree, Mass., as follows: the will of John Bass[3] (*Ruth*[2] *Alden, John*[1]), of Braintree; the will of Joseph Bass[3] (*Ruth*[2] *Alden, John*[1]), of Boston; the will of Joseph[3] Adams (*Joseph*[2], *Henry*[1]), of Braintree, who married three times, his second wife being Hannah Bass[3] (*Ruth*[2] *Alden, John*[1]); the will of Ephraim Thayer, of Braintree, who married, first, Sarah Bass[3] (*Ruth*[2] *Alden, John*[1]), and married, second, widow Mary Kingman.

The proper reference, to the original document on file, or to the record, is noted with each abstract.

[The Will of John Bass[3]]

[From original will] "John Bass of Braintree . . . . Yeoman" made his will on 10 July, 1723. Bequests were as follows:

To "Rebecca, my well beloved wife to be enjoyed by her during her natural life, that end of my dwelling house, next the Street, with the dary-Room; also one fourth part of the Lands, which my father left me by Will . further, I give to her, and to my Son Ebenezer after her Decease, one acre of Land adjoining to my orchard, which my father gave me, with my best feather-Bed, & furniture, and one pair new woolen blankets, Two pair Cotton & Linen Sheets . moreover, an Iron Kettle, a new Brass Skillet a warming-pan . foure chairs she brought with her, her Chest, the new Table, all Earthen, & glass weare of what Sort Soever, all peuter, not brought with my former wife, one Silver Spoone, a Tramel, Peal, Tongs & gridiron . all Spining Wheels for woolen or Linen, and utensils used about Spining &c with the half of all other moveables not above mentioned, in particular, excepting what came with my former wife. Further, towards her comfortable Subsistence, my will is, That my Sons, viz Samuel & Ebenezer, do provide for her, each of them (yearly & every year) five bushels of Indian corne, and three bushels of

Rye, Ten shillings in Beef, five Pounds of sheepswoll, & Three Pounds of flax . Each of 'em Two Cords of wood & and one Bushel of malt : and apples, what she needs for her own use . further I give to her, one Cow to be at her owne disposal . with all money or silver wear which I shall leave at my Decease, moreover, I give to her, and to my Son Ebenezer after her Decease . all that was given her by her father, whether money, or other moveables."

"To my Son John Bass, (who has had his full part of my lands already) I give in addition . . . . an equall part, with his Two Brothers, of my Cedar Swamp . also half of the Household, moveables, which came by his mother, the other half to be for his Brother Samuel, to be equally divided between them Two, only Reckoning what they have before my Death as a part, so to be proportioned."

To "my Son Samuel Bass . . . . my Dwelling-house Barne, and other Smal Edifices, with the Land about the house, and the orchard, with the half of all other the Lands I have power to Dispose of, (Excepting one acre of Salt Marsh, in the broad meadows.) with the half of the moveables which came by his mother as abovesaid".

To "my Son Ebenezer Bass . . . . besides what I have given to him to be enjoyed after the Death of his mother, one acre of Salt marsh in the broad-meadows, abovementioned, and, the remaining half of the Lands I have power to dispose of above mentioned also."

"further, my wills is, that my Malt-Mill, with all my shop-tools be equally divided between my three Sons abovementioned."

"all my Debts & funeral Charges shall be paid out of my Stock, and what shall remaine after this, shall be equally divided between my Son Samuel & my Son Ebenezer."

"whatsoever of household-provision either of graine or otherwise, shall be in the house at my decease, or of Cropps on the Ground, shall be for the use of my family that shall Survive."

"It is my desire and Will, that my Lands at the house Lot wch I value at Sixty Pounds; and that at home, in the orchard & stony field, valued at Ten Pound ℙ acre, and Pasture at Six Pounds an acre, If Samuel & Ebenezer See cause to sell one to the other, be Sold, at the value abovementioned."

"I do hereby constitute . . . . my Son Samuel Executor, & Rebecca my beloved wife Executrix"

The witnesses were Jonathan Webb, Jerusha Webb, and Benjamin Webb. They made oath to the will, at Boston, on 30 November, 1724. [The will was also recorded, 23 : 425.]

[From original petition] "These are to Signifie to your Honour, that it is my desire that you would admit of my Husband's Will being proved, tho' I am uncapable of appearing before your Honour, thro' bodily weakness at this Time &c" Signed "rebakca bass" and dated "Braintree Nov: 30, 1724."

[23 : 425] The will was probated on 30 November, 1724, and administration granted to "his Relict Widow Rebecca Bass and his Son Samuel Bass Executors".

[The Will of Joseph Bass[3]]

[From copy certified by Thaddeus Mason, Deputy Secretary]

On 25 February, 1733, "Alden Bass of Boston Wharfinger," petitioned the Governor and the General Court as follows:

"That on or about the latter End of October last Mr Joseph Bass your Petitioners Father made his last Will in Writing Whereby he devised to Your Petitioner Alden his Dwelling House reserving to his Wife one Chamber a Priviledge in the Garret and Celler and the Household Stuff in the Chamber during her Widowhood, and directed the s^d^ Alden to pay her for the Time afores^d^ Ten Pounds ℘ Annum . To his Son Joseph a Peice of Land lying between Mr Keyes and his Son Moses . And also devised to each of his Children fifty Pounds to be paid within five years after his Decease by your Said Petitioner, who thereupon was to hold a certain Wharff now in your Petitioner's Possession and by him formerly mortgaged to his Said Father for four hundred Pounds, which Legacies wou'd amount to three hundred & fifty Pounds being Seven Children (your Petitioner included) and the remaining fifty Pounds to compleat the Sum of £400 : as aforesaid was by him ordered to goe with the rest of his Personall Estate, and after paying Debts & Funeral Expenses to be equally distributed amongst all his Children, and he gave to his Son Benjamin all his wearing Apparel, and a Trunk to put them in, and devised to his Son Moses a Strip of Land behind his Brew House, Gave to his Daughter Miller his Silver Cup And to his Son Joseph and your Petitioner all the rest of his moveables or to the like Effect thereby constituting the Said Joseph and your Petitioner Executors ; That a month afterwards the Said Testator died, that about two Days after his Decease the Said Testator's wife & Children all met at S^d^ Dwelling House & being informed by the Testator in his Life Time that he had made his will and where the Same was deposited, they were desirous of having the Same opened & publickly read in their Hearing, in order to know if any Directions were given therein touching his Funeral, and accordingly your Petitioner's Brother Joseph having received the Key of the Trunk from their Mother where they were before informed the Will lay, went up in the Chamber and brought the same down & then openly read the Same Several Times to the Effect aforesd, That afterwards the s[d] Joseph being the Eldest Son, and first named Executor carry'd the Same and lockt it in the Trunk where he found it, and the next Day carried the Same to his House in the Country Where he read the Same in the Hearing of diverse Persons, That after the Funeral was over your Petitioner desired his Brother & Coexecutor to go to the Hono[ble] the Judge of the Probate of Wills &c for the County of Suffolk to prove the Same, and a time was accordingly appointed, but So it was, when the Said Joseph Appeared he acquainted the S[d] Judge that S[d] Will was lost, and by Some Means conveyed away & embezzel'd & concealed, and that your Petitioner has applied to the s[d] Judge to have the Same discovered the Same is without Effect no Law enabling the S[d] Judge to make a thorro Discovery of Such inhumane Practices as in a Court of Chancery in England, and thereupon the Said Joseph made Application to S[d] Judge as being the Eldest son to have Letters of Administration granted to him So as to proceed on said Estate as an Intestate Estate, notwithstanding all the Family wellknows, and he himself in particular That the Same is a Testate Estate, and that Such Attempts are a notorious Violation of the Will of the Deceased & detestable in the Sight of God & man, and loudly crys for the Interposition of your Excellency & Honours, otherwise no Person can dye with Assurance that his Will tho' made with the utmost Deliberation can take Effect.

"Wherefore your injured Petitioner most humbly prays your Excellency & Honours will in your great Wisdom & Justice take the Premises into consideration & enable the Said Judge alone or with Such a Committee as your Excellency & Honours Shall be pleased to appoint thoroughly to interrogate all Persons whatsoever Suspected in the Embezelment or Concealing the said Will, and to imprison Such as shall Stand in Contempt & also to examine Persons touching the Substance & Import of the said Will, and the Said Several Devises and when the Same is fully known to enable the Said Judge to prove the Substance thereof, and to grant Letters of Administration to your Petitioner who is the only Executor to whom no Fault can be imputed with the said Devises annexed, and that the Same Shall pass the Several Devises to the respective Devisees according to the Intent of the Testator to all Intents and Purposes as if the original Will that contained the same had not been embezelled & Concealed but duly proved, any Law Usuage or Custom to the Contrary notwithstanding, which will effectually discourage Such evil Practices for the future, when ill minded Persons perceive that the Wisdom of the Legislature justly frustrates their evil Intents, or that your Excellency & Honours will be pleased to afford your Petitioner Such further & other Relief as in your consummate Wisdom & Justice Shall Seem meet, and as in Duty will ever pray &c[a]

Alden Bass

"In the House of Represent[vs] Febru[a] 25 : 1733

Read & Ordered that the Petitioner forthwith Serve the Adverse Parties with a Copy of the Petition that they make answer thereto on Thursday the Twenty eighth Current.

Sent up for Concurrence

J: Quincy Spk[r]

"In Council Feb[r] 26 : 1733.

Read and Concurred

J Willard Sec[ry]

27 . Consented to, J. Belcher

"In Council, April 12th 1734.

Read again together with the answer of Joseph Bass & others, and Ordered That Thomas Hutchinson William Dudley & Francis Foxcroft Esq[rs] with Such as Shall be joined by the Hono[ble] House of Representatives be a Committee to consider of the Subject matter of this Petition, and report as soon as may be what may be proper to be done thereon, and that the Comittee have Power to send for Such Persons & Papers as they may think proper to give Light in the Affair.

Sent down for Concurrence

J: Willard Sec[ry]

"In the House of Represent[vs] April 16 : 1734.

Read & Concurred & Ordered That Samuel Welles Esqr, M[r] Bisby, John Choate & Will[m] Brattle Esqrs are joined in the Affair.

J: Quincy Spk[r]

Consented to J: Belcher

"In Council June 25th 1734.

Read and Ordered that this Petition be revived, and That Ezekiel Lewis, Francis Foxcroft & Jacob Wendell Esqrs with

Such as shall be joined by the Hono[ble] House of Representatives be a Committee to consider the Subject matter thereof & Report as Soon as may be what may be proper to be done thereon; and that the Committee have Power to Send for Such Persons & Papers as they may think proper to give Light in the Affair.

Sent down for Concurrence

J Willard Sec[ry]

"In the House of Represent[vs] June 25 : 1734

Read & Concurred & M[r] Welles M[r] Bisby Coll[o] Prescott & M[r] Cushing are joined in the Affair

J: Quincy Spk[r]

26 : Consented to J: Belcher

"The Committee appointed to consider of the Petition of Alden Bass pursuant to the Order of the 26th of June last met Several Times on that Affair, and Sent for the Widow & Children of the within named deceased Joseph Bass also for two of those Persons, namely Brice Eules & George Ray, who, the Committee was informed, were Witnesses to the Will within referred to (Miles Flood the other Witness being out of Town) and the Committee examined the Widow & Children Seperately, who all of them acknowledged that before the Funeral of the s[d] Dece'd they heard an Instrument read at his dwelling House which they apprehended to be his last Will & Testament; and Sundry of them heard the Same read again, at the House of his Eldest Son Joseph, who Said he had it In keeping for a considerable Time, and they all agreed that the Substance of the Devises therein made were truly set forth in the Petition, and Several of them declared that the said Instrument was of the s[d] Dece'd's own hand Writing: The said Brice Eules & George Ray declar'd that on or about the Twenty Second of September last, they (together with the said Miles Flood) Subscribed their names as Witnesses to an Instrument, which the said Dec'd executed before them, and declared to be his last Will and Testament, and was of his own Hand Writing, but that they knew Nothing of the Contents of it.

"Inasmuch therefore as from the Acknowledgments & Declarations of the Parties before named it appears very evidently that the beforenamed Dec[d] left a Last Will & Testament in Writing, the Substance whereof is Set forth in the s[d] Petition, and that Some Clandestine Methods have been made use of to Secrete & destroy the Same thereby to frustrate the Intent of the Decd as to the Disposition of his Estate after his Death, which ought Sacredly to have been Observed; The Committee are of Opinion, in order to discourage Such detestable Practices for the future, that the Several Devises and Legacies contained in the said Petition be deemed & taken as the last Will and Testament of the said Dec[d], and that the Judge for Probate of Wills &c[a] within the County of Suffolk be impowered & directed to approve & allow of the Same accordingly, and commit the Administration thereof, in all matters the same concerning unto his two sons Joseph & Alden Bass Executors therein named, if they See Cause to accept of the Same, and upon either of their Refusal, to him that will accept thereof, but upon both their Refusal to Such other Person or Persons as the Judge of Probate Shall think fit, taking Bond of Such Person or Persons with Sufficient Suerties to exhibit an Inventory of the Estate therein mentioned within three months from Such his Allowance, and for their faithful Administration: And that the Said Will so approved & allowed pass the Several Legacies & Devises therein contained to the respective Devisees & Legataries therein named as effectually to all Intents & Purposes, as if the original Will had not been destroyed but duly proved and allowed.

All which is humbly Submitted,

In the Name & by Order of the Committee

Sept[r] 14 : 1734. Eze: Lewis

"In Council Sept[r] 14 : 1734

Read & accepted.

Sent down for Concurrence

J: Willard Sec[ry]

"In the House of Represent[vs] Nov[r] 22 : 1734

Read & Concurred

J: Quincy Spk[r]

23 : Consented to J: Belcher

"A true Copy

Attest: Thad: Mason Dep[t] Sec[ry]"

[The petition etc. were also recorded, 32 : 59.]

[From original bond] On 11 February, 1734, "Joseph Bass of Dorchester Tanner Alden Bass Wharfinger & Thomas Webber Innholder both of Boston and Edward Breck Tanner of Dorchester" gave bond for £2000, "the above-bounden Joseph Bass & Alden Bass admitted admin[rs] . . . . of their Father

Joseph Bass late of Boston afores[d] Wharfinger Deced" The witnesses were John Payne and John Boydell, the Register of Probate.

[From original letter] On 11 February, 1734, "the Will Joseph Bass late of Boston aforesaid Wharfinger Deceased" was allowed, and administration granted to "his two Sons Joseph Bass & Alden Bass Executors"

[The Will of Joseph Adams]

[From original will] "Joseph Adams of Braintree" made his will 1 March, 1733/4. Bequests were as follows:

To "wife Elezebeth Adams thirty pounds in bills of Credit to be paid her at my decease by my Executor, and y[e] preveledge of y[e] three lower Roomes in y[e] East end of my house and so much of y[e] Celler as is for her Conveniancy during her life, and one Cow to be keept for her use, and y[e] income of one third of all y[e] Rest of my Estate all during her natural life: and all y[e] moveables she brought to me and y[e] irish wheel to be disposed of as she shall please"

To "my son Joseph Adams five pounds in good bills of Credit to be paid to him or his heirs in one year after my decease:"

To "my Son John Adams ten acers of meddow and upland in my homestead begining at y[e] lower end at y[e] Brook, and one quarter part of my wood lott in y[e] six hundred acers; and ten pounds in bills of Credit to be paid to him or his heirs in one year after my decease:"

To "my son Samuel Adams one half for quantity and quality of my Salt meddow lying at Rock Island and a Small peace of Swampy land lying betwen y[e] towns Common and his own land, he paying three pounds as is hereafter directed."

To "my Son Josiah Adams y[e] other half of my Salt meddow at Rock Island before mentioned; and a Small peace of Swampy land lying betwen y[e] towns Common and his own meddow, he paying three pounds as is here after directed,"

To "my daughter Hannah Owen twenty pounds in bills of Credit to be paid to her or her heirs in one year after my decease, and one half part of my household moveables"

To "my daughter Ruth Webb forty Shillings in bills of Credit to be paid to her or heirs in one year after my decease."

To "my daughter Bethiah Adams ninety pounds in bills of Credit to be paid to her or heirs in one year after my decease. viz Six pound by her Brothers Samuel Adams and Josiah Adams that is three pounds from each and eighty four pounds by her Brother Ebenezer Adams, and ye one half part of my household moveables"

To "ye heirs of my daughter Abagial Chaping Six pounds in bills of Credit to be paid to them in one year after my decease, to be equily devided amongst the three forty Shillings to each."

To "my Son Ebenezer Adams my dwelling house and barn orchad and all my lands and meddow and all my stock of Cattel of every kind, if any there be, and all my just debts and all my Estate what soever it is or where soever it shall or may be found, not before disposed of . he paying to his Brothers and Sisters and Sisters Children or to Such as leagaly Represent them all ye leagacyes before mentioned, excepting ye Six pounds that is to be paid by Samuel and Josiah Adams"

"Son Ebenezer Adams to be my Executor"

The witnesses were Thomas Baxter, Susanna Boylston and Richard Thayer. Thomas Baxter and Susanna Boylston made oath to the will, at Boston, 22 March, 1736, and Richard Thayer made oath on 29 April, 1737. [The will was also recorded, 33 : 83.]

[From original bond] On 10 June, 1737, "Ebenezer Adams Husbandman John Adams Cordwainer all of Braintry & Peter Boylston of Boston Shopkeeper" gave bond of £5000, the said "Ebenezer Adams Executor of the Last Will .... of his Father Joseph Adams Late of Braintree .... Deced" The witnesses were Daniel Goffe, Jr., and John Payne.

[33 : 82] On 22 March, 1736, the will was probated, at Boston, and administration granted to "his Son Ebenezer Adams Sole Executor"

[The Will of Ephraim Thayer]

[From original will] "Ephraim Thayer of Braintree .... Weaver" made his will 10 April, 1755. Bequests were as follows:

To "Wife Mary the Improvement of the best Room in my House and what priviledge She sees Cause to improve in My Garden if She Continues at my House During her Natural Life And also I order my Executors after Named to afford her a Comfortable maintainance but if she Sees Cause to Move Away then I give her all the household goods she brought and order my Executors to pay her yearly as much as she hath from her sons Kingmans during her Natural Life"

To "my Son Ephraim Thayer Twenty Shillings in money more that what he hath Already received to be paid in Two years after my wifes Decease"

To "my Son Philip Thayer the whole of my Wearing apparrell both Linnen & woolen to be Delivered him Immediately after my Decease And Also five pounds to be paid him in Two Years after my Decease"

To "my Son Joseph Thayer One pound to be paid him in Two years after my Decease — And also Two Barrels of Cyder p^r year for three years after my Decease"

To "my Son Shadrack Thayer my Ivory headed Cain and also half my Land in the first & Second Lott adjoining to the Land I gave to my Son Ephraim by deed."

To "my Son Naphtali Thayer the other half part of my Land in the first & Second Lott adjoining to the Lands I gave him by deed"

To "my Son Peter Thayer Twenty Shillings in money to be paid him in five years after my Decease"

To "my Grandaughter Ruth Vinton the daughter of my Daughter Sarah Dorman deceas^d a Cow to be delivered to her in one year after my decease"

To "my Daughter Hannah Blancher half An Acre of Land adjoining to my Son Blanchers Land also Two acres of Meadow bounded Westerly on James Pennimans Land to run of an equal Breadth . also my best Feather Bed & Furniture belonging thereto."

To "my Daughter Ruth Capen Five pounds to be paid in Two years after my decease She having received a Bed & Furniture thereto belonging already."

To "my Daughter Esther French a Feather Bed & furniture belonging to it"

To "my Daughter Priscilla Ford a Cow & Twenty Shillings in money"

To "my Daughter Abigail Richards my Silver Cup."

To "my five Daughters viz Hannah, Ruth, Esther, Priscilla, & Abigail all the Lands I Shall leave undisposed of Also all the household moveables I Shall leave undisposed off to be equally divided Among them"

To "my Two Sons Christopher Thayer & James Thayer the whole of my Homestead viz Housing & Barn with all the Lands both on the South & North Side the way Christopher to have the West part of the Land and James the East part to be equally divided between them for Quantity and Christopher to have the East end of the Barn & half the floor way and the Corn house to be divided equally between them and the Dwelling house to be divided as they Shall Agree to Suit them both. I also give unto my Son Christopher Two Acres & half of Meadow which I purchased of Captn Ebenezer Thayer. I Also give unto my Son James three Acres of Land which I bought of John Mills adjoining to Captn John Thayers Land. I Also give to my Son James my Cart & Wheels Yokes & Chains plows &c And Also my great Bible"

"I Constitute . . . . my Two Sons Christopher And James my Executors"

The witnesses were Isaac Newcomb, Elisha Niles, and Anna Niles. Isaac Newcomb and Elisha Niles made oath to the will, at Boston, on 15 July, 1757, before Thomas Hutchinson, Judge of Probate. [The will was also recorded, 52: 508.]

[From original] On 15 July, 1757, "Christopher Thayer Glazier & James Thayer Blacksmith Isaac Newcomb Housewright & Elisha Niles Gent^{n} all of Braintree" gave bond of £600, the said "Christopher Thayer & James Thayer Executors of the Last Will of their Father Ephraim Thayer late of Braintree afores^{d} Weaver dec^{d}" The witnesses were Jonathan Metcalf and John Payne.

[52: 507] On 15 July, 1757, the will was probated at Boston, and administration granted to "his Two Sons Christopher & James Executors"

THE WILL OF GEORGE VAUGHAN, SR.

ABSTRACT BY THE EDITOR

GEORGE[1] VAUGHAN died at Middleborough, Mass., on 20 October, 1694, in his seventy-third year, and his wife died there on 24 June, 1693, in her sixtieth year, according to the records of that town.* His will was made at Middleborough, on 30 June, 1694, and proved at Plymouth, on 10 November, 1694.

An exhaustive abstract of his will is here printed because two of his daughters had married descendants of Mayflower Passengers.

The oldest daughter, Elizabeth[2] Vaughan (*George*[1]), married Isaac[2] Howland (*John*[1]); and another daughter, Mary[2] Vaughan, married Jonathan Washburn[4] (*Elizabeth Mitchell*[3], *Jane*[2] *Cooke*, *Francis*[1]).

* Mayflower Descendant, 2: 159.

The original will and the original inventory, which are still preserved in the Plymouth County Probate Files, have been used in making the following abstracts.

[WILL OF GEORGE VAUGHAN, SR.]

[From original will] "George Vaughan S^r^", of Middleborough, made his will on 30 June, 1694. Bequests were as follows:

"To my son Daniell Vaughan .... the lot of land which he now lives on, with halfe my undevided meadow"

"To my son George Vaughan .... a twenty acre lot of land lying at ye head of ye lot of John Cob Junr with three acres and an halfe of meadow lying in ye meadow Commonly called the lower meadow. wth priviledges belonging thereunto, and an interest in all my undevided upland. my best bed wth 2 sheets a coverled a rugge and one blanket, two pillows with pillowbeers a bolster and curtains."

"To my daughter mary Wasborne .... ten acres of land lying where the house stands that I now live in, wth a bed & a rugge."

"All my upland & meadow except what is before mentioned I do give to my son Joseph Vaughan"

"To my daughter Elizabeth Howland .... my bigest brass Kittle."

"To my daughter Mercy Due .... A bed and a bolster."

"The rest of my estate I do give to my children (my debdts and necessary charges first being paid) equally to be divided amongst them except my son George Vaughan shall have a double share of all my iron & pewter vessels of my housholdstuff."

"my eldest son Joseph Vaughan to be my sole executor .... And I do .... request my son in law Isaac Howland to be helpfull to my s^d^ executor"

"My will is y^t^ what I give unto my youngest son George Vaughan shall be in my eldest son's Joseph Vaughans Custody untill he be setled." *

The witnesses were Samuel Wood and Ebenezer Tinkham, each of whom signed by a mark. The will was probated on 10 November, 1694, both witnesses being present and making oath

* This clause was written below the signatures of the testator and the witnesses.

"y[t] y[e] three lines under written were added by y[e] s[d] Testator at y[e] time of Sealing" [The will was also recorded, 1 : 210]

[From original inventory] An inventory of the personal estate was taken 27 October, 1694, by Samuel Wood and John Bennet, and was sworn to, on 10 November, 1694, by the executor. [It was also recorded, 1 : 211]

PLYMOUTH, MASS., VITAL RECORDS

(*Continued from p. 32*)

[p. 251] A purpose of mariage between Thomas Brace and Elisabeth Barnes both of Plymouth May 16 . 1741.

A purpose of mariage betwen Gideon Bradford of Plymton & Jane Paddock of Plymouth June 6th 1741

A Purpose of Mariage between Joseph Sachemus of Plym[o] & Lydia Peacken Sandwich June 6th 1741. Indians.

A purpose of mariage between Abraham Jackson of Plymouth & Mary Whiteing of Plymton Oct[o] 12 . 1741.

A purpose of Mariage between Sam[ll] Sepitt & Sarah Ryder both of Plym[o] Oct[o] 18 1741.

A purpose of mariage between William Wood & Eliz[a] Finney both of Plym[o] Oct[o] 25 . 1741.

A purpose of mariage between Tho[s] Clarke & Ruth Morton : both of Plym[o] Oct[o] 31 . 1741

A purpose of Mariage between Israel Clarke of Plym[o] & Deborah Pope of Sandwich Oct[o] 31 . 1741.

A purpose of Mariage between Josiah Churchell & Patience Harlow both of this Town Oct[o] 31 . 1741

A purpose of mariage between William Harlow jun[r] & Hannah Littlejohn both of Plym[o] Mar. 19 . 1741.

A purpose of mariage between Ephr[m] Holmes & Sarah Finney both of Plym[o] April 10 . 1742.

A purpose of mariage between Josiah Morton y[e] 3[d] & Experience Ellis both of this Town April 10 . 1742

A purpose of mariage between Seth Finney of Boston & Lydia Eames of Plym[o] April 16th 1742.

A purpose of mariage between m[r] Jn[o] Howland & m[rs] Patience Spooner both of Plym[o] april 16 . 1742

A purpose of mariage between Barzilla Stetson & Ruth Stutson * both of Plym[o] April 24 . 1742

* On original page 151, the marriage record reads "Barzillia Stetson, & Ruth Kempton, both of Plymo, Marryed at Plymo, Septr 6. 1742." See Mayflower Descendant, 14 : 160.

A purpose of mariage between Eleaz^r^ Holmes jun^r^ & Ester Ellis both of Plym^o^ May 8th 1742

A purpose of Mariage between Benj^a^ Barnes and Experience Rider both of Plym^o^ May 15 . 1742

a purpose of Mariage between Edward Tinkam of Plym^o^ & Sarah Ryder * of Plym^o^ & Lydia Ryder * of Kingston July 17th 1742

[p . 252] A purpose of mariage between Robt Shattuck & Ruhami Cook both of Plymoth Augt 14th 1742

a purpose of mariage between Zacheus Curtiss of Plym^o^ and Lydia Thomas of Dartmouth Augt 28th 1742

A purpose of mariage Ephr^m^ Paddock of Plym^o^ & Sarah Bradford of Plymton Septr 3^d^ 1742

A purpose of mariage between Ephraim Quoy & Mercy Peniss both of Plym^o^ Indians Septr 3 . 1742

A purpose of mariage between Theophilus Cotton & Martha Sanders both of this Town Oct^o^ 16 . 1742.

a purpose of Mariage between Josiah Cunnett & Hannah Quoy both of Plym^o^ Indians Oct^o^ 23 . 1742

a purpose of mariage between Joseph Shurtleff & Sarah Cobb both of Plym^o^ Oct^o^ 31 . 1742

a Purpose of mariage between Henry Sanders of Warham & Mary Hambleten of Plym^o^ Novr 21 . 1742

a Purpose of Mariage between Thomas Faunce 4th & Sarah Bartlett both of Plymouth Novr 27 . 1742

a Purpose of mariage between m^r^ Joseph Ruggles of Lambstown [Hardwick †] & m^rs^ Hannah Cushman of Plym^o^ Decr 4 . 1742

a Purpose of Mariage between Nath^ll^ Croade & Eliz^a^ Carte both of Plym^o^ December 11th 1742

a purpose of mariage between Peter Daniell & Hanah Ryder Indians both of Plym^o^ Janr^y^ 8 . 1742

a purpose of mariage between Job Hammond (Negro) & Hanah Quoy (indian) both of Plym^o^ Janr^y^ 30 . 1742.

A purpose of mariage between Noah Bradford and Hannah Clarke both of Plym^o^ Febr^y^ 13 . 1742

A purpose of Mariage between Archelaus Lane now resideing in Plym^o^ & Remembrance Walker of s^d^ Plym^o^ Febr^y^ 19 . 1742 spoke for p^r^ Isaac Little of Plym^o^ Febr^y^ 23 . 1742 s^d^ Lane came to my House & Declared s^d^ Publishment was Spoke for Contrary to his knowlege & Consent

A Purpose of Mariage Between William Keen and Ruth Serjeant both of Plym^o^ Febr^y^ 19 . 1742

A purpose of mariage between Gideon Gifford of Rochester and Lois Jackson of Plymoth Febr^y^ 27th 1742.

* The Kingston records show the intentions of Edward Tinkham of Kingston and Lydia Ryder of Plymouth, on 17 July, 1742, and the Plymouth town records [Mayflower Descendant, 17 : 4] show the marriage of Edward Tinkham of Kingston and Lydia Ryder of Plymouth, on 29 September, 1743.

† The word "Hardwick" has been interlined, in a different hand and ink.

[p . 253] 1746 Aug[st] 2 . A purpose of Marriage, Between Will[m] Jerman and Eleonar Thomas, both of Plymouth

30th A purpose of Marriage, Between Benj[a] Eaton of Kingston, & Mary Tinkcom of Plym[o]

Sep[t] 17th A Purpose of Marriage, Between David Wood of Plympton and Rebeckah Pratt of Plymouth

Sep[t] 13th A Purpose of Marriage, Between Benj[a] Churchell & Ruth Delano, Both of Plymouth.

27 . A Purpose of Marriage, between M[r] Peres Tilson & m[rs] Eliz[a] Doty . both of Plym[o]

oct[r] 11 . A Purpose of Marriage, between Will[m] Churchell and Susannah Clark . both of Plymouth

11th A Purpose of Marriage, between Nath[l] Bradford & Sarah Spooner, both of Plymouth.

18th A Purpose of Marriage, between [*] Dowty Randall of Scituate & [*] Eliz[a] Tilson of Plym[o]

25 . A Purpose of Marriage, between Nath[l] Goodwin & Lydia Le-Barron, both of Plym[o]

Nov[r] 22 A Purpose of Marriage, Between Eleazer Stephens, & Sarah Silvester, both of Plym[o]

29 A Purpose of Marriage, Between Joshua Finney, of Plym[o], & Elisabeth Pope of Sandwich

29 A Purpose of Marriage, Between Sam[l] Harlow, and Marcy Bradford, Both of Plymouth

Dec[r] 13 . A Purpose of Marriage, Between, Thomas Pattison & Susannah Beale, Both of Plymouth

27 . A Purpose of Marriage, Between Josiah Carver Jun[r], & Jerusha Sparrow . Both of Plymouth

Jan[ry] 3 A Purpose of Marriage, Between M[r] Joseph Le-Barron & m[rs] Sarah Leonard, both of Plym[o]

10 A Purpose of Marriage, between Edward Wright, & Elisabeth Decoster, both of Plym[o]

17 . A Purpose of Marriage, Between Jacob Tinkcom, & Lydia Donham, Both of Plymouth

24th A Purpose of Marriage, Between Tho[s] Spooner Jun[r] of Plym[o], and Deborah Bourn of Marshfield

Feb[ry] 14 . A Purpose of Marriage, Between James Clark Jun[r] and Hannah Swift, Both of Plym[o].

[p. 254] a purpose of marrage Between Elkanah Totman and Elisebeth Donham Both of plymouth July y[e] 7 1733

A Purpose of Marrage between Archibold Fisher and Elizabeth Decost both of Plymouth August 4th 1733

A Purpose of Marrage between Joslen Cepit & Desire Whood Indians both of Plymouth August 4th 1733

A Purpose of Marrage between m[r] Ebenezer Dogget & m[rs] Desire Rickard both of Plymouth August 11th 1733

* "Mr", before "Dowty", and "Mrs", before "Eliza", were crossed out, apparently in the same ink as the rest of the record.

A Purpose of Marriage between Ichabod Samson Junr of Duxberough and Marcy Savory of Plymouth August 17th 1733

A Purpose of Marriage between John Faunce Junr of Plymouth and Ruth Samson of Plimton September 15th 1733

A Purpose of Marriage between Ebenezer Sanders and Sarah Peters Indians both of Plymouth September 19th 1733.

A Purpose of Marriage between John Palmer of Scituate & Jean Doty of Plymouth Sepr 21th 1733.

A Purpose of Marriage Between John Valler and Mary May both of Plymouth September 22. 1733

A Purpose of Marriage between m^{r} Lazerus Samson and m^{rs} Abigal Shurtleff both of Plymouth October 6th 1733.

A Purpose of Marriage between Thomas Polden of Plymouth and Deborah Spooner of Dartmouth October 13 . 1733

A Purpose of Marriage between Nathaniel Thomas Junr Esqr of Plymouth and m^{rs} Elizabeth Gardner of Marshfeild . October 27th 1733.

A purpose of Marriage between Paul Cooke of Kingston and Joannah Holmes of Plymouth Novr 21th 1733.

A Purpose of Marriage between Robert Bartlett and Rebeckah Wood both of Plymouth Nov$^{r.}$ 21th 1733

A Purpose of Marriage between m^{r} Nathaniel Howland of Plymouth and Yetmercy Palmer of Bristol Novr 24 . 1733

A Purpose of Marriage between Samuel Hubberd and Hannah Polden both of Plymouth November 24th 1733

A Purpose of Marriage between m^{r} Barnebas Hedge of Yarmouth and m^{rs} Marcy Cole of Plymouth Decr 21 . 1733.

A Purpose of Marriage between Solomon Sepit and Sarah Farrow Indians both of Plymouth Decr 22 1733

[p. 255] A Purpose of Marriage Between Mr Jacob Tayler of Barnstable and m^{rs} Mary Atwood of Plymouth June 30th 1729.

A Purpose of Marriage Between Mr Nathaniel Thomas Junr of Plymouth & m^{rs} Hannah Robinson of Duxberough . Augt 16 . 1729

A Purpose of Marriage Between m^{r} Seth Doggett and m^{rs} Elizabeth Delano, both of Plymouth Augt 23 . 1729

A Purpose of Marriage Between Isaac King & Hannah Harlow both of Plymouth September 6th 1729

A Purpose of Marriage Between John Hambleton and Elizabeth Jones both of Plymouth October 24th 1729

A Purpose of Marriage between John Cushing Junr Esqr of Scituate & m^{rs} Mary Cotton of Plymouth Novr 1st 1729

A Purpose of Marriage between Thomas Ward & Joanna Donham both of Plymouth . Novr 1st 1729.

A Purpose of Marriage Between m^{r} Isaac Lothrop Junr of Plymouth and m^{rs} Hannah Freeman of Harwich . Novr 8th 1729.

A Purpose of Marriage between Joseph Treeble Residing in Plymouth and Ann Jones of s$^{d.}$ Plymouth Decr 6th 1729.

A Purpose of Marriage between Ebenezer Bryant of Plimton and Elizabeth King of Plymouth Decr 6th 1729

A Purpose of Marriage between Cornelius Brigs of Rochester and Thankfull Burges of Plymouth December 27th 1729.

A Purpose of Marriage between Ephraim Churchell and Priscilla Manchester both of Plymouth March . 14th 1729/30

A Purpose of Marriage between John Studly and Elizabeth Doty both of Plymouth March 28th 1730.

A Purpose of Marriage between Thomas Western and Prudence Conant Both of Plymouth April . 18th 1730.

A Purpose of Marriage between mr William Dyre of Boston and Mrs Hannah Phillips of Plymouth May 4th 1730

A Purpose of Marriage between mr John Atwood and mrs Experience Peirce both of Plymouth May 19th 1730

A Purpose of Marriage between mr Nathaniel Morton & mrs Meriah Clarke both of Plymouth June 17th 1730.

A Purpose of Marriage Between mr Thomas Kempton of Plymouth and mrs Esther Throop of Bristol . June 19th 1730.

A Purpose of Marriage between mr Nicholas Drew & mrs Lydia Doggett both of Plymouth . July 18th 1730.

A Purpose of Marriage between mr Ebenezer Finney of Barnsta[ble] and mrs Rebeccah Barnes of Plymouth August 1st 1730.

A Purpose of Marriage Between Nathaniel Thomas Esqr of Plymouth and Madam Anna Leonard of Norton August 8th 1730.

[p. 256] A Purpose of Marriage between Jabez Holmes and Rebecca Harlow both of Plymouth August 29th 1730

A Purpose of Marriage between Silas West & Mary Cob both of Plymouth Sepr 26th 1730

A Purpose of Marriage between Tobe and Dutch, negroes both of them Servants to Joseph Warren of Plymouth October 28 . 1730

A Purpose of Marriage between mr Jonathan Bartlet & Mrs Thankfull Barnes both of Plymouth December 5th 1730.

A Purpose of Marriage Between Samuel Cornish Junr and Meribah Clarke both of Plymouth January 16th 1730/31

A Purpose of Marriage between John Waterman and Hannah Cushman both of Plymouth . february 4th 1730/1

A Purpose of Marriage between Jacob Curtice and Fear Donham both of Plymouth March 6th 1730/1

A Purpose of Marriage between Joseph Donham of Plymouth and Jean Randel of Scituate March 13th 1730/1

we the Subcribers Select men of the Town of Plymouth declare that the above named Joseph Donham is not an Inhabitant in sd Town according to Law dated at Plymouth March 16 . 1730/1

Isaac Lothrop
Benja Warren
John Foster

A Purpose of Marriage between Jacob Johnson & Sarah Clarke both of Plymouth April 17th 1731

A Purpose of Marriage between Samuel Holmes of Plymouth and Mary Lewis of Falmouth April 24th 1731.

A Purpose of Marriage between Cato Negro Servant to m^r^ Thomas Foster and Jenne Negro Servant to Decon John Foster both of Plymouth May 6th 1731.

A Purpose of Marriage between Lemuel Fish of Rochester and Deborah Barden residing in Plymouth May 22th 1731

A Purpose of Marriage between Capt John Gould of Plymouth and m^rs^ Sarah Clark of Chilmark in Dukes County : May 29th 1731.

A Purpose of Marriage between William Kempton and Mary Brewster both of Plymouth July 3^d^ 1731

A Purpose of Marriage between Thomas Kempton Junr and Mary Holmes both of Plymouth July 24th 1731.

A Purpose of Marriage between Elnathan Holmes and Rebeccah Churchell both of Plymouth August 7th 1731.

A Purpose of Marriage between m^r^ Josiah Morton Junr of Plymouth and m^rs^ Maletiah Finney of Barnstable August 14th 1731

A Purpose of Marriage between Joseph Peach and Lydia Jeffry Indians both of Plymouth August 14th 1731

[p. 257] A Purpose of Marriage between John Harlow Junr and Mary Rider both of Plymouth Augt 28th 1731

A Purpose of Marriage between Benjamin Gifford of Plymouth and Mary Lawton of Portsmouth in Rhoad Island October 29th 1731.

A Purpose of Marriage between m^r^ Cornelius Clark of Rochester and Susanna Donham of Plymouth . October 30th 1731.

A Purpose of Marriage between Dolphin a Negro man Servant belonging to Nathaniel Thomas Junr and Flora a negro woman Servant belonging to m^rs^ Priscilla Watson both of Plymouth . November 6th 1731

A Purpose of Marriage between m^r^ Francis Curtis Junr & m^rs^ Elizabeth Barnes both of Plymouth . November 10th 1731.

A Purpose of Marriage between Dick a negro man Servant belonging to m^r^ Nathaniel Thomas Junr and Phebe a Negro Woman Servant belonging to Mr Haviland Torry both of Plymouth Dcember 4th 1731

A Purpose of Marriage between m^r^ Josiah Carver and m^rs^ Bethiah Churchell both of Plymouth Novr 20th 1731

A Purpose of Marriage between Ebenezer Bartlett of Plymouth and Rebekah Dimond of Rehoboth Plymouth february 5th 1731/2

A Purpose of Marriage between Samuel Burge of Plymouth and Jedidah Gibs of Sandwich . february 16th 1731/2

A Purpose of Marriage between John Blackmore Junr of Rochester and Sarah Holmes of Plymouth . Plymouth february 18th 1731/2

A Purpose of Marriage between Gyles Nash and Remembrance Jackson both of Plymouth february 19th 1731/2.

A Purpose of Marriage between Thomas Faunce the third of Plymouth and Hannah Damond of Scituate Plym^th^ March 25 : 1732

A Purpose of Marriage Between Micah Gibs & Sarah Sanders both of Agawam within the Township of Plymouth April 7th 1732.

A Purpose of Marriage between Mordecai Ellis and Desire Whood Indians both Residing in Plymouth April 14th 1732.

A Purpose of Marriage between Ebenezer Tinkcom of Plymouth and Mary Bonney of Plimpton Plymouth April 19th 1732.

A Purpose of Marriage between John Case Resident in Plymouth and Rebecah Peirce of Plymouth. May 6th 1732 *

A Purpose of Marriage between Quomeny a Negro Man Servant belonging to Josiah Cotton Esqr and Kate a Negro Woman Servant belonging to mr John Murdoch . both of Plymouth May 27 : 1732.

A Purpose of Marriage between mr Walter Rich of Boston and Rebeccah Morton of Plymouth June 16 . 1732

[p. 258] A Purpose of Marriage between Peter English and Alce Randel both of Plymouth June 24th 1732.

A Purpose of Marriage between Nicolas Spink of North Kingston in Naraganset and Mary Jackson of Plymouth . June . 30th 1732

A Purpose of Marriage between Barnabas Holmes & Abigal Shepherd both of Plymouth August 5th 1732

A Purpose of Marriage between Nathaniel Chubbuck Junr and Tabitha Besse of Agawam within the Township of Plymouth Augt 12th 1732

A Purpose of Marriage between Samuel Doty Junr and Joannah Bosworth Junr both of Plymouth September 9th 1732

A Purpose of Marriage between Joseph Lewen of Plymouth and Rejoyce Walker of Eastham Sepr 9th 1732

A Purpose of Marriage between John Wetherhead & Remember Bates both of Plymouth September 17th 1732

A Purpose of Marriage between Benjamin Rogers and Phebe Harden both of Plymouth September 17th 1732.

A purpose of Marriage between Quomeny a Negro Servant belonging to Josiah Cotton Esqr and Mary Hamshere Indian woman both of Plymouth Sepr 30th 1732

A Purpose of Marriage between Caleb Stetson and Deborah Morton both of Plymouth October 21 . 1732

A Purpose of Marriage between Benjamin Wanno Indian of Plymouth and Leah Tompom Indian of Barnstable Novr 4 . 1732

A Purpose of Marriage Benjamin Cole of Plimpton and Rebekah Harlow of Plymouth Novr 9th 1732

A Purpose of Marriage between James Winslow of Plymouth & Susannah Conant of midleberough November 14 . 1732.

A Purpose of Marriage between John Barker now residing in Plymouth and Meriah Cushman of Plymouth Novr 16 : 1732

A Purpose of Marriage between John Nelson & Mary Morton both of Plymouth November 25th 1732

A Purpose of Marriage between Cornelius Warren of Midleberough and Marcy Ward of Plymouth Decr 15 . 1732

A Purpose of Marriage between mr Isaac Lothrop Junr and Madam Priscilla Watson both of Plymouth Decr 23 . 1732

A Purpose of Marriage between mr Abiel Pulcifer and mrs Bethiah Cotton both of Plymouth January 20th 1732/3

* In the margin, opposite this entry, is written "June 10"

A purpose of marriage between Thomas Savery of Plimouth and Priscilla paddock of midlebourough march 10 1732/3

A purpose of Marrgie Betwen Samuell Bumpus of Barn[stable] and Sarrah Roggers now Residing in Plymouth March 2[*]

[p. 259] A Purpose of Mariage between Elisha Perry of Sandwich & Anna Sanders of Agawam within the Township of Plymouth Sepr 4th 1725

A Purpose of Marriage Between m^r^ Tomson Phillips of Jemaco In the West Indies & m^rs^ Hannah Cotton of Plymouth Sepr 9th 1725

A Purpose of Marriage Between Joseph Holmes & Phebe Churchell both of Plymouth October 9th 1725.

A Purpose of Marriage Between Allexander Malli[se] † and Bathsheba Hill both Residing in Plymouth Octr 9th 1725

A Purpose of Marriage Between Nathan Delano & Bathsheba Holmes both of Plymouth October 14th 1725.

A Purpose of Marriage Between Thomas Foster of Plymouth and Lois Fuller of Barnstable October 16th 1725.

A Purpose of Marriage Between Joseph Cornish of Plymouth and Patience Pratt of Scituate . October 30th 1725

A Purpose of Marriage Between m^r^ John Sparhawk of Plymouth and m^rs^ Hannah Jacob . of Scituate Octo^r^ 30th 1725.

A Purpose of Marriage Between Jacob Tinkcom and Judeth Hunt both of Plymouth Novr 2^d^ 1725.

A Purpose of Marriage between m^r^ Thomas Morton Junr & m^rs^ Hannah Nelson both of Plymouth . Decr 4th 1725.

A Purpose of Marriage between John Moore Resideing in Plymouth & Mary Shattuck of Plymouth . Decr 4th 1725

A Purpose of Marriage between Phillip Lee & Elizabeth Jackson Decr 11th 1725

A Purpose of Marriage between Nath^ll^ Howland & Abigal Billington both of Plym^th^ December 18th 1725.

A Purpose of Marriage between Silvanus Hall of Plymouth & Elizabeth Dogget of Marshfield . December 25th 1725.

A Purpose of Marriage between m^r^ John Winslow of Plymouth and m^rs^ Mary Little of Marshfield . January 21th 1725/6.

A Purpose of Marriage between William Foster of Sandwich and Hannah Rider of Plymouth January 21th 1725/6.

A Purpose of Marriage between Ebenezer Rider and Thankfull Silvester both of Plymouth february 12th 1725/6.

A Purpose of Mariage between Benjamin Besse and Martha Chubbuck both of Agawam within the Township of Plymouth March 20th 1725/6

Jonathan Barnes & Phebe Finny Published May 1726

A Purpose of Marriage between m^r^ Ebenezer Finney of Bristoll and m^rs^ Jean Faunce of Plymouth June 4th 1726.

* Illegible.

† See marriage on original page 141. [Mayflower Descendant, 14 : 71.]

A Purpose of Marriage between Peter Cole & Mary Marshall both of Plymouth July 16th 1726. mr Robert Brown forbid the bans July 18th 1726 by Reason the sd Mary Marshall is his Servant. Octor 20th mr Brown Consented

Left Josiah Finney Published to Mrs Marcy Thomas of Marshfeild Augt 6 . 1726

mr Isaac Little & mrs Sarah Church Published . Sepr 3 : 1726.

(*To be continued*)

EATON NOTES

BY THE EDITOR

(*Continued from Vol. XII, page 229*)

IN this issue we give exhaustive abstracts of all original documents and records, in the Plymouth County, Mass., Registry of Probate, relating to the estate of Samuel[5] Eaton (*Barnabas*[4], *Samuel*[3-2], *Francis*[1]), of Middleborough, Mass.

[SAMUEL[5] EATON'S WILL]

[From original will] "Samuel Eaton of Middleborough" made his will on 1 May, 1815. Bequests were as follows:

To "my two sons Israel Eaton and Enos Eaton all my Real estate with my money to be Equally divided; and also the Tanyard betwen them with this exception the Buildings of all kinds except the Cureing* Shop and Beckhouse I give to my Son Enos Eaton exclusive; by their paying out of my estate as hereafter mentioned which two Sons Israel & Enos I Constitute . . . . my Executors . . . . ; namely I give to my son Israel Eaton my Desk with one half of my Hetchel; to my Son Enos Eaton my watch and one bed with my Great Iron Kittle, and one half of my Hetchel together with my Fire tongs, I give to my Son Israel Eaton my Great Bible . I give to my Son Daniel Eaton one Hundred and fifty Dollars, I give to my Son Darius Eaton one Hundred and fifty Dollars I give and Bequeath to Each of the Children of my Son Samuel Eaton that may be living at my decease ten Dollars each I give to the Children of my daughter Mehitable Wood one Bed with one half my Household Furniture not above disposed of also I give to my Daughter Eunice Edy one Cow with the other half of my Houshold Furniture ; I give

* "currying" in the record.

to my Grandson Zenas Eaton ten Dollars to be paid him in leather, All which legasies Shall be paid .... after my just debts are paid within one year after my decease the rest and every part of my estate that may remain .... Shall be Equally Divided betwen my two Executors Israel & Enos Eaton"

The witnesses were Seth Eaton, Jr., Barnabas Eaton and Ziba Eaton.

The will of "Samuel Eaton late of Middleborough .... Gentleman deceased" was probated 21 February, 1820. [The will was also recorded, 50 : 501.]

[From original document] On 21 February, 1820, the executors, Israel Eaton and Enos Eaton, gave bond, with Samuel Morton and Solomon Richmond as sureties.

[From original document] On 21 February, 1820, letter testamentary was issued to Israel Eaton and Enos Eaton, Seth Eaton, Jr., and Barnabas Eaton, two of the witnesses to the will, being present.

[From original document] On 21 February, 1820, Israel Eaton and Enos Eaton, the executors, were ordered to give public notice of their appointment, by posting in Middleborough, and on 21 August, 1820, they both made oath that they had posted the notice as ordered.

NOTES BY THE EDITOR

Officers of the Massachusetts Society. At the Twentieth Annual Meeting of the Massachusetts Society of Mayflower Descendants, held at the Society's Rooms, 53 Mt. Vernon St., Boston, on Tuesday, 28 March, 1916, officers for the ensuing year were elected, as follows:

Governor,	Rev. Frederick B. Allen
Deputy Governor,	Arthur Perry
Secretary,	George Ernest Bowman
Treasurer,	Alvin P. Johnson
Historian,	Fred T. Field
Captain,	William B. H. Dowse
Elder,	Rev. Ernest M. Paddock
Surgeon,	Edwin A. Daniels, M.D.
Assistants,	Miss Mary F. Edson
	G. Andrews Moriarty, Jr.
	Mrs. Gordon Prince
	Mrs. Robert S. Russell
	Rev. Rufus B. Tobey
	Arthur C. Walworth
	Mrs. Leslie C. Wead

THE SOCIETY'S FIRST LEGACY. On 14 March, 1916, the Massachusetts Society of Mayflower Descendants received its first legacy. On that day Mrs. Fannie E. Long and Miss Emily A. Ransom, as executrices, turned over to the Society a check for five hundred dollars ($500.00), the amount of a bequest in the will of Mrs. Annie Humphrey (Trowbridge) Ward, a member of the Society from her election, on 21 February, 1899, until her death in Boston, on 26 December, 1915.

THE PROVINCETOWN MONUMENT. The illustration facing page 65 of this issue has been printed from a half-tone plate loaned by Mr. Edmund J. Carpenter, Secretary of the Cape Cod Pilgrim Memorial Association of Provincetown, Mass., and author of "The Pilgrims and Their Monument."

THE MAYFLOWER GENEALOGIES. During the past twenty years the Editor has received hundreds of communications claiming descent from supposed "Mayflower Passengers" who never saw "The Mayflower"; or claiming descent from actual Mayflower Passengers, but through children or grandchildren who died in infancy, or who died unmarried, or who never existed; and the number of such communications is steadily increasing, because of the growing interest in the Pilgrim Tercentenary in 1920.

For reference purposes in such cases, and to save a great deal of unnecessary correspondence, a preliminary outline of the first three generations of "The Mayflower Genealogies" will be printed in this Society's monthly magazine, "Pilgrim Notes and Queries," beginning with the Cooke and the Hopkins families in the issue for March, 1916.

HOBART — BROCK — BRADFORD. Three children of Francis Brock are recorded at Scituate, Mass.: Mary, born 15 December, 1699; Grace, born 27 July, 1701; Barsheba, born 21 May, 1703. The name of the mother is not given in connection with the births; but the death of Sarah, wife of Francis Brock, on 19 January, 1704/5, was entered on the Scituate records.

The will of Israel Hobart, of Scituate, dated 14 July, 1729, proves that his deceased daughter, Sarah Brock, was the mother of Francis Brock's three daughters, and proves that they all married.

The Plymouth Town Records [Mayflower Descendant, 14 : 38] give the marriage, on 7 September, 1719, of Elisha[3] Bradford (*Joseph*[2], *William*[1]) and Bathshua Brock.

The will of Israel Hobart is found in the Plymouth County, Mass., Probate Records, at Plymouth, Volume VI, page 111. The only original document in the files is the bond of the administratrix. An exhaustive abstract of the will follows:

[6 : 111] "Israel Hobart of Scituate .... Yeoman" made his will on 14 July, 1729. Bequests were as follows.

To "my son Israel Hobart Junr twenty shillings in Bills of Credit in full of his portion I having already Settled a Considerable Estate upon him in lands."

To "my Daughter Abigail Hobart twenty shillings in Bills of Credit in full of her Portion with what she has already Received"

To "my three Grand children ye children of my Daughter Sarah Brock Dec^d^ viz. Mary Witherton, Grace Davis & Bathsheba Bradford fifteen Shillings in Bills of Credit in full of y^r^ portion."

To "my Daughter Jael Hobart all my Estate Both Real & Personal.... She paying my Just Debts & Funeral Charge & ye Legacyes in this my will Given."

"Daughter Jael Hobart to be ye sole executrix"

The witnesses were James Torrey, John Cushing, Jr., John Holmes and Deborah Otis.

On 24 May, 1731, John Cushing, Jr., and Deborah Otis made oath to the will; and on 4 October, 1731, letter of administration was issued.

[From unrecorded bond] On 24 May, 1731, Jael Hobart gave a bond of £50, as executrix. Her surety was John Cushing, Jr. The witnesses were Cornelius White and Nicholas Davies.

THE VITAL RECORDS OF HALIFAX, MASS.

THE Town of Halifax, Mass., was incorporated in 1734, and included parts of the three towns of Middleborough, Pembroke and Plympton. The earliest birth entered on the Halifax records was in the year 1703; the earliest death occured in 1723; and the earliest marriage was in 1736.

The Massachusetts Society of Mayflower Descendants has printed, in a volume of over two hundred pages, a literal copy of every entry of a birth, intention of marriage, marriage, and death, prior to 1850, on the records of Halifax. A few entries of later date have also been printed, in order to include every vital record in the first four of the town's books. A complete index makes every name easily accessible.

Among the names found in this volume are: Alden, Allen, Barrows, Bearse, Bonney, Bosworth, Bourne, Bradford, Briggs, Bryant, Chandler, Chipman, Churchill, Cooke, Crocker, Curtis, Cushing, Cushman, Drew, Dunbar, Eaton, Eddy, Ellis, Fuller, Hall, Harlow, Harris, Hatch, Hathaway, Hayward, Holmes, Howland, Inglee, Jackson, Leach, Lucas, Lyons, Mitchell, Morton, Munroe, Palmer, Parris, Perkins, Pope, Porter, Pratt, Richmond, Ripley, Samson, Sears, Shaw, Smith, Soule, Standish, Sturtevant, Thomson, Tilson, Tinkham, Wade, Washburn, Waterman, White, Wood.

A copy of this book will be mailed to any one on receipt of three dollars ($3.00).

Remittances must be payable to "Massachusetts Society of Mayflower Descendants," and should be mailed to the Editor of this magazine.

THE MYLES STANDISH MONUMENT AT DUXBURY, MASS.

[See page 192]

THE MAYFLOWER DESCENDANT

Vol. XVIII JULY, 1916 No. 3

THOMAS[1] POPE'S WILL AND INVENTORY

TRANSCRIBED BY THE EDITOR

THOMAS[1] POPE of Plymouth and Dartmouth, Mass., married, first, Anne[2] Fallowell (*Gabriel*[1]) of Plymouth. She died leaving one daughter, Hannah[2] Pope, who became the wife of Joseph Bartlett[3] (*Mary*[2] *Warren*, *Richard*[1]) of Plymouth.

Thomas[1] Pope married, second, Sarah[2] Jenney (*John*[1]) of Plymouth, who died before her husband made his will. Thomas[1] and Sarah Pope appear to have had seven children: Susanna[2] Pope, who married Jacob Mitchell[3] (*Jane*[2] *Cooke*, *Francis*[1]); Seth[2] Pope, who married Deborah Perry and Rebecca——; Thomas[2] Pope, probably died young; John[2] Pope, probably died young; Sarah[2] Pope, married Samuel Hinckley; Joanna[2] Pope, married John Hathaway[4] (*Sarah*[3] *Cooke*, *John*[2], *Francis*[1]); Isaac[2] Pope.

Thomas[1] Pope made his will 9 July, 1683; and the inventory, in which he is called "of Dartmouth", was taken 4 August, 1683. The will appears to have been probated at Plymouth 2 November, 1683.

Literal copies of the will and inventory, and of the bond of the executors, are here printed, at the expense of a descendant. The proper reference, to the Plymouth Colony Wills and Inventories and the Plymouth Colony Court Orders, is given with each record.

The proof of the marriage of Hannah[2] Pope and Joseph Bartlett is found in a deed from Thomas[1] Pope to "my Son in law Joseph Bartlett", and in the will of the widow Katherine Fallowell, which mentions her grandchild "hannah the wife of Joseph Bartlett".

[Thomas Pope's Will]

[Plym. Col. Wills, 4:2:50] July the 9th 1683

The Last Will and Testament of Thomas Pope being aged and weake of body But yett in p^r^fect understanding and Memory wherin I have of my estate as followeth; I Give unto my son Seth as an adition to what I have formerly given him ten shillings in Mony alsoe I give unto my Grand son Thomas Pope all that my twenty five acrees of upland and two acrees of Meddow Lying and being on the west syde of Acushenett River be it more or lesse; and it is my Desire that his father may take the said Land into his hands, and make the best Improvement of it that hee can for the good of my said Grand son untill hee comes of age to Make use of it himselfe; alsoe it is my mind that my son Seth shall in consideration of the aforsaid Land pay three pound sterling unto my Grand son Jacob michell when hee Comes to age of twenty one yeers alsoe I give unto my Daughter Deborah Pope five pound in Mony and to each of my other Daugters five pound apeece in Mony alsoe my meddow Lying att the south Meddowes in Plymouth or the vallue of it I give to be equally Devided amongst all My sones and Daughters; alsoe I give and bequeath unto my son Isacke all my seate of Land where I now Dwell with all the Meddowes belonging therunto and all the privilidges therunto belonging To him his heires and assignes for ever; But an if it should please God that hee should Decease without an heire before hee comes to the age of twenty and one yeeres then my said seat of Lands shall belonge unto the sons of my son Seth, alsoe I give unto my son Isacke all my houseing and houshold Goods of all sorts alsoe all my Cattle, and horse kind and swine; alsoe all sorts of Provisions alsoe Cart and plowes with all the takeling belonging unto them alsoe I Give unto my son Isacke all my mony except that which I have Given to my Daughters and I order my said son Isacke to pay all my Just Debts and to receive all my Debts that are Due unto mee alsoe I order my Indian Lydia to live with my son Isacke untell hee is one and twenty yeers of age and my Indian Gerle I give to him During his life alsoe it is my mind and will that my son Isacke shall make Noe bargaine without the Consent of his overseers; untill hee be twenty yeares of age, I have made Choise of John Cooke and my son Seth and Thomas Tabor to be for overseers, To see this My will p^r^formed

Signed and sealed in p^r^sence of John Cooke and Thomas Tabor;

Thomas Pope his marke

[Thomas Pope's Inventory]

[p. 51] Agust The 4th: 1683

A true Inventory of the Lands goods and Chattle of Thomas Pope of the Towne of Dartmouth Late Deceased;

Impr: the housing and the seate of Land belonging therunto	100	00	00
Item 25 acrees of upland and 2 acrees of meddow lying on the west side of Cushenett River	10	00	00
Item 7 acrees of upland and 7 acrees of Meddow att Plymouth	20	00	0
Item 2 oxen and 2 steers	12	00	00
Item 5 Cowes and halfe a yeerling	11	10	00
Item 4 Calves	02	00	00
Item 1 horse and 1 mare	06	00	00
Item his swine	05	00	00
Item Cart & plow Tackling	03	00	00
Item for tooles of all sorts	02	00	00
Item 2 Guns	02	10	0
Item 3 bedds and the beding belonging to them	20	00	0
Item potts and kettles & puter	05	0	0
Item wearing Clothes	05	00	0
Item Chests and other houshold Lumber	05	00	0
Item Cotten woole & sheeps wool and yearne	05	00	0
Item Corn and other provision	07	00	0
Item this yeares Crope of Corn	10	00	0
Item in Mony	32	00	0
Item an Indian Gerle	10	00	0
Item Debts Due unto him	01	00	0
sume	274	00	0

Taken by us the Day & yeer abovewritten
Thomas Tabor
Arther Hathawey

[Court Orders, 6:2:1] Know all men by these prsents that I Isacke Pope and Seth Pope both of Dartmouth in the Govr-ment of New Plymouth Planders Doe heerby acknowlidge our-selves heerby to stand bound unto the Govr: and Court of Plym-outh aforsaid in the penall some of four hundred pound for the payment wherof well and truely to be made wee bind ourselves our heires executors and adminnestrators Joyntly and and sev-erall feirmly by these prsents; sealed and Given this second of November 1683

The Condition of the above written obligation is such That wheras the above bounden Isacke Pope and Seth Pope hath obtained Letters of Adminnestration To adminnester on the estate of Thomas Pope of Dartmouth aforsaid late Deceased; if therfor the said the said Isack Pope and Seth Pope; Doe pay all such Debts and Legacyes or Cause them to be payed as are Due or owing unto any from the said Estate; and keep a faire accoumpt of theire said adminnestration; and be redy to Give in an accompt therof when by them required; and save and keep harmles the said Gov[r]: and Court therof from any Damage that may accrew unto them by theire said adminnestration That then the above written obligation to be void and of Non effect or other to remayne in full force strength and vertue;

UNRECORDED BARNSTABLE COUNTY DEEDS

ABSTRACTS BY THE EDITOR

(*Continued from page 104*)

THE abstracts presented in this issue have been made from original documents now in the collection of the Massachusetts Society of Mayflower Descendants.

[SIPSON TO MAYO AND HOPKINS]

On 20 July, 1713, John Sipson and Tom Sipson, Indians, both of Harwich, for 38 shillings sold to "Samuel mayo & Joshua Hopkins both of Eastham . . . . Purchesars of the Land in the Township of Harwich above Said . . . . All that our flatts & Sedge Ground that now is or Ever hereafter Shall be Lying in the Township of Harwich above Said Lying Scituate between the main Chanil that Comes in at the Harbour Called Potonomoqut alias the middle Harbour and Runs up to namacoyek point and the Channel that Comes in at S[d] Harbour and Runs up Between Strongs Island and Esnue Island and So Runs up to the wadeing place that Goes over to Chatham that is all the flats and Sedge Ground that now is or Ever hereafter Shall between Said Two Channels up home to the main Land"

The grantors signed by marks. The witnesses were Elisha Hopkins, and Joseph Doane, Jr.

The deed was acknowledged, 20* July, 1713, before Joseph Doane, Justice of the Peace. It was recorded 11* July, 1713, by William Basset, Register.

* Sic.

"A True Coppy of the Record Taken from ye 6th Book of Evidences of Land for ye County of Barnstable page 61 and Comp^{d} Attest Edwd Bacon Reg^{r}. april 18th 1781"

[KNOWLES TO KNOWLES]

"I Willard Knowles of Sandisfield in the County of Berkshire* yeoman", for £40, "to me in hand paid by Seth Knowles 3^{d} and william Knowles both of Eastham in the County of Barnstable yeomans . . . . do forever Quit Claim to the following pieces of land lying in said Eastham which land was my honored fathers Willard Knowles Esq dec'd and in the first place all that piece of land which was my Said fathers lying at the Stage so called and all that piece of land which adjoins Nathaniel mayos land and Nathaniel mayos Cove and all that piece of land Called the Norset land lying near wher Mr Solomon Doane now dwells which pieces of land are Considered by the known and Customary bounds thereof"

The deed was dated 16 October, 1786, and was acknowledged the same day, before Elijah Knowles, Justice of the Peace. The witnesses were Elijah Knowles and Samuel Freeman. The deed was recorded, 4 April, 1787, in Barnstable County Deeds, Book 41, folio 3, by Ebenezer Bacon, Register, and has not been re-recorded, since the fire in 1827.

[RICHARD SEARS TO MULFORD HOWES]

On 6 March, 1823, "Richard Sears of Chatham . . . . Esqr in consideration of Two Hundred Dollars in Exchange of Lands" sold to "Mulford Howes of Chatham . . . . Yeoman . . . . the Cleard Land on Morrises Island, Called the Northerley or Stage Island and the Easterley Side of the wood Land on the South Island, so Called, with all my wright to the Cedar Swamp, that I Bought of Joseph Howes Executor to the Last Will and testament of Sam^{ll} Collings Deceased, Being a part of said Island formerley Laid out to said Saml Collings in the devition of the Land & Swamp by the Owners of said Island, Beginning at the South Side of said Stage Island at a Stone on the Bank, near the meadow that is Commonly discribed, Between the Islands, and running Northerley Over the Hill on the ridge of the Land made by their plowing & planting of their Severall Shares to a Stone on the Bank, above the meadows, then Southerley & Easterley as the Bank, & Lands Leads round, to the first mentioned Bounds also the Easterly half of said Collings Wright or

* Massachusetts.

Eighth in the Wood Land, on the South Island (so Called) Beginning at Richard Sears', South East Corner Bound of the Other Eighth or half of said Wood Land, on the South Island (so Called) at an Oak Trea & heap of Stones & Running Easterly Eleven Rods, to a Stake & heap of Stones by the Cleard Land, then Northerly as the s[d] Wood Lands Runs Round to North East Corner of said wood Land, then South westerly by s[d] wood Land to Richard Sears Northerly Corner Bounds of said wood Land with all my wright to the said Seader Swamp at the foot of the Cleard Land that the said Mulford Howes Conveyed to the said Richard Sears, all the above discribed premases Contains Six Acers, more or Liss . . . . I the said Richard Sears & Hitty his wife . . . . doth hereby quit Claim all her Wright & power of Thirds to the above discribed premases"

The deed was dated 6 March, 1823, and was signed by Richard Sears and Hitty Sears. It was acknowledged the same day, by Richard Sears only, before Richard Sears, Jr., Justice of the Peace. The witnesses were Richard Sears, Jr., and Watson Hinckley. The deed was not recorded.

ABSTRACTS OF BARNSTABLE COUNTY, MASS., PROBATE RECORDS

(*Continued from page 61*)

[Widow Mary Haughton's Will]

[p. 77] On 19 January, 1685/6, "mary Haughton widow y[e] Relict of James Haughton Late of y[e] Towne of Barnestable . . . . being Ancient and weake in Body" made her will. Bequests were as follows:

To "y[e] two Eldest Children of Joseph Potts my Brother Edward Potts his eldest Son five pounds apiece"

To "Thomas Hinckley Esq[r] twenty Shillings"

To "John Hinckley y[e] Son of y[e] abovesd Thomas Hinckley five pound"

To "Mercy Hinckely y[e] Daughter of y[e] sd Thomas Hinckley Esq[r] five pound"

To "Experiance Hinckley y[e] Daughter of sd Thomas Hinckley Esq[r] five pound"

To "Thankfull Hinckley y[e] daughter of sd Thomas Hinckley Esq[r] five pound and one Cow"

To "Abigail Hinckley ye Daughter of sd Thomas Hinckley Esqr five pound"

To "Ebeneazer Hinckeley ye Son of S^{d} Thomas Hinckley Esqr five pound"

To "Reliance Hinckley ye Daughter of S^{d} Thomas Hinckley Esqr five pounds"

To "Deacon Job Crocker twenty shillings"

To "Capt Joseph Lothrop twenty Shillings"

To "John Howland ye Son of Liu^{t} John Howland twenty Shillings"

To "Mary Fuller widow Relict of Samuel deceased twenty Shillings"

To "Mary Taylor ye Daughter of Henry Taylor twenty Shillins"

To "Ralph Haughton now Living att milton ten Shillings"

To "Liu^{t} John Howland a to year old and vantage Steere which is now in his keeping:"

"if ought of my Estate Remaine at my Decease more then Enough to pay my Debts and Legases here in mentioned to be Equally devided beetween the above mentioned Children of ye above sd Thomas Hinckley"

To "ye Church of Christ in Barnestable five pound to be Converted in to a peice of plate for ye use of sd Curch"

"Thomas Hinckley Esqr and ye said Deacon Jobe Crocker to be Joynt Executors"

The will was signed by a mark. The witnesses were Barnabas Lothrop, Sr., and James Whippo.

In October, 1687, "Mary Haughton desiered to have this following alteration in her will aforesaid viz that ye Cow mentioned to Thankfull Hinckley Shee Intended it for Abigail Hinckley and her will is that ye Leagase given to mary Taylor is Revoked and made null"

This codicil was witnessed by Thomas Hinckley, Sr., Samuel Hinckley, Jr., and Mary Jenkins.

On 5 April, 1693, "Barnabas Lothrop Esqr" made oath to the will, before Joseph Lothrop, Register; and Samuel Hinckley, Jr., and Mary Jenkins made oath to the codicil, "before Barnabas Lothrop Esqr" Judge of Probate. On 17 April, 1693, James Whippo made oath to the will, before Barnabas Lothrop, Judge of Probate, and the will was approved. It was recorded 18 April, 1693, by Joseph Lothrop, Register.

[p. 78] The inventory was taken, at Barnstable, 2 November, 1692, by John Howland, James Lewes and Samuel Hinckley. No real estate is mentioned. "m^{r} Thomas Hinckley" made oath to the inventory 5 April, 1693; and on 17 April, 1693, he added several items. John Hinckley, Jr., was indebted to the estate; and the estate owed "To Thomas Hinckley according to her account: 7$^{£}$: p year for diat and tendance 06: 10: 04". The other creditors were: "m^{r} Allin", "m^{r} Whippo" and "major walley".

[George Allen's Estate]

[p. 79] "where as Divers questions and Controversies have been, had moved, and continued between Caleb Allin of Sandwich .... and others his Natural Bretheren and Sisters, of ye one part and Sarah Allin Relict of Georg Allin Late of Sandwich afore Said deceased of ye other part .... concerning the .... moveable estate that ye sd Sarah Allin and George Allin was Seized of at ye time of his Death for the Appeasing where of the sd Caleb Allin for him self and other his Sd Bretheren and Sisters and ye sd Sarah Allin for her self have .... Chosen Barnabas Lothrop of Barnestable Capt John Thecher of yarmouth and Shearjashub Bourne of Sandwich .... Esq^{rs} Arbitrators .... and ye sd Caleb Allin .... And ye sd Sarah Allin .... are to meete with ye sd Arbitrators before Named att ye now Dwelling house of Capt Joseph Lothrop in Barnestable afore sd on ye first Tuesday in may next Insuing by ten of ye Clock in ye fore noone and there to make their Alligations on both sids and ye sd Sarah Allin then and there is also to present unto ye Arbitrators afore Named an Exact and true Inventory up on oath of all y^{e} .... Estate which Shee and ye Said George Allin was seized of at the time of his Death .... Now know yee that I ye s^{d} Caleb Allin do here by bind .... my self un to the sd Sarah Allin .... in the full sum of" £50 "that my Self and all my Natural Bretheren and Sisters .... will .... abide ye Award .... that shall be given .... under ye hands of ye sd Arbitrators with in three months after ye date of these presents or under ye hands of any two of them"

"And I ye said Sarah Allin do here by bind .... my self .... un to ye said Caleb Allin .... in ye Like Sum of fifty pounds that I will bring in .... a true Invintory as afore Said as also to .... abide ye award .... given in as aforesd"

This agreement was dated 22 April, 1693, and signed by Caleb Allin and Sarah Allin, the latter by a mark. The witnesses were William Bassett and John Otis.

On 2 May, 1693, "wee the sd Arbitrators having this day met togeather at ye house of Capt Joseph Lothrop in Barnestable and there heard ye Alligations on both sids and finding ye parties willing to Comply with this our Award do therefore order and determin that ye sd Sarah Allin Shall pay unto ye sd Caleb Allin or his assignes the full Sum of forty Shillings, . . . and that to be ye full proportion that sd Caleb Allin and his sd Bretheren and Sisters Shall have out of the sd Estate that Said Sarah and George Allin was seised of at ye time of his Death"

The award was signed by Barnabas Lothrop, John Thacher and Shearjashub Bourn, and was recorded 3 May, 1693, by Joseph Lothrop, Register.

[JOSEPH HOLLEY'S ESTATE *]

[p. 80] On 31 January, 1692/3, "Mary Holway Hannah Holway and Rose Holway all own Sisters ye Daughters of Joseph Holway Late of Sandwich deceased have all and every of us ye day of ye Date of these presents Received of Joseph Holway our Brother Administrator of ye Estate of Joseph Holway our Father . . . . the full Sum and Sums . . . . which by us . . . . was mutually agreed up on . . . . ye 5th of September: 1692: . . . . and is up on Record . . . . every one of us . . . . have Received . . . . Eighteen pownds apeice . . . . which wee do every one of us Acknowledg to be our full due & part of our sd deceased fathers Estate"

The witnesses were Thomas Ewer, Hannah Blish, Samuel Hilyer and Mary Hilyer.

The receipt was recorded 3 July, 1693, by Joseph Lothrop, Register.

[ROBERT DAVIS'S WILL]

[p. 81] Robert Davis of Barnstable made his will 14 April, 1688. His residence is not stated in the will, but he was "Late of Barnestable" when the inventory was sworn to.

Bequests were as follows:

To "wife Ann all my houshold goods of Iron and brass and pewter and all wooden ware and Linnen and Beding except it be ye bed that my son Joseph Lyieth on which I . . . . bequeath to him with ye Beding belonging to it"

To "my son Joseph Davis my Land that I bought of ye Indians Lying in ye Comon field"

"I will . . . . to my Son Josiah Davis and do also confirm to him a parcel of Land and swamp within ye Comon field fence nere about two acres butting on Samuel Cobs Land on ye North side and on James Gorehams Land that was on ye east sid and

* See agreement of heirs, printed in our sixteenth volume, pages 60 and 61.

butting westerly against my Improved Land and a parcel of Land that his house Stands up on of four Rod Squear lying on ye back side of his house and easter end faceing to ye highway not to come westerly above half a Rod of ye west end of his house with what he formerly had"

To "my son Joseph Davis all ye Rest of my Lands and ye housing Standing up on it .... he paying to his mother twenty shillings a year in Corne at Currant prise if shee hath need of it and his mother to have ye use of ye dwelling house during her Natural Life"

"I do confirm to my Daughter Deborah Geere what she hath alredy had"

"I do confirm to my two Daughters Sarah and marcy what they have alredy had"

To "my son Andrew Daves five shillings in currant pay"

To "my Daughter mary five shillings in currant pay"

To "my Daughter Hannah Dexter ten Shillings in currant pay"

To "my Son Robert Davis five shillings in Currant pay"

"after my Just Debts be paid I do give all my Stock of Cattel and Swine to my wife and Son Joseph to be equally devided between them two Except my Sheep them I .... bequeath to my wife"

"my Loving wife Ann and my Son Joseph Davis to be my executors"

The will was signed by a mark. The witnesses were James Gorham and John Gorham.

On 29 June, 1693, both witnesses made oath to the will, before Barnabas Lothrop, Judge of Probate.

[p. 82] "An Invintory of ye Estate of Robert Davis deceased ye 9 day of April 1693: taken ye 29 day of June 1693" by James Gorham and Jabez Lumburt. The total amount was £75, 13s. The only real estate was: "his house and Land" £30.

"Ann Davis vid Relict of Robirt Davis Late of Barnestable deceased and Joseph Daves Son of ye said deceased" made oath to the inventory, before Barnabas Lothrop, Judge of Probate, on 29 June, 1693.

The will and inventory were recorded 3 July, 1693, by Joseph Lothrop, Register.

(*To be continued*)

PLYMOUTH, MASS., VITAL RECORDS

(*Continued from page 125*)

[p. 260] John Bacon Esqr of Barnstable Publisht to m^{rs} Sarah Warren of Plymouth Sepr 10th 1726.

A Purpose of Marriage Between John White & Ruth Shepherd both of Plymouth September 17th 1726

A Purpose of Marriage between Joshua Larance of Rochester and Elizabeth Sprague of Plymouth : October 6th 1726.

A Purpose of Marriage between Lazerus Samson & Jemima Holmes both of Plymouth October 7th 1726.

A Purpose of Marriage between John Tommas & Abigal Donham both residing in Plymouth . October 15th 1726.

A Purpose of Marriage between Jonathan Bryant of Kingstone and Mary Eastland of Plymouth . November 12th 1726.

A Purpose of Marriage between Jedediah Hatch of Scituate and Sarah Churchell of Plymouth Novr 30th 1726 s^{d} Hatch ordered it to be taken down again ye Same day at night about 10 a clock

A Purpose of Marriage Between the Reverend m^{r} Robert Ward of Wenham and m^{rs} Margaret Rogers of Plymouth . December 16th 1726

A Purpose of Marriage between James Bumpass of Rochester and Marjery Norris of Agawam in the Township of Plymouth January 12th 1726/7.

A Purpose of Marriage between Joseph Bartlett and Sarah Morton both of Plymouth . January 21th 1726/7

A Purpose of Marriage Between Barnabas Shurtleff of Plimpton and Jemima Adams of Plymouth . feb^{ry} 10th 1726/7.

A Purpose of Marriage Between John Clarke of Plymouth and Rebecca Hathaway of Dighton in the County of Bristol . March 18th 1726/7

A Purpose of Marriage Between m^{r} Samuel Doty and m^{rs} Marcy Cob both of Plymouth . March 25th 1727.

A Purpose of Marriage Between Samuel Totman And Experience Rogers both of Plymouth March 25th 1727.

A Purpose of Marriage between Joshua Finney & Hannah Curtise July 29th 1727

A Purpose of Marriage between Elkanah Totman and Sarah Churchell both of Plymouth . August 26th 1727

A Purpose of Marriage between Nathan Whood Junr & Rachel Jeffry Indians both of Plymouth Sepr 23^{d} 1727.

A Purpose of Marriage between m^{r} Nehemiah Riply & m^{rs} Sarah Wood both of Plymouth November 8th 1727

A Purpose of Marriage Between Ebenezer Cob Junr & Lydia Stevens both of Plymouth . November 25th 1727

A Purpose of Marriage Between m^r^ Benjamin Lothrop Junr of Barnstable and m^rs^ Experience Howland of Plymouth December 1st 1727.

A Purpose of Marriage Between m^r^ Ebenezer Cob of Plymouth and m^rs^ Mary Thomas of Midleberough December 14th 1727.

A Purpose Marriage between John Smale of Provinceton & Hannah Barnebe of Plymouth february 24th 1727/8.

[p. 261] A Purpose of Marriage between m^r^ Joshua Freeman of Plymouth and m^rs^ Patience Rogers of Ipswich April 9th 1728.

A Purpose of Marriage between Thomas Scarrot and Alse Ward both of Plymouth . July 19th 1728.

A Purpose of Marriage between John Price and Esther Prat both of Plymouth August 9th 1728 . Daniel Prat forbid ye banes

A Purpose of Marriage between Thomas Ward Junr Residing in the Town of Plymouth And Marcy Ward of Plymouth August 26th 1728.

A Purpose of Marriage between Samuel Cole and Marcy Barnes both of Plymouth Sepr 7th 1728.

A Purpose of Marriage between Jonathan Freeman of Plimton and Sarah Rider of Plymouth Sepr 7th 1728.

A Purpose of Marriage between Jonathan Mory Junr of Plymouth and Elizabeth Swift of Sandwich Sepr 14th 1728.

A Purpose of Marriage between Elkanah Delano & Mary Sanders both of Plymouth October 12th 1728.

A Purpose of Marriage between Ephraim Samson of Duxberough & Ruth Shepherd of Plymouth October 18th 1728.

A Purpose of Marriage between Timothy Burbanks of Boston now residing in Plymouth and Mary Kempton of Plymouth Novr 2 . 1728

A Purpose of Marriage between Mathew Lemote & Marcy Billington both of Plymouth Novr 16th 1728.

A Purpose of Marriage between Thorton Gray & Katherine White both of Plymouth . Novr 20th 1728.

A Purpose of Marriage between James Holmes and Content Silvester both of Plymouth Decr 28th 1728.

A Purpose of marriage between Joseph Cole of Plimton & Mary Stevens of Plymouth January 28th 1728/9.

A Purpose of Marriage between Thomas Doan of Chatham in the County of Barnstable and Sarah Barnes of Plymouth february 15th 1728/9

A Purpose of Marriage between Elisha Doty Junr of Plymouth & Deborah Tubs of Duxberogh february 22th 1728/9

A Purpose of Marriage between Redolphus Hatch late of Province Town in the County of Barnstable now residing in Plymouth and Esther Holmes of Plymouth . March 1st 1728/9.

A Purpose of Marriage between Edward Stephens And Marcy Silvester both of Plymouth March 15th 1728/9

A Purpose of Marriage between Thomas Totman & Lucrecy Rose both of Plymouth May 10th 1729.

A Purpose of Marriage Between John Watson Esq[r] & m[rs] Priscilla Thomas both of Plymouth June 14th 1729.

A Purpose of Marriage Between Jacob Lewis & Bathsheba Mallis June 21th 1729.

[p. 262] Marriges Solemnized By y[e] Rev[d] M[r] Nath[l] Leonard.

1752 April 15 . James Howard of Plymouth, & Marcy Warren of Middleboro Marryed at Plymouth

June 13 . William Gammons & Fear Curtis, Both of Plym[o] Marry[d] at D[o]

July 14 . Joshua Totman & Johanna Scarret, Both of Plym[o] Mary[d] at Ditto

23 . Abijah Fisher of Norton, & Mary Washburn of Plymouth Marryed at Plymouth

Oct[r] 18 . Silvanus Morton & Mary Stephens, both of Plym[o] Marryed at Ditto

19 . Jabez Harlow & Experience Churchell, both of Plym[o] Marry[d] at D[o]

Joseph Rider of Province Town, & Thankfull Polden of Plymouth Marryed at Plym[o] July 13 . 1752

Nov[r] 9 . Thomas Hinckley Jun[r] of Barnstable, & Phebe Holmes of Plymouth Maryed at Plymouth

Rec[d] y[e] List March 2 . 1753 . & Entered

1753 Aprill 12 Zacheus Bartlett & Margaret Barnes Both of Plym[o] Marry[d] at Plym[o]

May . 24 Thomas Davis & Mercy Hedge Both of Plym[o] Marry[d] at Ditto

24 Eben: Ransom of Plimton, & Rebeckah harlow of Plym[o] Marry[d] at Ditto.

Aug[st] 13 M[r] Joseph Fulgham, & M[rs] Luranah Clark, Both of Plym[o] marry[d] at Ditto

Sept[r] 20 Benjamin Morton & hannah Faunce, Both of Plym[o] marry[d] at Ditto.

26 . Archipus Fuller of Plimton, & Mariah Churchell of Plym[o] marry[d] at Ditto

Nov[r] 13 Nathaniel Morton Jun[r] & Rebeckah Jackson ; Both of Plym[o] marry[d] at Ditto

15 Ichabod Bartlett Jun[r] & hannah Rogers, Both of Plym[o] marry[d] at Ditto

22 William Weston of Plimton, & Mary Westron of Plym[o] Marry[d] at Ditto

1754 Jan[ry] 3 . Samuell Jackson and Experiance Atwood Both of Plym[o] marry[d] at Ditto

March 14 John Bacon of Barnestable & Joanna Foster of Plym[o] marry[d] at Ditto

May . 30 The Rev[d] M[r] Elijah Packard, & M[rs] Mary Rider Both of Plym[o] marry[d] at Ditto

June . 20 Arthur Shepherd Resident in Plym[o] & Mary Morton of Plym[o] marry[d] at Ditto

July . 18 Samuel Torrey of Boston, & Deborah Torrey of Plym[o] marry[d] at Ditto

Septr 16 Zacheus Churchell & Mary Trask Both of Plym^{o} marry^{d} at Ditto
Octr 16 Elkanah Waterman & Mary West, Both of Plym^{o} marry^{d} at Ditto
Novr 28 Ephraim Dexter of Rochester, & Martha Wait of Plym^{o} marry^{d} at Ditto
Decr 5 Nathaniel Holmes & Lydia Churchell, Both of Plym^{o} marry^{d} at Ditto
12 Ebenezer Nellson, & Ruth Jackson, Both of Plym^{o} marry^{d} at Ditto
19 George Peckham, of Providence, & Jerusha Bartlett of Plym^{o} marry^{d} at Plymouth
Continued to Book ye 2nd page 252
To the Honerable Isaac Lothrop Esqr

Whereas the Province Law makes provition that all births & deaths shall be registred by the Town Clerk in the Several Towns within said Province These are to Informe your Honner that Josiah Sturtevant of Plymouth in ye County of Plymouth in New England had a child born in or about the month of April Last past and the s^{d} Sturtevant neglecteth to give Notice thereof as according to the direction of the Law . I do therefore pray your Honner to give forth a Warrant to cause S^{d} Sturtevant to appear before your Honner that he may be dealt withall as according to ye direction of the Law
Plymouth Decr 30th 1724 John Dyer
Town Clerk

[p. 263] Ebenazar Holmes publeshed to patiene ffiney on ye first of agust 1719
Elisha Holmes published To Suzanna Clark August 7 1719
John Johnson Publeshed To Elisabeth Goold august . 21 1719
Elish Bradford published to Bathsheba Brock agust 22 : 1719
Job Prince of plimouth published to abigail Cimbol of plimptown September ye 5 — 1719
Joseph King publisht To ye Widow Marcy Spooner october 3 1719
David Turner publisht To Ruth Jacson october . 5 : 1719
Josiah Sturdefunt publisht to Hannah Church of Sittuate october 9th 1719
Gidion Ellice & Anna Clarke published octobe 10th 1719
Mr John Mordow to phebe Morton october 24th 1719
Ichabod Standish publisht to phebe ring october y^{e} 30 — 1719
Joseph Pearce was Publisht to Elezebeth Ring on y^{e} 20 of november 1719
Ebenazar Dunham was published to Abigaiel Smith Desem 12 1719
Joseph vahan & Elizabeth Shurtlif Janewary 14 170$\frac{9}{10}$
John Barse to Sarah Holmes published January 23^{d} 170$\frac{9}{10}$
Benjam Rider to hannah Stephens of marshfeild published february 29 1719/20
John Goole published to Mary Coombs March 28 1720
Nathanel Morton published to Recka Ellece Aprill 2^{d} 1720
Nathaniel Jackson Jun published to Reeckah Powin Aprill 8th 1720
lazaros labaron published to lidia Bartlet Aprill 16 1720

Nathaniel Cobb published to Mary Waterman Aprill 23[d] 1720
Thomas Branch published to lidiah Barrow April 23 1720
Ebenazar Doged published to Elizabeth Rickard on y[e] 14 Day of May 1720
James Rickard published to hanna howland May 14th 1720
Tobe and Billa published May 20th 1720
Eleazar Harlow published to Hannah pratt of plimton on y[e] 21st Day of May 1720
Richard Church & anna stirtvent published June 18 : 1720
Rasteling Bruster of plim & Hannah Thomas of Duxbero Agust 17 1720
[p. 264] Ase Beale was publisht to Rhoda Lathle y[e] 1 day of october 1720
Peter Hopkins was publisht to priscilla prat Y[e] 3 day of october 1720
Ebenazar Morton of Middlebery published to Marsy Foster 24 december 1720 y[e] 24
Elkana Churchill publeshed to suzanah Manchester Jannuary 28 1720
John Churchill published to Bethya Sponer January 28 1720
Elish holmes Jun: published to Sarah Bartlett February 16 : 170$\frac{20}{21}$
Thomas Woshbon published to Elizabeth Howland february 18th 170$\frac{21}{20}$
Eben fuller published to Joanna Gray March : 17th 1721
Thomas peters & Rebecka Shepard March 18 1721
M[r] Joseph Stace to M[rs] patien Warren March 25 : 1721
John finney of plimton To Rebekah Bryant May 13 1721
peleg Durfey publisht to Mary Cole May y[e] 27 1721
Anthoney Coast Marrener and Elisabeth bacon both now residing In plymouth publisht June y[e] 10 1721
Joseph Silvester publisht to mercy holmes July y[e] 7 day 1721
Seth Chitman* publisht to priscilla bradford august y[e] 7 day 1721
Thomas Rogers published to picila Churchill october 12 1721
Jacob Tinckham published To hanna Cobb october 14th 1721
Ichabod Bartlet published to Suzanna Sponer octobe 23 1721
Nath: Holmes published to pricilla prat November : 9 : 1721
ffrances Labaron publ: to Sarah Bartlet November 9th 1721
Samuel Bartlet Published to Elizabeth Latherop ; on the first Day of December 1721
John finey published on y[e] first Day of Decembe to Sarah Bartlet 1721
Joseph Sangerele Published To Mary Thomas of Duxberouh february 17 1721
George Barrows Ju: published To Desir Doty March 10th 1721/22
Seth Swift published To Meriah Morey March 17 : 1721:/22
Seth Barns to Sarah Wooden March 24 1722
Edmond tilson publisht to Elisabeth Coper : aprel y[e] 17 1722
James Clark published to Anna Rider Aprill 21 1722

* An error of the town clerk. The name should have been "Chipman", as shown by the marriage, on the Kingston church records, and by the will of Priscilla's father, Maj. John[3] Bradford (*William*[2-1]).

John pratt publish to pricila Bryant Aprill 21 1722
Joseph Warren to allatheah Chi[tten]ton * Aprill 18 1722
[p. 265] Isral Ferren published to Martha Gibbs May 2d 1722
William Lucust publisht to mehetible doty may : ye 4 : 1722
Nathaniel Thomas published to hope Warren July 7th 1722
July 21st 1722 Richard Weight published to marey Barnes of plimouth
Ebenazar Cobb published to Ruth Tinckham July 28th 1722
Jesiah Feney publisht to abigaiel briant august ye 11 1722
Robert Jones published to Mary Stuard Agust 18 1722
Johnathan barns : publisht to ye widow Mercy Doty august 25 1722
James Clarke Junio published to Meriba Tuper of Sandwich September first 1722
Joseph Rider published to abigaill Warren September first 1722
James young & rebecker Shepard was publisht ye 6 September 1722
Samuel Rider published to Marey Silvester September 15th 1722
Josiah Rider published to Experiance Jenney or Jennes october : 4 : 1722
Thomas Philips Published to abigaiel Rider october 20th 1722
Thomas Morton published to Abigaiel pratt November 3d 1722
Jams Cushmon published to Sarah Hatch November 3d 1722
Nath Wood published to Mary Adams November 17th 1722
Thomas Stoormy published to Rebeckah philips November 23 1722
Thomas Western published to Mary Howland Desembe 18 1722
James Howard A Strainger published to Sarah Billenten Desember 22d 1722
Edward Crowly published to Jane Rich Desembe 27th 1722
Samuel Foster published To Margeret Tilden Desember 29 : 1722
John Bartlett published To Sarah Cobb January 5th 1722/23
Addam Jones of plymouth publisht to Mary Cran of diten January ye 30th 1723
John Sturtavant publisht to ye widow Sarah bartlit fabuary ye 9th 1723
John Stirtevant published to the Widow Sarah Bartlet ffebruary 9th 172$\frac{3}{2}$
Joshua Dunham Published To Sarah Pratt ffebruary 16th 1722/23
Samuel Norrice published to Marcy Jones March 8th 1722/3
Caleb Cooke published To Abigaill Howland Aprill 11th 1723
Richard Bagelet published to Elizabeth polon Aprill 27th 1723
Israel Jackson published to Marcy Dunham on ye [†]1 of may 1723
Joseph lewing published to hanna Rogers July 3d 1723
Jacob lewes publisht to Sarah Reavis September : 25th 1723
beniamin Elis publisht to hannah gibs october ye 29 1723
David Stirtevant published To Sarah holmes november first 1723
James Warren publisht to penelepe winslow december ye 27th 1723
Samuell baker publisht to Susaner mitchel ye 5th of January 1723/24
Joseph Jackson to Rembrance [Jackson ‡] february first [1]723/24

* See marriage record, in Mayflower Descendant, 14:39.

† The first figure is doubtful – probably "1".

‡ "Jackson" has been interlined in a modern hand. See marriage, in Mayflower Descendant, 14:70.

[p. 266] The Children of Richard & mingo his Wife both servants to Mr Josep[h *worn*]

1 Margeret born on ye 9th of January 1701 She was baptized 1708

2 Mary born on ye 22 of June 1708 } these 2 Children was both baptized

3 Marth born June 22 1708 } the 27 of Jun. 1708

George Jonson the son of hanna Jonson was born at plimouth on the 16 Day of february 170 8/9

Eleazer Faunce & Hannah Warren * Published March 30th 1724

Elkanah Morton & Elizabeth Holmes Published March 30th 1724

Samuel Morton & Lydia Bartlett Published may 16 — 1724.

Caleb Tinkcom & Marcy Holmes Published Augt 8th 1724

Benjamin Bartlett Published to Lydia Morton [†] 1724

mr Robert Brown Published to Priscilla Johnson of Boston Sepr 12 . 1724

Thomas Jackson Published to Hannah Woodward of Little Compton Sepr 22 . 1724

Isaac Jackson Published to Sarah Bridgett of Scituate October 17 — . 1724

The Reverend mr Nathaniel Leonard Published to mrs Priscilla Rogers of Ipswich Nov: 7 . 172[4]

Eleazer Martin Junr & Deborah Delano Published . November 21th 1724.

Nathaniel Donham & Rebeccah King Published Decr 18th 1724

mr John Cooke Published to mrs Hannah Morton Decr 19th 1724

Ichabod Delano & Elizabeth Cushmans Publishment Sot up . Decr 26th 1724.

Francis Allen & Jane Kirk Publishment Sot up January 2d 1724/5

Consider Howland & Ruth Bryant Publishment Set up March 13 . 1724

Nathaniel Bartlett & Abigal Clarke Published March . 13th 1724/5

Ichabod Washborn & Bethiah Phillips Published March . 13th 1724/5

Robert Cushman Junr & Marcy Washborn Published April 17th 1725

mr John Barnes Junr and mrs Dorcas Corben of Haverill April . 28th 1725

John Peirce & Rebecca Donham Published May 22th 1725

A Purpose of Marriage between Barnabas Seabury of Bridgwater and Abigal Cooke of Plymouth . May 29th 1725

A Purpose of Mariage between Stephen Barden Junr of Midleboro & Deborah Prat of Plymouth June 26th 1725. Quinten Crimble forbid the banes by reason he had an Indenture on sd Barden Since agreed

A Purpose of Marriage between Samuel Bartlett & Hannah Churchel both of Plymouth June 26th 1725.

A Purpose of Marriage between Samuel Dexter of Falmouth and Elizabeth Burg of Agawam within ye Township of Plymouth July 31th 1725.

* "Morton" was first written, but was crossed out and "Warren" interlined, in the same hand and ink. See marriage, in Mayflower Descendant, 14 : 70.

† The month and day were omitted.

A Purpose of Marriage between Benjamin Cornish & Experience Gibs both of Plymouth August 19th 1725

A Purpose of Mariage between Elkanah Shaw of Plimpton & Hanna[h] Cushman of Plymouth . August 28th 1725

[p. 267] 1754 Janry 19 . A Purpose of Marriage, Between John Robinson of Plymouth, And Elizabeth Studley of Hannover Daughter of Mr Eliab Studley.

Febry 2. A purpose of Marriage, Between The Revd Mr Elijah Packard, & Mrs Mary Rider, Both of Plymouth

9 A purpose of Marriage, Between, Mr John Bacon of Barnstable, & Mrs Joanna Foster of Plymouth

March 16 A purpose of Marriage, Between Joshua Pocknot Indian Man, & Sarah Adams Indian Woman both of Plym

16 A purpose of Marriage Between Simon Mahomon, & Phebe Robbin Indians, both of Plymo

30 A Purpose . of . Marrage . Between . Edward . Lanman . of . Plymouth And Joan Tobey . of Sandwich

Ap: 27 A purpose of Marriage, Between Mr Seth Barnes Jun & Mrs Elizabeth Rider, both of Plymouth

May . 4 . A purpose of Marriage, Between Mr Job Brewster of Duxboro, & Mrs Elizabeth Elles of Plymouth

18th A . Purpose . of . Marriage Between Elkanah Waterman And Mary . West . Both of . Plymouth

25 A purpose of Marriage Between Mr Arthur Shepherd Resident in Plymouth & Mrs Mary Morton of Plymouth

June 1 . A purpose of Marriage, Between Nathl Holmes and Lydia Churchell both of Plymouth

June 1 . A purpose of Marriage, Between Thomas Morton & Mary Morton Daughter of Mr Nathl Morton Both of Plymouth

8 A purpose of Marriage, Between Mr Joseph Watson Resident in Plymo & Mrs Marcy Wadsworth of Duxboro

15 A purpose of Marriage, Between Mr Saml Torrey of Boston, and Mrs Deborah Torrey of Plymouth

20 A purpose of Marriage, Between Elisha Witon Jun of Plimton, and Betty Holmes of Plymo

Ded the Çertificate To Edward Doten Novr 9th

Augst 2 . A purpose of Marriage, Between Noah Penes & Patien[ce] Wampom both of Plymouth Indians

3 . A purpose of Marriage, Between Mr Ebenezer Nel[son*] and mrs Ruth Jackson

10 A Purpose of Marriage, Between Lemuel Fish, Joanna Doten, both of Plymouth

Augst 17th A purpose of Marriage, Between Zacheus Churchell and Mary Trask Both of Plymouth

[On fly-leaf, at back of book.] Abigal Cornish . deceased ye Last day of May . 1724

[End of Volume I of original records. — *Editor.*]

* See marriage, on original page 262.

FRANCIS[3] COOKE'S WILL AND INVENTORY

TRANSCRIBED BY GEORGE ERNEST BOWMAN

FRANCIS[3] COOKE (*Jacob*[2], *Francis*[1]) was born at Plymouth, on 5 January, 1662. He married, on 2 August, 1687, according to the Plymouth town records, Elizabeth Latham[4] (*Susanna Winslow*[3], *Mary*[2] *Chilton*, *James*[1]), who was born about 1664 and died at Kingston on 16 November, 1730.*

Francis[3] Cooke of Kingston, Mass., made his will 28 October, 1732, and added a codicil 15 May, 1736. The will was probated 18 September, 1746; and his inventory was made on 6 October, 1746; but the date of his death has not been found.

Six children were mentioned in the will: Caleb[4] Cooke, who married Hannah Shurtleff; Robert[4] Cooke, who married Abigail Harlow and Lydia Tilden; Elizabeth[4] Cooke, who married David Leach; Francis[4] Cooke, who married Ruth Silvester[5] (*Ruth* [*Turner*[4]] *Prince*, *Mary*[3] *Brewster*, *Jonathan*[2], *William*[1]); Susanna[4] Cooke, who married James Sturtevant; Sarah[4] Cooke, who married Ephraim Cole.

Three of these children, Robert[4], Francis[4] and Sarah[4], died before their father, all leaving children, referred to, but not named, in their grandfather's will.

Literal copies of the will and inventory and all records relating to the estate, in the Plymouth County, Mass., Registry of Probate, are here printed, at the expense of Hon. William S. Harris, of Geneva, O., a descendant of Caleb[4] and Hannah (Shurtleff) Cooke.

There are no original documents remaining in the probate files.

[FRANCIS[3] COOKE'S WILL]

[10: 328] "In the Name of God Amen I Francis Cooke of Kingston in the County of Plimouth in New England Yeoman being of a Disposeing Mind & Memory blessed be God for it & Calling to mind that it is appointed for all Once to die Do make & ordain this my last Will and Testament in manner & form following.

"In the First place I Give and bequeath my Soul to God that Gave it me and my body to the Earth with a Decent Christian Burial in hope of a Blessed Resurrection: and as to

* Mayflower Descendant, 7: 26, 13: 204, 17: 183.

the Outward and temporal Estate that it hath pleased God to bless me with I dispose of the same in the following order

[p. 329] "Imprimis I Give and Bequeath unto my loving son Caleb Cook and to his heirs and assigns forever and to the Children of my loving Son Robert Cook deceasd and their heirs & assigns forever all that my landing place that I bought of Major John Bradford at Jones River in Kingston: and allso I Give unto my son Caleb Cook all my Oxen of four years old and upwards with all my Carts plows Chains and all my Implements for Carting & plowing allso half my Sheep with my Mare for four years and at the End of s[d] four year then if there is no Increase to have half y[e] mare If there is Increase of the Mare then only half the Increase

"Item I Give and bequeath unto my loving daughter Elizabeth Cook Seventy pounds to be paid out of my Estate and what She hath in her Chest and hath had for some time past

"Item I Give and bequeath unto my loving Grand Children the Children of my loving son Francis Cook Deceasd five Shillings I haveing allready Given them their Portion

"And after my Just Debts are paid and my funeral Charge Discharged and the Afores[d] Legacies paid My mind is that y[e] remainder of all my Estate Real & personal whatsoever or wher-soever it is or may be found Shall be Equally divided between my three daughters or such as Legally represent those that are Dead that is to say my Loving Daughter Susanna Stertevant the Children of my loving Daughter Sarah Cole and my loveing Daughter Elizabeth Cook to have Equal as aforesaid of the remainder of my Estate. And lastly I Do Nominate and appoint my Loving son Caleb Cook the Sole Executor Of this my last will & Testament Hereby Declaring all other Will or Wills by me heretofore Made void & Confirming this and no other to be my last will and Testament as witness my hand and Seal this 28th day of October 1732.

Signed Sealed Declared and Pronounced by the Aboves[d] Francis Cook to be his Last will and Testament Before us Witnesses — Francis Cook (seal)

Elisha Washburne
Ephraim Washburne
Francis Adams

"Plim[o] Ss, Sep[r] 18th 1746, This will being Presented by the Exec[r] within Named for Probate Francis adams & Ephraim

Washburne made oath that they Saw s^d^ Fra Cook Sign Seal & heard him declare this Instrument to be his last will & Testam^t^ and that they together with s^d^ Elisha Washburne in his presence Subscribed as witnesses at ye Same time & y^t^ he ye s^d^ Testator was then of Sound mind

Before me Jno Cushing Judge of Prob^t^

[p. 330] "Notwithstanding any thing in the aforesaid Will To the Contrary My Mind is that my son Caleb Cook have Only one pair of Oxen If I leave any with my Carts & wheels & tackling therto belonging and I do hereby Give & bequeath unto my daughter* Before mentiond my part in a Furnice for makeing of Iron begun in Kingston to be Divided to them as is in this will afores^d^ is Declared In witness hereof I have hereunto Set my hand and Seal this fifteenth day of May annoq Dom. One thousand seven hundred & thirty Six 1736.

Signed Sealed published & Francis Cook (seal)
Pronounced By the Afors^d^
Francis Cook to be a
Codicill to the Afores^d^ Will
Before us
Ichabod Washburne
Bethiah Washburne
Francis Adams

"Plim^o^ Ss, Sepr 18th 1746. The above Codicil being presented also by the within Named Exec^r^ for prob^t^ the s^d^ Francis adams & Bethia Washburne made oath that they Saw s^d^ Francis Cook Sign & Seal and heard him declare the above Codicil to be part & parcel of his afores^d^ will and that they with s^d^ Ichabod Washburne Subscrib^d^ as witnesses at the Same time in his the Testators presence & that he was then of sound mind

Before me Jno Cushing Judge of prob^t^

"Province of the Massachusets bay Plimouth Ss, John Cushing Esqr appointed & Commissioned by the Govr with the advice & Consent of the Council of said province to be Judge of the Probate of Wills and for Granting of Letters of Administration on the Estates of persons Deceas^d^ haveing Goods Chattles rights or Credits in the County of Plimouth within the province Aforesaid.

"To all unto whom these presents Shall Come Greeting

"Know ye that upon the day of the date hereof Before me

* Sic. Probably should be "daughters".

at Plimouth in the County Aforesaid The will of Francis Cooke late of Kingston in the County of Plimouth yeoman Deceasd to these Presents Annexed was Proved approved and allowed who haveing while he lived and at the time of his Death Goods Chattles Rights or Credits in the County Aforesaid . and the probate of the said Will and power of Committing administration of all and Singuler the Goods Chattles rights and Creditts of the s[d] Deceasd . [p. 331] By Vertue therof Appertaining unto me. The administration of all and Singuler the Goods Chattles rights and Credits of the said Deceasd and his will in any manner Concerning is hereby Commited unto Caleb Cook of Kingston in the County Afores[d] Yeoman Executor in the Same will named well and faithfully to Execute the said will and to administer the Estate of the said Deceasd according thereunto . and to make a true and perfect Inventory of all and singuler the Goods Chattles rights & Credits of the said Deceasd and to Exhibit the Same into the Registry of the Court of Probate for the County Aforesaid at or before the Eighteenth day of December next Ensuing . And allso to render a plain & true Acco[t] of his said administration upon Oath within twelve months next Comeing . In Testimony wherof I have hereunto Set my hand and the Seal of the said Court of Probate . Dated at Plimouth the 18th day of September Annoque Domini 1746.

Jn[o] Cushing

"An Inventory of the Estate of M[r] Francis Cooke of Kingston in the County of Plimouth Deceasd taken by us the Subscribers October the Sixth A.D. 1746.

	old tenour
Imprimis To One Blew Straite Bodyed Coat & Jackett	3 . 10 . 0
To a Blew Great Coat 10s a Straite Bodyed Coat & Jacket	1 . 5 . 0
To a Morticeing Ax 2 Augurs & 1 Adds	1 . 1 . 0
To 1 Scyth 4[s] One Crow barr 20s To Sheep Shears 5s	1 . 15 . 0
To 1 Sixteenth part of a Furnice in Kingston	75 . 0 . 0

Gersham Bradford
Francis Adams
William Ripley

"Plim[o] Ss, Dec[r] 18th 1746. Caleb Cook adm[r] on s[d] Estate made oath this Inventory Contains s[d] Dec[ds] Estate as far as he knows & that when he Shall know of more he'l Give it in s[d] Apprizers viz. Fra[s] Adams & will[m] Ripley being under oath at the Same time

Before Jn[o] Cushing Judge of Prob[t]"

MIDDLEBOROUGH, MASS., VITAL RECORDS

(Continued from page 85)

[p. 34] Elias Thomas the Son of Noah Thomas by Mary his Wife: Was born January the 19th 1746/7.

hannah Thomas the Daughter of Noah Thomas by Mary his Wife: Was born January the 9th 1748/9.

Sarah Tinkham the Daughter of Samuel Tinkham by Malatiah his Wife Was born June the 18th 1748.

Ebenezer Tinkham the Son of Joseph Tinkham by Agnus his Wife Was born July the 28th 1748. who Departed this Life September ye 19 1749

Peter Thacher the Son of Samuel Thacher by Deboroah his Wife was born September ye 19th 1749.

William Tupper the Son of Thomas Tupper by Rebeckah his Wife Was born September the 14th 1735.

Ichabod Tupper the Son of Thomas Tupper by Rebeckah his Wife Was born april the 4th 1737.

Joseph Tupper the Son of Thomas Tupper by Rebeckah his Wife Was born august the 25th 1739.

Mary Tupper the Daughter of Thomas Tupper by Rebeckah his Wife Was born May the 14th 1741.

Susanna Tupper the Daughter of Thomas Tupper by Rebeckah his Wife Was born January the 10 and is Deceast 1742.

Rebeckah Tupper the Daughter of Thomas Tupper by Rebeckah his Wife Was born august the 26th 1743.

Nathaniel Tupper the Son of Thomas Tupper by Rebeckah his Wife Was born September the 4th 1745.

Thomas Tupper the Son of Thomas Tupper by Rebeckah his Wife Was born March the 12th 1747.

Susanna Tupper the Daughter of Thomas Tupper by Rebeckah his Wife was born March the 6th 1749.

Ephriam Thomas the Son of Ephriam Thomas by Sarah his Wife Was born January 21st 1740:

Sarah Thomas the Daughter of Ephriam Thomas by Sarah his Wife was born May the 9th 1743.

[p. 35] Elisha Thomas the Son of Ephriam Thomas by Sarah his wife was born March the 27th 1747.

Jacob Thomas the Son of Ebenezer Thomas by Anna his Wife Was born September the 16th 1794.

Nathaniel Tomson the Son of Caleb Tomson by Abigail his Wife was born September ye 13th 1750.

Mary Tupper the Daughter of Thomas tupper by Rebeckah his Wife was born October ye 23rd 1750. and Deceasd November the: 6th 1750.

Corneliues tinkham the Son of John Tinkham Jur by Jerusha his wife was born October the 20th 1745.

Daniel Tinkham the Son of John Tinkham Jur by Jerusha his wife was born January the 26th 1746.

Susanna Tinkham the Daughter of John Tinkham Jur by Jerusha his wife was born November the: 27th 1748.

Joseph Tinkham the Son of John Tinkham Jur by Jerusha his Wife was born august the: 18th 1750.

Ichabod Tupper the Son of Thomas Tupper by Rebeckah his wife was born January the 21st 1752

Caleb Tomson: the Son of Caleb Tomson by Abigail his Wife was born October the 18th N: S 1752.

Prisscilla Thomas the Daughter of Noah Thomas by Mary his Wife was born November the 2nd 1751:

Zebulun Thomas the Son of Samuel Thomas Jur by Mehetabel his wife was born May the . 11th 1750.

Thankfull Thomas the Daughter of Samuel Thomas Jur by Mehetabel his wife was born April the . 9th 1752.

Betty Thomas the Daughter of Israel Thomas by Phebe his Wife was born September the 30th 1750

John Tinkham the Son of John Tinkham Jur by Jerushah his wife: was born april the 16th 1754.

[p. 36] Amos Barrows the Son of Robert Barrows by Fear his Wife was born Aprel the 27th 1750.

Peter Bates the Son of Joseph Bates Junr by Eunice his Wife was born December the 22: 1750.

Joshua Benson the Son of Joshua Benson: by Sarah his Wife was born august the 7th 1746

Elizabeth Benson the Daughter of Joshua Benson by Sarah his wife: was born July the 4th 1749.

Marcy Barrows the Daughter of Robert Barrows by Fear his wife was born June the 17th 1752.

Nehemiah Bennett the Son of Jacob Bennett by Hope his Wife : was born March the 25th 1753.

Nathan Backus the Son of Isaac Backus by Susanna his wife was born June the 18th 1752.

Isaac Backus the Son of Isaac Backus by Susanna his wife was born february the 21st 1754.

Solomon Barden the Son of Ichabod Barden by Bethiah his Wife: was born October the 13th 1754.

Joanna Bates Daughter of Joseph Bates Jr by Eunice his wife, was born August 2d 1752

Elizabeth Bates Daughter of Joseph Bates Junr By Eunice his wife, was born July 20th 1754

Lydia Bumpas Daughter of Nathaniel Bumpas by Abijah his Wife was born November the 13th 1752

Joseph Bumpas Son of Nathaniel Bumpas By Abijah his Wife was born Feby [*] 1754

* The day of the month was omitted.

Nathaniel Bumpas Son of Nathaniel Bumpas by Abijah his Wife was born Decr the 18th 1755

James Barden Son of Isaac Barden by Experiance his was born November the 15th 1755

Sarah Bates Daughter of Joseph Bates Junr by Eunice his wife was born Feby the 26th 1756

[p. 37] Joseph Warteman the Son of Joseph Warterman by Joanna his Wife was born November the 12th 1750.

Deliverance Wood Daughter of Henery Wood by Lydia his Wife was born march the 25th 1755

Silas Wood Son of Silas Wood by Priscilla his wife was born April the 16th 1755

Joshua Wood Son of Edmond Wood by Patience his Wife Was born December 27th 1753

Robart wood Son of Josiah Wood by mary his Wife was born February the 25th 1753

Noah Waterman the Son of Joseph Waterman by Joanna his wife was born march the 3^{d} 1754

Ruth Waterman Daughter of Joseph Waterman by Joanna his Wife Was born february the 24th 1756

anna Wood Daughter of Nathaniel Wood by mary his wife was born January the 15th 1756

mary wood Daughter of Ephraim wood by mary his Wife was born august the 8th 1756

mary Wood Daughter of Henery Wood by Lydia his Wife Was born may the 16th 1756

Susanah Weston Daughter of Edmond Weston Junr by mary his Wife was born august the 17th 1756

Frances Wood Son of Edmond Wood by Patience his Wife Was born September the 6th 1756

Thomos wood Son of abiel wood by Dorcas his wife was born at Freetown august the 5th 1751

Priscilla wood Daughter of Silas by Priscilla his wife was born January 5th 1757

Abner Washburn Son of Jonah Washburn by Huldah his Wife was born October 12th 1757

[p. 38] Elizabeth Wood the Daughter of Nathaniel Wood by Mary his Wife was born May the 12th 1751.

Priscilla Wood the Daughter of Edmond Wood by Patience his Wife was born Jenuary ye 4th 1752

Joanna Waterman the Daughter of Joseph Waterman by Joanna his wife was born June the 14th 1752.

Samuel White the Son of Benjamin White by Betty his Wife was born Janauary : 23rd 1746/7.

Benjamin White the Son of Benj^{a} White by Betty his wife was born October : 22nd 1749.

Silas White the Son of Benja White by Betty his Wife Was born Octo N : S 16th 1752.

Lusana Weston the Daughter of James Weston by Abigail his was born August : 25th 1749.
Samuel Weston the Son of James Weston by Abigail his wife : was born March . 18th 1751.
Andrew Weston the Son of James Weston by Abigail his wife : was born february 27th 1753.
Ezra Wood the Son of Ephraim Wood by Mary his Wife was born June the 28th 1753.
Sarah Wood the Daughter of Nathaniel Wood by Mary his Wife ; was born August the 31st 1753.
Sarah Wood the Daughter of Siles Wood by Priscilla his was born December the 10th 1753.
[p. 39] Sasanna Smith the Daughter of Samuel Smith by Rachel his Wife was born January the 20th 1752
abishai Samson the Son of Nathaniel Samson by Martha his Wife was born March the 7th 1752
Mary Severy the Daughter of Thomas Severy by Mary his wife was born May N : S ye 14th 1753.
John Soul the Son of John Soul by Mary his Wife was born May the 9th 1751.
Samuel Snow the Son of Samuel Snow by Deborah Tinkham was born May the . 10th 1753.
Mary Strobridge the Daughter of William Strobridge Jur by Jane his wife was born august the 10th 1749.
Thomas Strobridge the Son of William Strobridge Jur by Jane his wife was born May the 30th 1751.
Martha Soul the Daughter of James Soul by Deborah his Wife Decased March the 26 1754.
Rachel Soul the Daughter of James Soul by Deborah his wife was born March the 26 1754.
Bathsheba Sproutt the Daughter of Ebenr Sproutt by Bathsheba his wife was born July the 11th 1754
Nathanael Samson the Son of Nathll Samson by Martha his Wife was born . July the 10th 1754
Lucia Shurteliff the Daughter of Jonathan Shurteliff by Elisabeth his wife was born October the 9th 1751.
Mary Shurteliff the Daughter of Jonathan Shurteleff by Elisabeth his wife was born June the 7th 1753.
Hannah Smith Daughter of Samuel Smith by Rachal his wife was born may the 24 1754
martha Simmons Daughter of David Simmons by Priscilla his Wife was born September the 2d 1754
[p. 40] Samuel Cobb the Son of Jonathan Cobb by Pataince his Wife was born January 24th 1752.
Susanna Cobb Daughter of James Cobb by Susanna his wife was born November the 22d 1754
Priscilla Cushman Daughter of William Cushman By Priscilla his Wife was born October the 23d 1751

Isaac Cushman Son of William Cushman by Priscilla his Wife Was born february the 27th 1754
Ezra Clap Son of Elijah Clap by Hope his Wife was born febuary the 26 1751
Hope Clap Daughter of Elijah Clap by Hope his wife was born April the 3d 1754
Sarah Canedy Daughter of John Canedy by Anna his Wife was born august the 16th 1737
Betty Canedy Daughter of John Canedy by Anna his Wife was born february the 1st 1739
Martha Canedy Daughter of John Canedy by Anna his wife was born July the 4th 1741
Hugh Canedy Son of John Canedy by Anna His wife was born June 6th 1744
Isaac Canedy Son of John Canedy by Anna his Wife was born December the 6th 1746
Alexander Canedy Son of John Canedy by Anna his Wife was born September the 24th 1747
Moley Cushman Daughter of Ichebod Cushman by Patience his wife was born April the 20th 1754
Susanna Cushman Daughter of William Cushmas by Priscilla his wife was born Janr 13th 1756
[p. 41] Sarah Ransom Daughter of William Ransom By Sarah his Wife was born April the 14th 1752
Samuel Ransom Son of William Ransom By Sarah his Wife was born march the 9th 1755
hannah Redding Daughter of moses Redding by Joanna his Wife was born april the 5th 1746
hannah Raymond Daughter of Samuel Raymond by Diniah his Wife was born Feby 13th 1758
Mercy Redding Daughter of William Redding by Bennett his Wife Was born Janaury 21st 1740
Thankfull Redding Daughter of William Redding By Bennett his wife was born December 13 1735
Moses Redding the son of William Redding by Bennett his wife was Born December 16 1741
Zachriah Redding son of william Redding by Bennett his wife was Born December the 23 1744
fear Redding the Daughter of william Redding by Bennett his wife was Born November the 5 1746
Experance Raymond Daughter of Barnabas Raymond by Allice his Wife was born may the 28th 1748
Silveanus Raymond Son of Barnabas Raymond by Allice his wife was born may 2d 1752
Elizabeth Raymond Daughter of Barnabas Raymond by Allice his wife was born april the 20th : 1755
John Redding Son of Thomas Redding by Sarah his wife was born november 4th 1754

Deborah Redding Daughter of Thomas Redding by Sarah his wife was born may 25th 1757

Lemuel Rider Son of Isaac Rider by Bridget his wife was born august the 29th 1758

[p. 42] Ziba Eaton Daughter of Barnabas Eaton by Elizabeth his Wife was born September the 14th 1750

Nathan Eaton Son of Barnabas Eaton By Elizabeth his Wife was born august the 11th 1753

Welthy Eaton Daughter of Barnabas Eaton by Elizabeth his Wife was born June the 19th 1755

Jabez Eddy Son of Jabez Eddy J^{r} by Paitence Eddy his Wife was born april the 5th 1744

Eliphalet Elmes Son of Elkanah Elmes by Sarah his wife was born December 14th 1753

Mary Elmes Daughter of Elkanah Elmes by Sarah his Wife was born December 28th 1755

Ruth Elmes Daughter of Elkanah Elmes by by Sarah his Wife was born march 14th 1758

Thomas Eddy Son of Lieu^{t} Zechariah Eddy by mercy His Wife Was born march 28th 1756

Lucy Eddy Daughter of Lieu^{t} Zechariah Eddy by mercy His Wife Was born March 25th 1758

Samuel Eddy Son of Lieu^{t} Zechariah Eddy by mercy his Wife was born april 29th 1760

Deborah Elmes Daughter of John Elmes by Lydia his Wife was born January 11th 1757

Olive Elmes Daughter of John Elmes by Lydia his wife was born July the 9th 1759

Keziah Eaton Eaton Daughter of Barnabas Eaton by Elisabeth his Wife was born October 8th 1757

Meribah Eaton Daughter of Barnabas Eaton by Elisabeth his Wife was Feby 10th 1760

Charles Ellis Son of Charles Ellis by Barsheba his wife was born august the 9th 1760

Thomas Ellis Son of Thomas Ellis by Ruth his wife was born September 22^{d} 1757

William Ellis Son of Thomas Ellis by Ruth his wife was born march 10th 1760

[p. 43] Susanna Pratt Daughter of Eleazer Pratt Junr by Hannah his wife was born april the 3^{d} 1731

Hannah Pratt Daughter of Eleazer Pratt Junr by Hannah his wife was born march 3^{d} 1734

Kimbil Pratt Son of Eleazer Pratt Junr by Hannah his wife was born february 20th 1737

Paul Pratt Son of Eleazer Pratt Junr by Hannah his wife was born november 10th 1739

Lucy Pratt Daughter of Eleazer Pratt Junr by Hannah his wife was born October 88th* 1742

* Sic.

Noah Pratt Son of Eleazer Pratt Junr by Hannah his wife was born January 18th 1746

Zurashaddai Palmer Son of James Palmer by marabah his wife was born June 23^{d} 1754

Thomas Palmer Son of James Palmer by Marabah his Wife was born march 22^{d} 1757

Jerusah Pratt Daughter of Nathan Pratt by Margret his wife was born July 10th 1751

Nathan Pratt Son of Nathan Pratt by margret his wife was born July the 9th 1752

Betty Pratt Daughter of Nathan Pratt by margret his wife was born may the 21st 1755

Micah Pratt Son of Nathan Pratt by Margret his wife was born June the 14th 1758

Eli Peirce Son of Hilkiah Peirce by Hannah his wife was born august the 24th 1760

Silvanus Pratt Son of Nathan Pratt by margret his wife was born Feby 23^{d} 1761

Zebedee Pratt Son of Phinehas Pratt by Sarah his wife was July 16 1744

Abner Pratt Son of Phinehas Pratt by Sarah his wife was born may 2^{d} 1746

Hannah Pratt Daughter of Phinehas Pratt by Sarah his wife was born February 29 1748

John Paddock Son of Zechariah Paddock by Martha his wife was born June the 3^{d} 1763

Peter Paddock Son of Zechariah Paddock by Martha his wife was born July 3^{d} 1765

[p. 44] Plim^{o} Ss Middleborough February 6 . 1752 This may certifie that Nathanael Bumpas and Abijah Vaughan both of Said Middleborough were on the above Date joined in marriage according to Law by me Peter oliver Just ad Pace

Plimouth Ss: Middleborough Novr 24 . 1752. This Certifies that Silas Wood & Priscilla Cob both of Middleborough were joined in Marriage according to Law on the Day of the Above Date by me Peter Oliver Just . ad Pace :

Plimouth Ss This may Certifies that m^{r} Ebenezer Morton & m^{rs} Sarah Cob both of Said Middleborough Were on ye 23^{d} Instant Joined in Marriage by me Peter Oliver Just a^{d} Pacs Middleborough July 24th 1753.

Plimouth Ss: This Certifyes that m^{r} William Canada and m^{rs} Charity Leonard ware this Day joined in Marriage by me Peter Oliver Jus^{t} a^{d} Pac Middleborough December . 6 : 1753.

June . 27 : 1751. Samuel Thrasher of Taunton and Susanna Prat of Middleborough was Marred by me Benjamin Ruggles

July 27 . 1751 then John Dugglas & Mary Brayley both of the Town of Middleborough was maryed by me Benj^{a} Ruggles

March the 12 . 1752 . John Booth and Lydia Richmond both of the Town of Middleborough was Marred by me Benj^{a} Ruggles

april 9th 1752 : Thomas Peckins of Middleborough and Abigail Briggs of Taunton was marred by me Benja Ruggles
May . 7 : 1752 . Joseph Leonard the . 3rd and Abigail Raymond both of the Town of Middleborough was marred by me Benja Ruggles
June . 5 : 1752 . Joseph Downing and Dorothy Niles both of the Town of Middleborough was marred by me Benja Ruggles
September . 24 : 1752 . Jonathan Donham of Middleborough and anna Elicit* of Raynham was marred by me Benja Ruggles
September 26 : 1752 . Jedidiah Wood & Keziah Samson both of the Town of middleborough was marred by me Benja Ruggles.

(*To be continued*)

ELEAZER CROCKER'S ESTATE

By George Ernest Bowman

Eleazer[2] Crocker (*William*[1]) of Barnstable, Mass., married, first, Ruth Chipman[3] (*Hope*[2] *Howland, John*[1]) of Barnstable, by whom he had ten children: Benoni, Bethiah, Nathan, Daniel, Sarah, Theophilus, Eleazer, Ruth, Abel, Rebecca. Two of these, Benoni and Daniel, died without issue, before their father, therefore are not mentioned in the settlement of his estate.

Eleazer[2] Crocker married, second, Mercy Phinney[4] (*Mary*[3] *Rogers, Joseph*[2], *Thomas*[1]) of Barnstable, by whom he had one child, Mercy. Both mother and child are mentioned in the settlement of the estate, in 1723.

The four daughters of Eleazer and Ruth (Chipman) Crocker married as follows: Bethiah Crocker married John Whiton of Plympton, Mass.; Sarah Crocker married Joseph Bursley of Barnstable; Ruth Crocker married Samuel[5] Fuller (*Barnabas*[4], *Samuel*[3-2], *Edward*[1]) of Barnstable; Rebecca Crocker married Jeduthan Robbins of Plympton.

An exhaustive abstract of all records relating to the settlement of Eleazer Crocker's estate, from the Barnstable County, Mass., Probate Records, will be found in the following pages, published at the expense of Mr. John W. Churchill of Plymouth, Mass., a member of the Massachusetts Society, and a descendant of John Howland through Bethiah (Crocker) Whiton.

The reference to the volume and page of the original record is given with each abstract.

* This name is spelled "Ellicet" in the intention.

[Appointment of Administrator]

[4 : 136] "To Nathan Crocker and Theophilus Crocker both of Barnstable within the County of Barnstable yeomen Greeting

"Whereas Eleazer Crocker Late of Town of Barnstable [p. 137] In the County aforesd Deceased, having while he Lived and at the Time of his Decease goods Chattels Rights or Credits In the County aforesd, lately Dyed Intestate .... I Do by these presents Commit unto you full power to administer all and Singular the goods Chattles Rights and Credits of the said Deceased Eleazer Crocker .... Dated at Barnstable aforesaid the 17th day of September Annoque Domini 1723"

[Inventory]

[4 : 142] "A True Inventory of all and singular the goods Chattels Rights and Credits of Mr Eleazer Crocker Late of Barnstable Deceased prized this 6th day of September 1723 by Joseph Smith Joseph Hinckly and John Bacer being impowered and sworn theretoo as followeth

Imprimus	£		
To . purs and apperial	24	10	6
To . arms 2 . 6 0 To books . 18/6	03	04	6
To . one bed and beding with it	12	17	0
To . one bed and beding	09	08	0
To . one rug	03	10	0
To . 3 sheets and 4 pillow Coats	03	07	0
To . New Lining Cloth	05	11	0
To . Table Lining	00	15	0
To . 5 yards of Osted Stuff	01	00	0
To . Osted wollen Lining and Cotton Yarn	02	15	0
To . flax Middelns Tow and Cotton woole	01	10	0
To . Sheeps wool	04	07	0
To . Baskets	00	08	0
To . Brass and pewtur	06	04	0
To . Iron potts Kittels and Other Utensiells	07	08	0
To . Earn-wear and Glass bottles	00	17	0
To . one Trunk	00	10	0
To . Chist Chears barrells and other household wear	06	02	0
To . Chees-press sives and Some other tools	00	10	0
To . Meal bags	00	06	0
To . English and Indian Corn In the house and barn	06	04	6
To . meat Butter and Chees	03	18	0
To . Husbandry Tacklin	09	13	0
To . Carpenturs Tools and Old Iron	02	16	0
To a horse and horstacklen	17	10	0
To Neat Cattle	58	00	0

To . Sheep	13	00	0
To . swine	04	00	0
To . Muslen Sheep Shears and Other Smale things	01	00	0
To one barrill of Salt	00	18	0
To . Lime and hay	18	00	0
To . Indian Corne on the ground	13	00	0
To . feathers and hopes	00	10	0
To the homestead with the houseing	470	00	0
To one peice of Land and Marsh adjoyning to Col. Otis's Land	328	00	0
To One peice of Land and marsh formerly Phillip Dexters . viz the half of it	136	00	0
To . one peice of Land at the green hole	066	00	0
To . half 111 Lot In the Second Division	030	00	0
To . 12 Shears ½ in 42 wood Lot In the Second Corse	010	00	0
To . ½ the 30th wood Lot In the Lower Corse	020	00	0
To . 6 Shears and ½ In the Last Division wth Shobal Howland	005	00	00
[p. 143] To : one wood Lot	30		
To : ½ the 128 Lot In the Second Division	20	00	00
To . ½ the peice of Marsh adjoyning to Joseph Smiths upland	20	00	00
To . a peice of Marsh at the mouth of the Dock	18	00	00
To . ½ the Second Lot of Marsh	20	00	00
To one peice Near Scoton Creeck	15	00	00
To . ½ the Twenty third Lot of Marsh	18	00	00
To . the 18th Lot of Marsh and 3 acres Joyning	70	00	00
To . half a Lot at Sandy Neck	02	00	00
To . the Lands Convayed to Daniel Crocker Late deceased To be paid to his sisters Ruth and Rebecca	40	00	00
To . Debts owing to the Estate	02	03	00
To . part of a dock Landing & upland ajoyning to the dock	07	10	00
To . Chain	00	08	00
To Claboards	00	18 .	00

Joseph Smith
Joseph Hinckly
John Baker"

"Barnstable Sep. 17 . 1723 Then Nathan Crocker and Theophilus Crocker made Oath to the Truth of the within written Inventory so far as they Know, and that if any Thing further of ye Estate of the Said Deceased shall Come to their Knowlidge (if it be valuable) they will allso bring it to this Inventory.

"Sworn before me John Otis Judge of Probate

"Debts Due more to the Estate.

From Able Crocker	14	00	00
from Nathan 4/6 he had of Capt Otis	00	04	06"

[ALLOWANCE TO WIDOW]

"Whereas Eleazer Crocker Late of Barnstable Died Intestate . Leaveing a widow and one Smale Child; Do therefore pursuant to the Direction of the Law for makeing allowances for Necessary beding &c: for the Upholding of Life; do set out unto Mercy Crocker widow of the Late deceased for the Use aforesaid

Imprimis	£		
To one bed and beding with it	12	17	00
To money given to her In his Life Time to bey Apparil . not Laid out 3£	03	00	00
To Meat butter and Chees	03	18	00
To Chees-press sives and Some other tools	00	10	00
To . Table Lining 15/ meal bags 6/	01	01	00
To one third of the Indian Corne and English In the house and barn 2 1 6	02	01	06
To . One Trunk	00	10	00
To ½ the Iron potts Kittels & other Utensalls	03	14	00
To . a Rugg 3 10 0	03	10	00
	31	01	6

John Otis"

[APPOINTMENT OF GUARDIAN]

[4 : 145] "To M[rs] Mery * Crocker of the Town of Barnstable and County aforesaid, Greeting

"Whereas Mercy Crocker a minor, being aged about [†] years Daughter of M[r] Eleazer Crocker Late of the Town of Barnstable now Deceased, hath Occasion for a guardian, In her Minority . I Do therefore hereby Authorize and appoint you Guardian to the said Mercy Crocker . . . . Dated at Barnstable the 26th day of Sep[br] In the Tenth Year of His Majestys Reign Annoque Domini 1723 John Otis"

[DOWER SET OFF]

[4 : 144] "To Joseph Hinckly John Baker and Ichabod Hinckly all of the Town and County of Barnstable Gen[t] Greeting &c:

"Whereas Eleazer Crocker Late of the Town of Barnstable aforesd Now Deceased Died Intestate and Left a widow Namely

* Sic. Clearly an error for "Mercy".

† The age was omitted.

Mercy who Desiers and hath applyed her self to me That her dower or one third part of all the Houseing and Lands which her Late Husband Eleazer Crocker Dyed Seized off In his own right may be Set out and allotted to her During the Term of her Natural Life. These are therefore to Authorize and impower you the said Joseph Hinckly John Baker & Ichabod Hinckly to allot set out and Divide unto her the Said Mercy the widow of the said Deceased the one third part of all ye houseing and Lands for Quantite and Quallity which the said Eleazer Crocker Seized off In his own Right or of which She is Indowable off at the Comon Law, and this Shall be your sufficent Warrant for so doing. Given under my hand and seal of the Court of Probate this Second Day of Oc^br^ In the Tenth Year of his Maj^tes^ Reign. Annoque Domini. 1723 John Otis

"Oc^br^ 2^d^ 1723 Then the Above Named Joseph Hinckly John Baker and Ichabod Hinckly were Sworn to the faithfull performance of their Trust Committed to them as above written before John Otis

"P:suant to the power and Directions above written given to us the subscribers we have and hereby do allot and sett out to the widow Mercy Crocker above written the one third part of all the housing and Lands which her Husband Eleazer Crocker died seized off (viz) the house She now dwells In and the Land adjoyning to it bounded from a stake standing within the wall to the Southward of said house seting Northerly from said Stake on a straight Line to a Mapel Saplin marked standing In the fence between the orchard and Neck of Land and then Setting westward by said fence as it runs Down to the River and as the River runs to the End of said Neck and then as the other River Leads to the Lain or highway and then by sd way to the said stake Except that part within said bounds which was Convayed To Jonathan Crocker and allso half the 30th wood Lott In the Lower Corse and half the Second Lott of marsh and a peice of marsh at the mouth of the Dock and the southard half of a peice of Marsh Near Scoton [p. 145] Creeck . and allso the Privilidge of the Dock to Land the hay She Shall Cut on the abovesaid Marsh or so much of it as She Shall see cause and allso one third part of the fruit of the Old Orchard

Joseph Hinckly
John Baker
Ichabod Hinckly"

[Settlement of Estate]

[4 : 216] "To all to whom these presents Shall Come Greeting Whereas application is made to me Said Judge to Settle the Estate of Eleazer Crocker Late of Barnstable within the County of Barnstable who died Intestate, The real and P.sonal Estate . being prized by Sufficent freeholders under Oath, wch amounts to fifteen hundred Eighty Nine pounds fourteen shilling and Two pence; after the Debts were paid, and the widow allowance and her third of the personal Estate being allready Delivered unto the widow, there remains to be Divided, before ye widows Decease one thousand three hundred & Twenty five pound; To be Settled as the Law Directs, And there [p. 217] Childeren of said Deceased. It remains (the Eldest son having a Double Portion) That said Estate be divided Into Ten Shears That is to say to Nathan Crocker the Eldest Son Two hundred and Sixty five pounds; he having allready Recd one hundred pounds their remains Due to him one hundred and Sixty five pounds; To Theophilus, One hundred thirty Two pounds and Ten shillings, he having Recd one hundred and Twenty four pounds; To Able Crocker one hundred and Thirty Two pounds and Ten Shillings, he having Recd Ninty Six pounds : To Eleazer Crocker one hundred Thirty Two and Ten Shillings, he having Recd one hundred Twenty four pounds To Bethiah Whiteing one hundred thirty Two pounds and Ten shillings she having Recd Sixty Two pounds Including the fourty pounds Due from Theophilus by deed; To Sarah Bursley one hundred thirty Two pounds and Ten shillings, she having Recd Sixty Two pounds Including the fourty pounds Due from Eleazer by deed : To Ruth Fuller one hundred Thirty Two pounds and Ten shillings she having Recd Sixty Two pounds Including the fourty pounds Due from Able Crocker by deed, To Rebacca Robins One hundred thirty Two pounds and Ten Shillings she having Recd Sixty pounds Including fourty pounds Due from Able by Deed, And to Mercy the youngest Daughter one hundred and thirty Two pounds and Ten shilling, she having Recd No part, Their remains Due unto Theophilus Eight pounds and Ten Shillings To Able Crocker thirty Six pounds and Ten shillings. To Eleazer Eight pounds & Ten shillings To Bethiah Whiteing Seventy pounds and Ten Shillings, To Sarah Bursley Seventy pounds and Ten shillings. To Ruth Fuller Seventy pounds and Ten Shillings, To Rebecca Robins seventy Two pounds and Ten Shillings, and to Mercy Crocker one hundred thirty Two pounds and Ten Shillings. I Do therefore hereby Sett out unto Nathan Crocker the Eldest Son of the said Deceased ; the homestead viz the house and Land where he dwelt, prized at four hundred & seventy pounds ; half the Eighteenth Lott of Marsh and three acres adjoyning, prized at fifty four pounds, the halfe of Two acre right In marsh near Scoton prized at Seven pounds and Ten Shillings : The half of the second Lott of Marsh prized at Twenty pounds ; half one peice of marsh adjoyning to Joseph Smiths upland prized at Twenty pound, a quarter of a Lott at the round pond prized at fifteen pounds ; half a Lott at Sandy Neck prized at Two pounds, half of the wood Lott In the Lower Course prized at Twenty pounds . and allso a third of a Small bit of Land and the one third of the Privilidge of a Dock and sd Land ; w[ch] belonged unto the said Deceased prized Two pounds and Ten Shillings . w[ch] in y[e] whole amounts to Six hundred and Eliven pounds. To have and to hold the respective part and parcells of Houseing Land and Meadow ground to him the said Nathan Crocker his heirs and asigns for Ever. He paying unto Ruth Fuller the Sum of fifty three pounds and Ten Shillings, and allso pay unto her the said Ruth Twenty Six pounds Nine Shillings and four pence after the Decease of the widow Mercy Crocker. To pay unto Rebacca Robins the Sum of Sixty five pounds and Ten Shillings, and Twenty Six pounds Nine Shillings and four pence after the decease [p. 218] To Sarah Bursley the Sum of Seventy pounds and Ten Shillings, and allso Twenty six pounds Nine Shillings and four pence after the Decease of the widow, and To Mercy the youngest Daughter of Said Deceased, the Sum of one hundred Thirty Two pounds and Ten Shillings To be paid when She arrives to the age of Eighteen years or Marriage, To gether wth five ℔ Cent Interest In the mean Time, and, allso pay unto her y[e] Said Mercy the Sum of Twenty Six pounds Nine Shillings and four pence . after the Decease of Said widow, and allso to pay unto his Brother Eleazer Twenty Six pounds Nine Shillings & four pence. To Theophilus The Sum of Eight pounds Nine Shillings and four pence, and To bethiah Whiteing the Sum of Twenty Six pounds Nine Shillings and four Pence all after the Decease of the widow. To Able Crocker the Sum of Twenty Six pounds Nine Shillings and four pence After the Decease of sd widow. To Theophilus Crocker I do Sett out one peice of meadow at the docks mouth prized at Eighteen pounds one peice of Land at the green hole prized at Sixty Six pounds To a quarter of a Lott at the round pond In the Second Division Prized at fifteen pounds Six Shears and an half with Shobal Howland prized at five pounds, To one third of the Privilidge of the Land and Dock for Landing prized at fifty Shillings To him the said Theophilus Crocker his heirs and asigns for Ever, He the Said Theophilus paying unto Bethiah Whiteing the Sum of Seventy pounds and Ten Shillings, and allso pay unto Rebacca Robins ye Sum of Seven pounds: and Eighteen pounds, wch will be Comeing to him after the Decease of his Mother wch will then be In his own hands. To Able Crocker Son To Said Deceased I do sett out Twelve Shears In the fourty Second wood Lott In ye Second Course, prized at Ten pounds, half the Eighteenth Lott of Marsh prized at Sixteen pounds To half a Lott of Marsh at Sandy Neck prized at Twenty pounds, half a Two acre right lying Near Scoton Creeck prized at Seven pounds and Ten Shillings, and the third part of the Privilige of the Dock and upland prized at fifty Shillings with his Two Brothers. viz Nathan & Theophilus to him the said Able Crocker his heirs and assigns for Ever He paying unto Ruth Fuller his sister the Sum of Seventeen pounds, all wch Sums above Expressed. The Said Nathan Crocker Theophilus Crocker and Able Crocker, having Given bonds to pay Each one their Respective Shears, and when Said money is paid It is In full to Each Child their portion or part of the Estate of said Deceased, And I do further Order and Reserve unto Mercy Crocker widow of said Deceased her right of Dower or use of one third of the real Estate of Said Deceased, as was bounded & Sett out unto her by three sufficent freeholders under oath, as ℘ Record may appear Dated October 2^{d} 1724. In Testimony whereof I have hereunto sett my hand & seal of ye said Court of Probate. Dated at Barnstable the [p. 219] Ninteenth Day of November. In the Eliventh year of his Maj^{tes} Reign Annoq^{e} Domini 1724 John Otis"

[Appointment of Guardian]

[5 : 47] "To Isaac Hinkly of Barnstable in ye County of Barnstable in ye Province aforesd Yeoman Greeting—Trusting In Your Care & Fidelity I do by these Presents .... Nominate & Appoint You to be Guardian unto Mercy Crocker a minor & daughter of Eleazer Crocker Late of Barnstable .... Dated at Barnstable The Eighth Day of July Anno Domini 1731

M Bourn"

PLYMOUTH COLONY VITAL RECORDS

(*Continued from page 70*)

[p. 41] Taunton Regester of Beirthes Marriages and buria[ls] p^{r}sented to the Court anno 1668

Sarah the Daughter of John Bundy borne the 4th of March 1668 *

Samuell the son of Thomas Caswell borne the 26 of January 1662 *

Elizabeth The Daughter of Thomas Casewell borne the 10th of January 1664*

Abigaill the Daughter of Thomas Caswell borne the 27th of october 1666

Richard son of Richard Briggs borne the 7th of Aprill 1668

Sarah the Daughter of John Dean borne the 9th of November 1668

John the son of John Lincon borne the [*16 of Novem* †] 11th of octob: 1665

Thomas the son of John Lincon borne the 15th of September 1667

Hannah the Daughter of Daniell Fisher borne Febru: ye first 1666

John the son of Daniell Fisher born the last of Novemb: 1667

John the son of Jabez Hackett borne the 26th of December 1654

Jabez the son of Jabez Hackett born the 12th of Septem: 1656

Mary the Daughter of Jabez Hackett borne the 9th of January 1659

Sarah the Daughter of Jabez Hackett borne the 13th of July 1661

Samuell the son of Jabez Hatckett borne the 29th of July 1664

Hannah the Daughter of Jabez Hackett borne the 25 of January 1666

Mary the Daughter of John Richmond borne att Bridgwater June 2^{cond} 1654

John the son of John Richmond borne att Bridgwater the 6th of June [*1654* †] 1656

Thomas the son of John Richmond born att Newport on Rhode Iland the 2^{cond} of February 1658

Sussanna the Daughter of John Richmond borne att Bridgwater the 4th of Noember 1661

Josiah Richmond the son of John Richmond borne att Taunton the 8th of December 1663

Edward the son of John Richmond borne the eight of February 1665

Samuell the son of John Richmond born the 23 of September 1668

This was taken out of Taunton Towne Record Attested by Shadrach Wilbore Towne Clarke, march 1 : 1668:69

* These three children were entered immediately under the heading of the page; but the recorder, having made errors in the third entry, crossed out all three and began again, as here printed.

† Crossed out in the original.

Taunton Register of Mariages beirth and burialls 1667
James the son of John Bundy borne the 29th of December 1664
Patience Daughter of John Bundy Died the 27th of March 1665
Hannah the Daughter of Samull Smith borne the 17 of Septem 1662
Sarah the Daughter of Samuell Smith was borne the 25 of January 1664
Sarah Daughter of Samuell Smith Died the 18th of July 1665
Samuell the son of Samuell Smith borne the 15 of october 1666
Steven the son of Thomas Casewell borne the 15 of february 1648
Thomas the son of Thomas Casewell was [*born* *] borne 22 of February 1650
Peter the son of Thomas Caswell was borne the Last of October [*borne the last of October* *] 1652
Mary the Daughter of Thomas Caswell was borne the Last of august 1654
John the son of Thomas Casewell was borne the last of July 1656
Sarah the Daughter of Tho: Caswell borne the last of November 1658
Willam the son of Thomas Casewell borne the 15 of September 1660
Mary the Daughter of Shadrach Wilbore borne the 18th of March 1661
Samell the son of Shadrach Wilbore was borne the first of Aprill 1663
Rebeckah the Daughter of Shadrach Wilbore was borne the 13 of January 1664
Hannah The Daughter of Shadrach Wilbore borne the 24th of February 1667
Samuell the son of Samell Hall was borne the 11th of December 1664
John the son of Samuell Hall was borne the 19th of October 1666
Johanna Thayer the Daughter of Nathaniell Thayer borne 13 of December 1665
[p. 42] Edward Shove son of Mr Gorge Shove was borne the 28th of Aprill 1665
Edward Shove the son of Mr Gorge Shove Died buried the 7th of August 1665
Elizabeth the Daughter of Mr Gorge Shove was Borne the 10th of august 1666
Seeth the son of Mr Gorge Shove was borne the 10th of December 1667
Elizabeth the Daughter of John Smith was borne the 7th of [*December* *] September 1663
Henery the son of John Smith was borne the 27th of May 1666
Hannah the Daughter of Samuell Hallowey was borne the first of March 1667
Willam the son of Willam Briggs was borne the 25 of January 1667
Gared the son of Garett Talbutt was borne the [*was borne* *] the 20th of March 1667
Mary Eedy the Daughter of John Eedey was borne the 14th of March 1666

*** Crossed out in the original.**

Willam the son of Richard Briggs was borne the [*25 of January 1661* *] 21 of November 1663
Rebecka the Daughter of Richard Briggs borne the 15th of August 1665
Samuell the son of John Dean born the 24th of January 1666
Samuell the son of Samuell Lincon borne the first of June 1664
Hanna the Daughter of Samuell Lincon borne the the 24th of March 1666
Tamisen the Daughter of Samuell Lincon born the 27th of October 1667
John the son of Robert Crosman borne the 16th of March 1654
Mary the Daughter of Robert Crosman borne the [*3 of august* *] 16 of July 1655
Robert the son of Robert Crosman borne the third of august 1657
Joseph the son of Robert Crosman borne the 25 of Aprill 1659
Nathaniell the son of Rober Crosman borne the 7th of August 1660
Eliezer the son of Robert Crosman borne the 16 of March 1663
Elizabeth the Daughter of Robert Crosman born the 2cond of May 1665
Samuell the son of Robert Crosman borne the 25 of July 1667
Eliezer the son of Robert Crosman Died the 26 of October 1667
Ester Allin the Daughter of Jonah Allin Junir was borne the 3 of January 1662
Mary the Daughter of Jonah Allin was borne the 12 of May 1663
Sarah the Daughter of Jonah Allin was borne the 4th of November 1665
Jonah Allin the son of Jonah Allin borne the 17th of August 1667
[p. 43] Thomas Auger Married to Elizabeth Packer of Bridgwater the 14th of November 1665
Thomas Lincone senir: married to Elizabeth Street widdow the 10th of December 1665
Agnis Smith wife† of Francis Smith Died the sixt of January 1665
Willam Briggs Married to Sarah Macomber of Marshfeild the sixt of November 1666
Samuell Hallowey Married to Jane Brayman the 26th of March 1666
Garett Talbutt Married to Sarah Andrewes the first of Aprill 1664
John Eedey Married to Sussannah Padducke of Dartmouth the last of November 1665
Richard Briggs Married to Rebecah Hoskins of Lakenham the 15th of August 1662
John Dean Married to Sarah Edson of Bridgwater the 7th of November 1663
Joseph Gray Married to Rebecka Hill the 25th of February 1667
Constant Allin the wife of Jonah Allin senir Died the 22cond of Aprill 1667
Jonah Allin senir Married Francis Hill of unketey the 14th of December 1667

* Crossed out in the original.

† "Daughter" was first written, but it was crossed out and "wife" interlined, in the same hand and ink.

Timothy Poole the son of Mr Willam Poole Died the 15 of December 1667 hee was Drowned in a little pond att Wesquabenansett where it was thought hee Did swime after a fowle which hee had shott

John Parker Died the 14th of February 1667

This is a true Coppy Drawne out of Taunton Regester the first of March 1667:or68 and Attested by Shadrach Wilbore Clarke ;

Taunto Regester of Beirthes Marriages and Burialls March 1670 :

Anna Burt the wife of James Burt Died the 17th of August 1665

Elizabeth Wilbore the wife of Joseph Wilbore ; Died the 9th of November 1670

John Dean the son of John Deane Died the sixt of august 1670

Sussanna the Daughter of Samuell Smith [*Died* *] was borne the 20th of July 1669

Samuell the son of Samuell Bundey was borne the 4th of october 1670

Easter the Daughter of Thomas Casewell was borne the 4th of June 1669

Joseph the son of Shadrach Wilbore was borne the 27th of July 1670

Nicholas Hall the son of Samuell Hall was borne the 28th of October 1670

Thomas the son of Willam Brigges was borne the 9th† of September 1669

Sarah the Daughter of Willam Briggs was borne the 10th† of September 1669

John the son of John Deane was borne the 28th of July 1670

Elizabeth the Daughter of Thomas Lincolne was borne the 24th of Aprill 1669

Mercye the Daughter of Robert Crosman was borne the 20th of March 1669

Mercy Hoare the Daughter of Hezekiah Hoar was borne the last of January 1654

[p. 44] Nathaniell the son of Hezekiah Hoare was borne the last of March 1656

Sarah the Daughter of Hezekiah Hoare was borne the first of Aprill 1658

Elizabeth Hoare the Daughter of Hezekiah Hoar was borne the 26 of May 1660

Edward the son of Hezekiah Hoar was borne the 25 of [*December* *] September 1663

Lydia the Daughter of Hezekiah Hoar was borne the 24th of March 1665

Mary the Daughter of Hezekia Hoare was borne the 22cond of September 1669

Mehittabell the Daughter of Joseph Gray was borne the 21 of February 1668

* Crossed out in the original.

† Sic.

Jonathan the son of Jonathan Briggs was borne the 15th of March 1668 *
David the son of Jonathan Briggs was borne the sixt of December 1669 *
Mary Lincon the Daughter of Thomas Lincon was borne the 12 of May 1652
Sarah the Daughter of Tho: Lincon was borne the 25 of September 1654
Thomas the son of Thomas Lincon was borne the 21 of Aprill 1656
Samuell the son of Thomas Lincon was borne the 16th of March 1658
Jonah the son of Thomas Lincon was borne the 7th of July 1660
Hannah the Daughter of Thomas Lincon was borne the 15th of March 1663
Constant the Daughter of Thomas Lincon was borne the 16th of May 1665
Marcye the Daughter of Thomas Lincon was borne the 3 of Aprill 1670
Unis the Daughter of James Leanard Jnir: borne att Braintree the 25 of November 1668
Prudence the Daughter of James Leanard Junir was borne the 24th of January 1669
Edward the son of Edward Bobbit was borne the 15 of July 1655
Sarah the Daughter of Edward Bobitt was borne the 20th of March 1657
Hannah the Daughter of Edward Bobbitt was borne the 9th of March 1660
Damaris the Daughter of Edward Bobbitt was borne the 15th of September 1663
Elkana the Daughter * of Edward Bobbitt was borne the 15th of December 1665
Dorcas the Daughter of Edward Bobbitt was borne the 20th of January 1666
Ester the Daughter of Edward Bobbitt was borne the 15th of Aprill 1669
James the son of James Phillips was borne the first of January 1661
Nathaniel the son of James Phillipps was borne the 25 of March 1664
Sarah the Daughter of James Phillipps was borne the 17th of March 1667
Willam the son of James Phillipps was borne the 21 of August 1669
Elizabeth the Daughter of Joseph Williams was borne the 30th of July 1669
Jane the Daughter of James Bell was borne the 4th of Aprill 1658
John the son of James Bell was borne the 15th of August 1660
[*page 45 is blank*]
[p. 46] James Bell the son of James Bell borne the 10th of July 1663
Nathaniel the son of James Bell was borne the seaventh of January 1664

* Sic.

Sarah the Daughter of James Bell was borne the 15th of September 1666

Elizabeth the Daughter of James Bell was borne the 15th of November 1668

Mary the Daughter of James Bell was borne the seaventh of July 1669

John the son of Joseph Staples was borne the 28 of January 1670

This is a true Coppy of what was brought to mee ; Taken out of Taunton Regester this sixt of March 1670/71

Attested by Shadrach Wilbore the Towne Clarke of Taunton ;

(*To be continued*)

PLYMOUTH COLONY DEEDS

(*Continued from page 94*)

[Constant Southworth to Ralph Allen]

[p. 129] 1663 Prence Govr:

A Deed appointed to bee Recorded

To all people to whom these prsents shall come mr Constant Soutworth of the Towne of Duxburrow in the Jurisdiction of Plymouth in New England in America yeoman sendeth greeting &c

Know yea that I the said Constant Southworth for and in consideration of the full and Just sume of forty pounds sterling to mee in hand payed by Ralph Allin of the Towne of Sandwich in the Jurisdiction aforsaid Wheelwright; wherwith I Doe acknowlidge my selfe sufficiently satisfyed contented and fully payed ; and therof and of every pte and pcell therof Doe exownarate acquite and Discharge the said Ralph Allin hee his heires exequitors adminnestrators by these prsents have bargained sold allianated enfeofed and Confeirmed and by these prsents Doe bargaine allianate sell enfeofe and Confeirme from mee the said Constant Southworth and my heires to him the said Ralph Allin and his heires and assignes for ever ; all that my portion or lott of land lying and being att the place or places Comonly Called Acushena Coaksett and places adjacent in the Jurisdiction aforsaid : viz : one hundred acrees of upland lying on the westerly necke of Coaksett aforsaid and forty acrees of upland lying att a place Comonly Called and knowne by the name of Barnes his Joy the said forty acrees of upland lying and being bounded on the westerly side with the land of mistris Allice Bradford senir: and on the Easterly side with the land of Nathaniel Warren with all the rest and remainder of my lands in the places foremencioned both upland and meddow with all and singulare the appurtenances privilidges and emunities belonging to the said hundred acrees and forty acrees and all other my lands or rightes of land in the said Acushena Coaksett and places adjacent To have and to hold the aforsaid tract of one hundred acrees of land and forty acrees of land bounded and lying as aforsaid with all other my rightes of lands in the places foremencioned both upland and meddow with all and singulare the woods waters and all other appurtenances belonging therunto or to any pte or pcell therof unto the said Ralph Allin hee his heires exequitors adminnestrators and assignes for ever to bee holden as of his Matie his Mannor of East greenwich in the Countey of Kent in free and Comon Soccage and not in Capite nor by Knights service by the rents and services therof and therby Due and of right accostomed In Witnes wherof I the said Constant Southworth have heerunto sett my hand and affixed my seale this 29th of June one Thousand six hundred sixty and three 1663

Signed Sealled and Delivered — Constant Southworth (and a seale)
in the p^rsence of — Elizabeth Southworth
Willam Collyare
Benjamine Bartlett

Elizabeth Southworth owned this as her Consent before mee Willam Collyare Assistant;

[John and Alice Hoare to John Saffin]

[p. 130] 1663 Prence Govr:

A Deed appointed to bee Recorded

To all people to whom these p^rsents shall come; John Hoare of Concoard in the Gov^rment of the Massachusetts in New England in America sendeth greet &c

Know yea that I the said John Hoare and Allis my wife for Divers and valluable causes and Considerations us therunto moveing; and especially for and in consideration of one hundred and fifty pounds sterling money; that is to say the full vallue therof in good and marchantable New England goods to us in hand payed by John Saffin of Boston in the Gov^rment aforsaid Marchant wherwith the said John Hoare and Allis his wife Doe acknowlidge themselves fully satisfyed contented and payed and therof and of every pte and pcell therof Doe exownarate acquitt and Discharge the said John Saffin hee his heires exequitors and adminnestrators for ever by these p^rsents have given graunted bargained and sold enfeofed and Confeirmed; and by these p^r^sents Doe give graunt bargaine sell enfeofe and Confeirme unto the said John Saffin his heires exequitors adminnestrators and assignes for ever all that our Dwelling house out houses and barne together with fifty eight acrees of upland bee it more or lesse; and is lying and being in Scittuate in the Gov^r^ment of New Plymouth in New England; att a place there comonly called and knowne by the Name of Conihassett and adjoyning to a pond there Comonly Called and knowne there by the Name of Musquashcutt pond; all which said Dwelling house out houses and barne with the fifty eight acrees of upland are bounded in manor and forme following; that is to say att a great stake and heape of stones by the Cart way that comes from the aforsaid pond: near the turning away of the way to the great necke; from the aforsaid stake with a straight line through the swamp towards the south untill it comes to a marked oake att the great mersh; and from the said marked oake it is bounded with the great mersh as the mersh trencheth; untill it cometh to the pond called Musquashcutt pond aforsaid and soe as the pond trencheth untill it cometh to the way of the watering place and from thence to the highway that leads to the great necke and soe on a straight line by the said way untill it comes to the aforsd stake and heape of stones; and alsoe all the tryangles nookes and strapps of mersh which lyeth between the said upland and the said pond; together with a smale strapp of meddow that lyeth from the pond aforsaid along by the mersh of John Williames; and the Easterly side of the aforsaid upland untill it cometh to a little Iland or spott of upland in the mersh; likewise all the mersh from the said strapp of mersh; which is bounded with the said Iland untill it comes to John Stockbridges mersh; and from thence with a smale trench alonge by the mersh of John Williams and soe with the same trench into the Creeke that is by the great rocke in the great mersh; and by the said Creeke it runs untill it comes to John Stockbridges mersh att a stake over against the point of hooppole necke and from that stake alonge [p. 131] by John Stockbridges to a little point or nooke of upland in the mersh; and on the same line to a marked tree on the great necke and from thence alonge towards the east alonge by the upland untill it comes to the strapp of mersh att the little Iland; all which said mersh is by Computation fifty acrees bee it more or lesse; as alsoe twenty and five acrees of upland adjoyning to the westerly end of the aforsaid fifty and eight acrees of upland att the marked oake tree alonge by the aforsaid mersh untill it comes to the aforsaid marked tree by the point of upland that points towards the point of hooppole necke as aforsaid; likewise one quarter of an acree of mersh lying and being in the mersh neare hooppole necke swamp; lying between the mersh of John Williams and the mersh of m^r^ Timothy Hatherley on an equall breadth from hooppole necke to the Creeke in the mersh neare the bridge in the great mersh; likewise one share and an halfe of all the undevided land belonging to Conihassett aforsaid; According to the tenor and graunt of the Court of New Plymouth aforsaid To have and to hold the aforsaid house out houses and barne together with all the aforsaid severall pcells of upland and mershes and share and halfe of the undevided land as it is before specifyed and bounded with all and singulare the appurtences rightes and privilidges therunto belonging or any way appertaining; unto the said John Saffin his heires and assignes for ever To the onely use and behoofe of the said John Saffin his heires and Assignes for ever; And the said John Hoare and Allis his wife Doth Covenant promise and graunt unto the said John Saffin his heires exequitors adminnestrators and assignes by these p^r^sents that hee the said John Hoare and Allis his wife are lawfully seized of and in the said p^r^mises and every pte therof with the appurtences therof in theire owne right and to their owne use of a good estate of Inheritance in free simple and are the true and proper owners therof; and have in them selves full power and right and lawfull authoritie to graunt bargaine sell and Convey and assure the same unto the said John Saffin his heires exequitors adminnestrators and assignes in such manor as before in these p^r^sents is mencioned and Declared: for any acte or thing Done or Comitted by him the said John Hoare or Allis his said wife and for warranty of the said p^r^mises the said John Hoare and Allis his wife Doeth for themselves theire heires exequitors and adminnestrators further Covenant promise and graunt to and with the said John Saffin his heires exequitors adminnestrators and assignes by these p^r^sents; that the p^r^mises now bee; and att all time and times heerafter shalbee remaine continew and abide unto the said John Saffin his heires and assignes freely acquitted exownarated and Discharged or otherwise from time to time and att all times heerafter well and sufficiently saved and kept harmles of and from all and all manor of former and other bargaines and sales givfts grauntes feofments Joyntures Dowers titles of Dowers estates morgages forfeitures seasures Judgments extents executions and all other actes and Incomberances whatsoever had made Done acknowlidged or comited by the said John Hoare or Allis his wife or any other pson or psons claiming or haveing any title or Interest of in; or to the said p[r]mises or any pte therof or any the appurtenances therof [p. 131a] therof by from or under him the said John Hoare or Allis his wife or theire Assignes lawfully claiming any state right title enterest to the before mencioned bargained p[r]mises or any pte therof; wherby the sd John Saffin his heires or assignes shall or may any wayes bee molested or lawfully evected out of the posession or enjoymen therof or any pte therof And the said John Hoare and Allis his wife for themselves theire heires exequitors adminnestrators and for every of them Doth covenant promise and graunt to and with the said John Saffin his heires exequitors and adminnestrators; that from time to time and att all times; Dureing the space of seaven yeares next after the Date heerof; att and upon the reasonable request of the said John Saffin his heires exequitors adminnestrators or assignes; to to make better and more full Asurance att the Cost and charges of the said John Saffin his heires or assignes; To and for the true pformance of the aforsaid p[r]mises wee the said John Hoare and Allis his sd wife bind us; our heires exequitors and Adminnestrators In Witnes wherof wee the said John Hoare and Allis my wife have sett our hand and seales; Memorandum it is agreed before the sealing and Delivery heerof that Jeremiah Hatch and Thomas Hatch; tenants on the said land; shall enjoy the use therof according to theire agreement with the said John Hoare; they paying theire full rent to the said John Saffin or his assignes; and alsoe that m[r] Timothy Hatherley of Scittuate is to have the use of five acrees of the said mersh Dureing his naturall life; Dated the one and twentieth Day of August in the yeare of our Lord one Thousand six hundred and sixty 1660:

Signed Sealed and Delivered
in the p[r]sence of
Amos Richison
Richard Garrett
Nathaniel Laurance
John Laurance his marke

John Hoare (and a seale)
The marke of Allis Hoare
and a (seale)

This was by mistris Allice Hoare sealed and Delivered before us on the 28[th] Day of August 1661

[Alice Bradford, Sr., to Ralph Allin]

[p. 131b] 1663 Prence Govr:

A Deed appointed to bee recorded

To all people to whom these p^{r}sents shall Come; mistris Allis Bradford seni^{r}: of the Towne of Plymouth in the Jurisdiction of Plymouth in New England in America sendeth greet &c

Know yea that I the said Allis Bradford for and in consideration of the full and Just sume of twenty pounds sterling to mee in hand payed by Ralph Allin of the Towne of Sandwich in the Jurisdiction aforsaid wheelwright; wherwith I Doe acknowlidg my selfe satisfyed contented and fully payed; and therof and of every pte and pcell therof Doe exownarate acquite and Discharge the said Ralph Allin hee his heires exequitors and adminnestrators by these p^{r}sents, have bargained and sold enfeofed and confeirmed; and by these p^{r}sents Doe bargaine sell enfeof and Confeirme from mee the said Allis Bradford and my heires To him the said Ralph Allin and his heires and Assignes for ever; the one halfe of my whole Intire pte portion or share of land being the one half of a purchsers share of land, lying and being att the place or places Comonly Called and knowne by the names of Acushena Coaksett and places adjacent: viz: the one halfe of one hundred acrees of land lying att Barnes his Joy which said hundred acrees is bounded on the Easterly side with the land that was somtimes the land of m^{r} Constant Southworth and on the North and west with the Common and abuting on the south on the marsh; and the one halfe of forty acrees of land lying on the easterly side of Coaksett River; which said forty acrees of land is bounded on the North with the land of Nathaniell Warren and on the south with the land of Mr John Aldin and on the west with the river and on the east with the Comon; with all the one halfe of all the rest or remainder of my lands in the places forementioned both upland and meddow with all and singulare the appurtenances privilidges and emunities belonging to the one halfe of the said hundred acrees and the one halfe of the said forty acrees and the one halfe of all the remainder of my said lands or rights of lands in the said Acushena Coaksett and places adjacent, I the said Allis Bradford haveing given the other halfe of the said hundred acrees of land; and the other halfe of the said forty acrees of land with the other halfe of all my rights of lands in the said Acushena Coaksett and places adjacent with all and singulare the appurtenances belonging therunto; unto my son Mr John Bradford; To have and to hold all my said one [p. 131c] one halfe of the said hundred acrees of land and my said one halfe of the forty acrees of land and my said one halfe of the remainder of my rights in the said Acushena Coaksett and places adjacent with all and singulare the the appurtenances privilidges and emunities belonging therunto or to any pte or pcell therof unto the said Ralph Allin hee his heires and Assignes for ever unto the onely proper use and behoofe of him the said Ralph Allin hee his heires exequitors adminnestrators and assignes for ever; To bee holden as of his Ma[tie] his mannor of East greenwich in the Countey of Kent in free and Comon Soccage and not in Capite nor by Knightes service; by the rents and services therof and therby Due and of right accustomed; In witnes wherof I the said Allis Bradford have heerunto sett my hand and Affixed my seale this fifteenth Day of the month Called october Ann[o]: Dom: one Thousand six hundred sixty and three 1663

Signed sealled and Delivered in the p[r]sence of
Nathaniel Morton
Hugh Cole
Willam Nelson

the marke
A B (seale)
of Allis Bradford

[End of Volume II of original records.—*Editor.*]

THE WILL OF BENJAMIN BARTLETT[4] OF DUXBURY AND THE DIVISION OF HIS REAL ESTATE

Communicated by Miss Ethel Bradford Davis

Benjamin Bartlett[4] (*Benjamin*[3], *Mary*[2] *Warren*, *Richard*[1]), of Duxbury, by his will, dated 10 December, 1717, bequeathed all his real estate to his wife Ruth, for her life, but at her death it was to be equally divided between his seven daughters, Sarah Bradford, Rebecca Bradford, Ruth Murdock, Mercy Turner, Priscilla Bartlett, Deborah Bartlett, Abigail Bartlett, and his granddaughter Ruth Bartlett, daughter of his son William Bartlett deceased.

The date of Benjamin Bartlett's death is unknown, but it was before 10 April, 1724, when one of the witnesses to the will was sworn. The will was probated 6 July, 1724.

Ruth Bartlett, the widow, made oath to her husband's inventory on 25 April, 1724, but she died before 27 March, 1725, the day on which the real estate was divided, in accordance with the terms of the will. Ruth Bartlett, the granddaughter, evidently died before her grandmother, as the real estate was divided between the seven daughters.

By means of three deeds, abstracts of which are here given, we prove that Benjamin Bartlett's seven daughters married, as follows: Sarah married Israel^{3} Bradford (*William*$^{2-1}$); Rebecca married John^{4} Bradford (*John*^{3}, *William*$^{2-1}$); Ruth married John Murdock, Jr.; Mercy married John Turner^{5} (*Benjamin*^{4}, *Mary*^{3} *Brewster*, *Jonathan*^{2}, *William*^{1}); Priscilla married John^{3} Samson (*Stephen*^{2}, *Henry*^{1}); Deborah married Josiah Thomas; Abigail married Gamaliel^{4} Bradford (*Samuel*^{3}, *William*$^{2-1}$).

Benjamin Bartlett^{4} was descended from William Brewster and Richard Warren; his wife, Ruth Pabodie, was descended from John Alden; and five of their seven daughters married descendants of Mayflower Passengers, as shown in the preceding paragraph.

Gamaliel^{4} Bradford, who married Abigail Bartlett^{5}, was a descendant of Gov. William Bradford, John Alden and Thomas Rogers. Seth^{5} Bradford, son of Gamaliel^{4}, married Lydia Southworth, a descendant, in two lines, from John Alden. The children of Seth^{5} and Lydia (Southworth) Bradford, therefore, had eight lines of Mayflower descent: four from John Alden, one from Gov. William Bradford, one from Elder William Brewster, one from Thomas Rogers and one from Richard Warren. Seth^{6} Bradford, son of Seth^{5} and Lydia, was the great-grandfather of the present writer.

The will of Benjamin Bartlett^{4} is recorded in the Plymouth County, Mass., Probate Records, Volume IV, page 440. The only original paper now remaining in the probate files is the inventory.

In the following abstract of the deed of division, dated 27 March, 1725, the complete descriptions of the lots set off to Gamaliel and Abigail (Bartlett) Bradford have been given, as these lots are identical with the lots sold by Gamaliel and Abigail in 1729.

[Will of Benjamin Bartlett^{4}]

[Plym. Co. Prob., 4:440] "I Benjamin Bartlett of Duxboro .... Bequeath unto my Loving wife Ruth : all my Estate in Duxboro & Else where, whether Houses, uplands medows or moveables (During Her Life) only obliging Her to Pay to my three youngest Daughters . Priscilla . Deborah & Abigail . the vallue of thirty Pounds a Peice at their marriage in Consideration of So much given to Each of my other Daughters already married

Item : my will is that after ye decease of my Loving wife Ruth all my uplands meadows & Houses with all my moveable Estate be Equally divided amongst my Daughters ; viz. Sarah Bradford, Rebeckah Bradford : Ruth murdoch, mercy Turner, Priscilla Deborah & Abigail . and also my Grand Daughter Ruth Bartlett ye Daughter of my Son William Dec^d^ by this my last will & Testament : I Bequeath unto my sd Grand : Daughter of all my aboves^d^ Lands meadows Houses & moveables an Equall Part : with my other aboves^d^ Daughters; but with this Proviso that She doth not Sue at Law for ye Farm in Duxboro that I now live upon . Item . my will is that if my s^d^ Grand:daughter or Her overseers Doe Sue at Law, my s^d^ Loving wife or Daughters for s^d^ Farme (that I now live upon) She may Have one shilling & no more,"

His wife Ruth was made sole executrix. The will was dated 10 December, 1717. The witnesses were Peleg Wiswall, John Wadsworth and Ebenezer Wormall. They were sworn as follows: Ebenezer Wormall on 10 April, 1724, John Wadsworth on 11 April, 1724, and Peleg Wiswall on 11 June, 1724. The will was probated on 6 July, 1724. The original will is not now in the files.

[From the original inventory.] "A true Inventory of all .... personal Estate of Benjamin Bartlit late of Duxborough .... Cooper . Dec^d^ prised at s^d^ Duxborough ye 15th day of April . Anno Domini . 1724 . by James Partridge Thomas Southworth & John Wadsworth". The inventory was sworn to by "Ruth Bartlet Executor" on 25 April, 1724. [The inventory is also recorded, 4:441.]

[Division of Real Estate]

[Plym. Co. Deeds, 18:225] "Benj^a^ Bartletts Childrens Division" "We Israel Bradford and Sarah his Wife Rebekah Bradford Widow & Relict of John Bradford Deceased & John Murdoch jun^r^ & Ruth his Wife of the Town of Plymouth John Turner & Mercy his Wife John Samson & Priscilla his Wife & abigail Bartlett of ye Town of Duxborough in ye County afores^d^ & Josiah Thomas & Deborah his Wife of ye Town of Marshfield in ye County afores^d^ being ye Heirs of our Hon^d^ Father m^r^ Benj^a^ Bartlett late of Duxborough afores^d^ deceas^d^ Have by mutual agreement Divided amongst Us all the Lands & Salt marsh belonging to ye Homestead whereon our s^d^ Father last Dwelt ; and which he dyed Seized lying & being in Duxborough afores^d^ as followeth, Namely first We Divided all the Salt marsh into Seven Lots as followeth .... The fifth Lot is bounded on ye South

West End thereof by the fourth Lot, & on ye North West Side thereof it is bounded from ye North Corner of the fourth Lot being a Stake & Stones North 60 . Degrees Easterly 32 . Pole to a Stake & Stones, & from thence East three Degrees Southerly four Pole & a half to a Stake & Stones and from thence ye North East End thereof rangeth South Ten Degrees Easterly unto a Stake in ye Marsh near the Bay & so on ye Same Course down to ye Bay . . . . We divided all ye Uplands belonging to sd Homestead into fourteen Lots as followeth: The first of sd Lots lyeth at ye Southerly Corner of sd Land & Containeth about Six acres & a half & is bounded from ye North Corner of the first Lot of Marsh being a great forked Walnut tree marked at ye Range of John Wadsworths Land, Ranging by [fol. 226] by the Fence next to sd Wadsworths Land unto ye East Corner of ye Fence at ye East Corner of sd Wadsworth Land & from thence North 75 : Degrees Easterly 30 . Pole to a Stake and Stones & from thence South 23 . Degrees Easterly 24 . Pole to a Stake & Stones by ye marsh Side at ye Range of ye Sixth Lot of marsh & from thence bounded by ye Bounds of ye Lots of marsh unto ye forked Walnut tree marked first mentioned . . . . The thirteenth Lot being about Nine Acres is bounded on the South East by the twelfth Lot, & at ye South West End thereof it is Bounded by the Sixth Lot from the West Corner of the 12th Lot 33 . Degrees Westerly about Eight Pole to the Bound between the Sixth & Seventh Lots being a Stake & Stones & from thence on ye Same Range by ye Seventh Lot 25 : Pole to the Bound between the Seventh & eighth Lots, being a Stake & Stones & from thence on ye Same Range by the eighth Lot Two Pole to a Stake & Stones & from thence the North West Side thereof rangeth North 61 . Degrees Easterly unto a Stake & Stones in ye Range of John Wadsworth's Land, and from thence the North East End thereof is bounded by sd Wadsworths Range South 30 . Degrees Easterly 34 . Pole to ye North Corner of ye 12th Lot being a Stake & Stones . . . . We do mutually agree that ye tenth Lot & the twelfth Lot of Upland & the Sixth Lot of Salt meadow shall belong unto Israel Bradford & Sarah his Wife . . . . the aforesd Second Lot with the orchard thereon & Eighth Lot of Upland & the Second Lot of Meadow or Marsh shall belong unto the aforesd Rebekah Bradford . . . . the Sixth Lot & Eleventh Lot of Upland, & the first Lot of Meadow or Marsh shall belong unto the aforesd John Murdoch junr & Ruth his Wife . . . . the third Lot and the fifth Lot of Upland and the fourth Lot of Marsh shall belong unto the aforesd John Turner & Mercy his Wife . . . . ye Seventh Lot & Ninth Lot of

Upland & the Seventh Lot of Marsh shall belong unto the afores^d^ John Samson & Priscilla his Wife . . . . the first Lot & the thirteenth Lot of Upland and the fifth Lot of Marsh shall belong unto the afores^d^ Abigail Bartlett . . . . the fourth Lot & the fourteenth Lot of Upland with the Buildings & Orchards on s^d^ fourth Lot of Upland [fol. 228] Upland & the third Lot of Marsh shall belong unto the afores^d^ Josiah Thomas & Deborah his Wife . . . . The s^d^ Josiah Thomas having already paid a valuable Consideration for s^d^ Buildings & Orchards"

The deed was dated 27 March, 1725, and signed by all the grantors, Sarah Bradford and Rebecca Bradford signing by marks, and was acknowledged by all, on that date, before Jacob Tomson, Justice of the Peace. The witnesses were Jacob Tomson and Isaac Cushman, Jr. The deed was recorded 27 April, 1725.

[GAMALIEL AND ABIGAIL BRADFORD TO JOSIAH THOMAS]

[Plym. Co. Deeds, 34:31] "Gamaliel Bradford of Duxboro . . . . Husbandman, & Abigail Bradford his Wife" for £100, "in money" sold to "Josiah Thomas of s^d^ Duxborough Housewright . . . . All our whole Right Title & Interest in & unto that Farm both Upland and Meadow lying & being within ye Township of Duxborough abovesaid whereon our Honoured Father Mr Benjamin Bartlett late of s^d^ Duxborough Dec^d^ dwelt & was Seized of at the Time of his Decease Our s^d^ Right in s^d^ Farm being One Seventh Part thereof both in ye s^d^ Upland & Meadow & is Comprehended in three Lots as ye s^d^ Farm is now divided into twenty one Lots by ye Heirs thereof which s^d^ Division by Record may appear, and s^d^ three Lots wherein our s^d^ Right is Contained or Comprehended is the fifth Lot in ye s^d^ Meadow & ye first & ye thirteenth Lots in ye s^d^ Upland which are bounded as followeth viz the said Fifth Lot is bounded on ye South West End thereof by ye fourth Lot in s^d^ Meadow and on ye North West Side thereof it is bounded from the North Corner of ye s^d^ fourth Lot being a Stake & Stones North 60 Degrees Easterly 32 . Pole to a Stake & Stones & from thence East three Degrees Southerly four Pole & a half to a Stake & Stones, & from thence the North East End thereof rangeth South ten Degrees Easterly unto a Stake in ye Marsh near ye Bay & so on ye Same Course down to ye Bay, & ye said first Lot in ye Upland lyeth at ye Southerly Corner of s^d^ Farm and Containeth about Six Acres & an half & is Bounded from the North Corner of ye first Lot in ye s^d^ Meadow being a great forked Walnut tree marked at ye Range of John Wadsworth's Land Ranging by ye Fence next to s^d^ Wadsworth's Land unto ye East Corner of ye Fence at y^e^

East Corner of sd Wadsworth's Land and from thence North 75. Degrees Easterly 30. Pole to a Stake & Stones, & from thence South 23. Degrees Easterly twenty four Pole to a Stake & Stones by ye Marsh Side at ye Range of ye Sixth Lot in sd meadow & from thence bounded by ye Bounds of ye Lots of ye sd Meadow unto ye forked Walnut tree first mentioned, & ye sd thirteenth Lot in ye sd Upland being about nine acres is bounded on ye South East by ye twelfth Lot in sd Upland, and at ye South West End thereof it is bounded by ye Sixth Lot in sd Upland from ye West Corner of ye sd Twelfth Lot North 33. Degrees Westerly about eight Pole to ye Bound between ye Sixth & Seventh Lots in sd Upland being a Stake & Stones & from thence on ye Same Range by ye sd Seventh Lot 25. Pole to ye Bound between ye Seventh and eighth Lots in sd Upland being a Stake & Stones & from thence on ye Same Range by ye sd eighth Lot two Pole to a Stake & Stones & from thence the North West Side thereof rangeth North 61. Degrees Easterly unto a Stake & Stones in ye Range of John Wadsworth's Land, & from thence ye North East End thereof is bounded by sd Wadsworths Range South 30. Degrees Easterly 34. Pole to ye North Corner of ye sd Twelfth Lot being a Stake & Stones."

The deed was dated "the twenty fith Day of April in the Year of Our Lord one thousand Seven hundred & twenty eight* or twenty nine" and was signed by Gamaliel Bradford and Abigail Bradford. The witnesses were Thomas Loring and Joseph Freeman. The deed was acknowledged, by both grantors, on 25 August, 1729, before Edward Arnold, Justice of the Peace. It was not recorded until 28 February, 1740.

[BRADFORD, MURDOCK, TURNER AND THOMAS TO SAMSON]

[Plym. Co. Deeds, 41:14] "We, to wit, Israel Bradford and Sarah Bradford his Wife both of Kingston and Rebekah Bradford Widow Relict of Mr John Bradford late of sd Kingston deceased John Murdoch and Ruth Murdoch his wife of Plimton John Turner and Mercy Turner his Wife both of Scituate Josiah Thomas and Deborah Thomas his Wife Captain Gamaliel Bradford and Abigail Bradford his Wife of Duxborough and all in the County of Plymouth .... in Consideration of the Sum of fourty and two Pounds in Currant Money of New England or in the Old Tenour to Us well and truly in hand Pay'd by John Samson of Duxborough aforesaid Yeoman" sold to said John Samson "one certain Lot of Land lying and being in the Township of Dux-

* As Gamaliel Bradford and Abigail Bartlett were not married until 30 August, 1728, this deed must have been made in the year 1729.

borough aforesaid and s^d^ Lot is the Eighty Second Lot in Number in the Second Division of the Commons of Upland which belonged to the Townships of Duxborough and Pembroke in the County abovesaid and is bounded as follows, viz, on the South West by the Eighty first Lot from the East Corner thereof being a red oak Tree marked by the North Side of the Road Way Ranging North fifty Degrees Westerly 106. Pole to the North Corner of the said Eighty first Lot being a Great white Oak marked in the Range of the fourty acre Lot of Israel Silvester and from thence the North West End thereof is bounded by said fourty acre Lot North thirty Seven Degrees Easterly fifty eight Pole and a half to a great white Oak hollow Stump marked and a Stone Set into the Hollow of it and from thence the North East Side rangeth South fifty Degrees Easterly one hundred and twenty Pole to a red oak marked by the Road Way and from thence the South East End thereof is bounded by said Road Way unto the East Corner of the Eighty first Lot being a red Oak marked first Mentioned Said Lot being about fourty one Acres. To Have and to Hold all the Above granted and bargained Eighty Second Lot of Land bounded and described as aforesaid or at least all Our Parts of s^d^ Lot which is [fol. 14] is Six Sevenths of the Whole of said Eighty Second Lot"

The deed was dated 28 December, 1742, and was signed by all the grantors, Rebecca Bradford and Ruth Murdoch signing by marks.

The witnesses were Seth Chipman, Mercy Chipman, Benjamin Bradford, Zeresh Bradford, George Barrow, James Murdoch, Hezekiah Ripley, Joshua Thomas, Thomas Clap, Deborah Turner and Joseph Freeman.

The deed was acknowledged before Thomas Clap, Justice of the Peace; by John and Mercy Turner, on 22 March, 1747; by Gamaliel and Abigail Bradford and Josiah Thomas, on 28 March, 1748; by Israel and Sarah Bradford, on 29 March, 1748.

It was acknowledged before Samuel Bartlett, Justice of the Peace; by John Murdoch on 3 August, 1749; by Ruth Murdoch on 28 February, 1749; by Rebecca Bradford on 2 March, 1749.

It was acknowledged before Thomas Foster, Justice of the Peace, by Deborah Thomas, on 25 October, 1750.

The deed was recorded 5 November, 1750.

INCREASE IN SUBSCRIPTION PRICE OF "PILGRIM NOTES AND QUERIES"

Beginning with January, 1917 (Vol. V, No. 1), the subscription price of "Pilgrim Notes and Queries" will be increased to one dollar and fifty cents ($1.50) per year, payable in advance.

At the close of the year 1917, a title-page, with indexes of subjects, of persons and of places, will be sent, without extra charge, to all who have paid cash subscriptions for that year.

[*Subscribers should note particularly that, as in the case of the first three volumes, an extra charge of fifty cents will be made for the title-page and indexes for Volume IV (1916), when completed.*]

Beginning with the issue for January, 1917 (Vol. V, No. 1), the price of single copies of current issues will be increased to twenty cents each. [*"Pilgrim Notes and Queries" is not issued for the months of June, July, August and September.*]

Special Combination Rate for 1917

"Pilgrim Notes and Queries" & "The Mayflower Descendant"

"Pilgrim Notes and Queries" for 1917 (Volume V, including the Title-page and Indexes) and "The Mayflower Descendant" for 1917 (Volume XIX) will be mailed to one address for four dollars ($4.00), *provided remittance accompanies the order.* [The regular subscription price of "The Mayflower Descendant," which is issued quarterly, is $3.00 per year.]

All remittances must be made payable to "Society of Mayflower Descendants" (*not to the Editor*) and mailed to 53 Mt. Vernon St., Boston, Mass.

FREEMAN GENEALOGY

A Freeman Genealogy, including descendants of Edmund Freeman, of Sandwich, and Samuel Freeman, of Watertown, Mass., compiled by Rev. Frederick Freeman, was published in 1875.

The unsold remainder was presented to the Massachusetts Society of Mayflower Descendants, in 1909, by a member, to be sold for the benefit of its research work.

The Society still has for sale a few copies of this book of 457 pages, bound in cloth, at five dollars ($5.00) each, postage prepaid.

Remittances must be made payable to "Society of Mayflower Descendants," and may be sent to the Editor of this magazine.

PLYMOUTH COLONY WILLS AND INVENTORIES

BY GEORGE ERNEST BOWMAN

(*Continued from page 77*)

ABSTRACTS OF THE RECORDS IN VOLUME III

A LITERAL copy of the entire first book of the Plymouth Colony Wills and Inventories, transcribed by the Editor from the original records, was printed in the first eleven volumes of this magazine, and exhaustive abstracts of all the records in the second book of Wills and Inventories, made from the original records, were begun in our twelfth volume and completed in our last issue.

The present article begins a series of abstracts of all the records in the third book of the Plymouth Colony Wills and Inventories.

[CAPTAIN THOMAS SOUTHWORTH'S WILL]

[3:1] The will of "Captaine Thomas Southworth Deceased" was probated at Plymouth, 1 March, 1669,* on the oaths of John Morton and George Bonum, the witnesses.

The will was dated 18 November, 1669, and bequests were as follows:

To "my Daughter Elizabeth Howland all my housing and Lands both upland and meddow within the Township of Plymouth to her and her heires Lawfully begotten upon her owne body; To them and theire heires for ever"

"I Give all my other Lands out of the Township of Plymouth unto my said Daughter Elizabeth; and unto her husband Joseph Howland; Towards the payment of my Debts; to be Done with the advise of the Supervisors of this my last will"

"my Rapier and belt to my sonne in Law Joseph Howland"

"to Thomas Faunce" 40s., "in sheep or neate Cattle"

"unto Deborah Morton" 40s., "in sheep or neate Cattle"

"unto Willam Churchill a sheep to be Delivered to him the next Springe following the Date heerof"

"That lott and halfe of Land which is att the Eelriver which was exchaunged by m^r^ Willam Bradford Deceased: with John

* This is old style. In new style the date would be 11 March, 1670.

Faunce for a Lott att Jonses River I Doe yeild up all my Interest in the said Lott; & halfe; of Land To Thomas Faunce"

"The Rest of my estate I leave in the hands of my son Joseph Howland and my Daughter his wife & my brother Constant Southworth To be Disposed of as they shall see reason: for the supply of my wife in her poor Condition"

The inventory, taken by George Watson, John Morton and Ephraim Morton, was exhibited to the court at Plymouth, 1 March, 1669, on the oath of Joseph Howland. No real estate is mentioned. The estate was indebted to: "Capt: Fuller"; George Watson; John Morton; Thomas Lettis; John Wood, Sr.; Gyles Rickard, Sr.; "Mr Barnes"; William Harlow; "Clarke the Iron Munger att Boston"; Thomas Whitney; Patience Whitney; "Samuell Fuller of Plymouth"; Jabez Howland.

[Widow Alice Bradford's Will]

[The Will and Inventory of Alice Bradford, Sr., widow of Gov. William Bradford, taking up the next four pages of the original record, were printed in full in our third volume.—*Editor*.]

[Joseph Tilden's Will]

[p. 6] The will of "Mr Joseph Tilden of Scittuate .... yeoman" was probated at Plymouth, 5 July, 1670, on the oaths of "Captaine James Cudworth and Richard Curtice"

The will was dated 12 May, 1670. Bequests were as follows:

To "wife Elizabeth Tilden" £100 in silver money, also £100 "in Movable goods; shee to take her choise of what shee best liketh"

"wheras I have settled my lands upon my sonnes Nathaniel: John Stephen Samuell and Benjamine by Deeds of feofment and a letter of Atturney to put each and every of my said sonnes into posession of what by Deed is settled upon each of them: when each of them shall attaine the full age of twenty one yeares; which Letter of atturney and Deeds of feofment beare Date" 16 April, 1670, "wherfore .... all the rents proffitts benifitt and use fruite of all my said Lands; my beloved wife Elizabeth Tilden shall take to her selfe .... untill each of my said sonnes shall attaine to the age of twenty one yeares; and the thirds of the proffitts of all my lands after theire attainment to the age aforsaid During her Naturall life; and incase .... any of my said sonnes one or more should Depart this life before hee shall attaine the full age of twenty one yeares or after the attaining the age of twenty one yeares; Die without Issue Lawfully begotten .... his p^rte and portion of Land shalbe equally Devided amongst all my Children surviveing both males and feamales"

"my loveing wife shall have the Care and Charge of bringing up all my Children; and to have the use and benifitt of all the Legacyes or portions untill each of them Come to full age"

To "my Daughter Rebeckah Tildin twenty pounds in silver mony and one bed furnished"

To "my Daughter Elizabeth Tilden ten pounds in silver mony"

To "my Daughter Lydia Tilden ten pounds in silver mony"

To "my sister Lydia Garrett five pounds in Currant Country pay; and Doe acquitt and Discharg her of all Debts and accoumpts betwixt us"

"I Doe acquitt and Discharge my brother Stephen Tilden of all Debts and accoumpts betwixt us"

Debts and legacies being paid the remainder is to be equally divided "amongst my Children Nathaniel: Tilden: John: Tilden: Stephen Tilden Samuell Tilden Benjamine Tilden Rebeckah Tilden Elizabeth Tilden and Lydia Tilden" to the sons at twenty-one, and to the daughters at twenty-one or at earlier marriage. If a son dies before twenty-one, or a daughter before marriage or before twenty-one, that child's share is to be divided among the survivors.

Wife Elizabeth Tilden is made sole executrix.

The witnesses were John Sutton, Richard Curtice and James Cudworth.

The inventory was taken, at Scituate, 31 May, 1670, by Isaac Buck, Isaac Chettenden and James Cudworth, and exhibited at court at Plymouth, 5 July, 1670, on the oath of "Elizabeth Tilden Widdow"

At the end of the inventory the following items were added:

"belonging to the estate on Anualtie of p^r annum	17	00	00
after mistris hatherlyes Decease the Reversion of	06	p^r annum	
after the Decease of old Beare the Reversion of	06	p^r annum"	

[William Macomber's Inventory]

[p. 9] The inventory of "Willam Macomber of Marshfeild Deceased" was taken 27 May, 1670, by Thomas King, William Ford, Sr., and Mark Eames, and exhibited to the court at Plymouth, 7 June, 1670, "on the oathes of Ursilla Maycomber Thomas Macomber and Mathew Maycomber". No real estate is mentioned.

[Samuel Sturtivant's Will]

[p. 10] Samuel Sturtivant of Plymouth made his will 1 August, 1669, and it was probated at Plymouth, 29 October, 1669, on the oaths of the two witnesses. Bequests were as follows:

To "my soninlaw John Waterman the one halfe of that my share of Land that I bought of Edward Gray which lyeth neare Namassakeesett ponds Called the Majors purchase"

To "my sonnes Namly Samuell James John and Joseph and to the Child my wife now goeth with (if a boy) after my wifes Decease; all my house and Land that I now Dwell upon: and all other Lands and meddowes; with all Rightes belonging therunto; That I have in any place whatsoever; To be equally Devided to all or soe many of my aforsaid sonnes as shalbe alive att my wifes Decease; and incase my wife thinketh it meet; to settle and give my son Samuell a Doubble share of the said housing and lands; then it is my will that hee shall have it; that is two shares and the Rest Liveing one share apeece; and incase any of my sonnes are minded to sell their p^rtes after theire Devison; my will is that hee sell it to one of his brothers incase any of them will give as may bee thought meet by two Indifferent men"

To "my . . . . wife all my Cattle goods and estate whatsoever" and she is "to be the sole exequitrix"

The witnesses were William Crow and John Smith, the latter signing by a mark.

The inventory was taken 22 October, 1669, by "serjeant Ephraim Tinkham Joseph Howland and Willam Crow; and exhibited to the Court held att Plymouth" 29 October, 1669. The only mention of real estate is: "As for his housing and lands wee leave the valluation therof;"

The estate was indebted to "John Rogers of Duxburrow"; John Dunham; Jabez Howland; John Moses; James Cole, Sr.; James Barnabey; Edward Gray; William Nelson; "the widdow Dunham"; "John Shaw of Boston"; "Elizabeth Combes of Boston"; "mistris Sarah Paine"; "m^r Thomas Clarke of Boston"; John Wood; "serjeant Willam Harlow"; Andrew Ring; "John Hubbard"; Thomas Lucas; John Smith.

(*To be continued*)

THE WILL OF BENJAMIN HIGGINS

WITH NOTES BY THE EDITOR

THROUGH the courtesy of Mr. George C. Higgins, the owner of the original document, we are allowed to present here a copy of the will of Benjamin[3] Higgins (*Benjamin*[2], *Richard*[1]) of Eastham. This will was made 1 July, 1760; but for some unknown reason was never probated. It is here printed because of its genealogical importance in connection with "The Mayflower Genealogies", all of the children of the testator being descendants of Elder William Brewster, through their mother.

Benjamin[3] Higgins was the son of Benjamin and Lydia (Bangs) Higgins, and was born at Eastham, 15 September, 1681. He married, first, at Eastham, on 22 May, 1701, Sarah Freeman[5] (*Edmund*[4], *Mercy Prence*[3], *Patience*[2] *Brewster, William*[1]), who was the mother of all his children, and died at Eastham, 21 January, 1743/4.

Benjamin[3] Higgins married, second, at Truro, 28 June, 1749, Mercy (Freeman) Hopkins, who was mentioned in his will. She was the widow of Caleb[4] Hopkins (*Caleb*[3], *Gyles*[2], *Stephen*[1]) of Truro.

"The Treat Family", published in Salem, Mass., in 1893, states that the Benjamin Higgins who married Mercy (Freeman) Hopkins was born 19 April, 1701, and was "a son of Isaac and Lydia Higgins"; but the will of this Isaac Higgins, dated 12 February, 1760, contains a bequest to the heirs of his deceased son Benjamin. Isaac's son Benjamin, therefore, died more than four months before Benjamin[3], son of Benjamin[2] and Lydia Higgins, made his will, in which he named all but three of his children by his wife Sarah, and mentioned his wife Mercy in a way which proves that she was a second wife.

The marriage of Benjamin Higgins and Sarah Freeman, and the births of their fourteen children, were printed in the Eastham records in our seventh volume. All but three of these children, viz. Reliance, Thankful and Solomon, were mentioned in their father's will.

This will is about eleven and three-fourths inches in height, and about seven and one-fourth inches in width. It is badly broken in the creases, but no part of it has been lost.

A literal copy of the will, transcribed by the Editor, from the original document, is here presented.

[Will of Benjamin Higgins]

In the name of God Amen the first day of July anno Domini: 1760 I Benjamin Higgens of Eastham in the County of Barnstabel in New England yeoman being inferm of Body but yet of disposing mind and memory coling to mind the mortallity of my body and knowing that it is apointed for all men once to Dye do make and ordaine this my last Will and testement in maner following first I give my soul into the hands of God that gave it and my Body I Recommend to the Earth to be buried at the discresion of my Executer and after my Just depts and funerel Charges are paid and discharged out of my personal Estate I Give Devise and dispose of all my Estate borth Real and personal as hear after Exprest

Imprim I gvie and bequeath to my beloved Wife mercy Higgens one hundred and sixty ounses of silver for har Right of dour to be paid out of my Real Estat as I shall here after Expres I also give unto my s^d^ wife one feather bead with Convenant furniture there unto and also one Cow with a prevelege of pastering one Cow on my land and to Cut hay on my meadow to winter one Cow so long as she lives my widow I allso give unto my s^d^ wife convenant house roome in the Easterly part of my Dwelling house and fire wood for har to burn brought to har dore as I shall heare after order solong as she shall live my widow and my s^d^ wife shal have leberty to carry of all the personal Estate she brought with har when I married har

Ittm I give unto my son Thomus Higgens his note of hand that he gave me for fifteen pounds lawful mony and also Eight pounds lawful mony to be paid out of my Real Estate as I shall hear after order

Ittm I give to my son paul Higgens his note of hand that he gave me for mony I allso give unto him my s^d^ son paul Eightteen acors of land to be measured of to him of my land that lays by Ralphs pond and of that end that joins to said pond I also give unto him my s^d^ son my two lots of meado on monnement plane and one right in the undivided sege ground in that propriete all which land and meadow I give unto him my s^d^ son pawl and to his heirs and asings for Ever

Ittm I give unto my son Benjamin Higgens that my lot of land whare his house now stands and also all my land at Robbens hill and also four acors of land at Ralphs pond next to my son paul his land and also my two lots of meadow at the old ship and also one Right in the undevided sege ground in that propriate all which lands and meadow I give unto him my s^d son Benjamin and to his heairs and assings for Ever

Ittm I give unto my three sons namely Zaccheus higgens Isaac higgens and freeman higgens all my lands and meadows in Eastham and in the town of Harwich not yet disposed of in this my Will they paying to my wife the silver I have given har and also procure har fire wood and alow har the prvelege of keeping har cow as is with in mentioned and that they also pay to my son Thomus the Eight pounds I have given him viz one thurd part of the above said lands and meadows I give to my son Zaccheus higgens and to his heairs and assings for Ever, and one thurd part of s^d lands and meadows I give unto my son Isaac higgens and to his heairs and assings for Ever and one thurd part of the above s^d lands and meadows I give unto my son freeman higgens and to his heairs and assings for Ever

Ittm I give unto my son freeman higgens and to his heairs and assigns the westerly halfe part of my dweling house

Itm I give unto my two sons Zaccheus higgens and Isaac higgens the Easterly halfe part of my dweling howse they allowing my wife Convenant fire rome solong as she lives my widow

Ittm I give to my three sons Zaccheus higgens Isaac higgens and freeman higgens my barn in Equil proportion alike

Ittm I give to my son freeman higgens my Cart and wheales and Scow and all my farming tackling

Ittm I give all my personal Estate not yet disposed of in this my Will to my daughters and grand children and theire heairs and assings namely to my daugter Presiller smith one fifth part and to my daughter Sarah smith one fifth part and to my daughter Experens fohy one fifth part and to my daughter Lois Cirkum one fifth part and to my Grand Children namely solomon young anne young Eunis young sarah young Elesebeth young and and hennery young one fifth part or to somany of them as shall survive at my deceas

Lasty I Constitute and ordaine my son Zaccheus Higgens of Eastham to be the Exacutor of this my Will Ratifying and Conferming this and no other to be my last will and testement in Witnes whare of I have here unto set my hand and seal the day and year on the other side above Ritter

Signed sealed and declared Benjmin Higgens (seal)
to be his last will and testement
in presens of us
Richard Sparrow
Moses Higgens
Elnarthan Higgens

FORM FOR A BEQUEST

I GIVE and bequeath to the Society of Mayflower Descendants, a corporation organized under the laws of the Commonwealth of Massachusetts, the sum of .... dollars.

NOTES BY THE EDITOR

COMMITTEES OF THE MASSACHUSETTS SOCIETY. The Board of Assistants has appointed Committees for the year 1916–1917, as follows:

Committee on Membership: Edwin A. Daniels, M.D., Mrs. Albert S. Apsey, Rev. Rufus B. Tobey, Mrs. C. Peter Clark, Mrs. Micajah P. Clough.

Committee on Publication: Rev. Frederick B. Allen, Arthur Perry, Alvin P. Johnson, Frederick Foster, George Ernest Bowman.

Committee on Finance: Arthur Perry, Winthrop J. Cushing, Horace H. Soule, Benjamin A. Delano, Curtis Chipman.

Committee on Library: Miss Mary F. Edson, Mrs. Theodore P. Gooding, Miss Ellen Chase, Mrs. John F. Eliot, Miss Mary Alden Thayer.

Committee on Annual Dinner: William B. H. Dowse, Rev. Frederick B. Allen, Mrs. Robert S. Russell, Frank W. Stearns, Mrs. Gordon Prince.

Committee on At Home Days: Mrs. Gordon Prince, Miss Grace W. Geer, Mrs. Lorenzo D. Baker, Jr., Mrs. George A. Burdett, Mrs. Edward W. Baker.

Committee on Mary Chilton Memorial: Lew C. Hill, Mrs. Robert S. Russell, Charles F. Cutler, Mrs. Frederick A. Turner, George Ernest Bowman.

THE STANDISH MONUMENT AT DUXBURY. The illustration facing page 129 has been printed from a half-tone plate loaned by Myles Standish, M.D., compiler of "The Standishes of America".

THREE GENERATIONS OF THE MAYFLOWER GENEALOGIES. In the March, 1916, issue of "Pilgrim Notes and Queries" the Editor began A Preliminary Outline of the First Three Generations of The Mayflower Genealogies.

Three generations of the Cooke and Hopkins families were given in the March issue; the Brewster family was in the April issue; the Rogers and Winslow families were in the May issue.

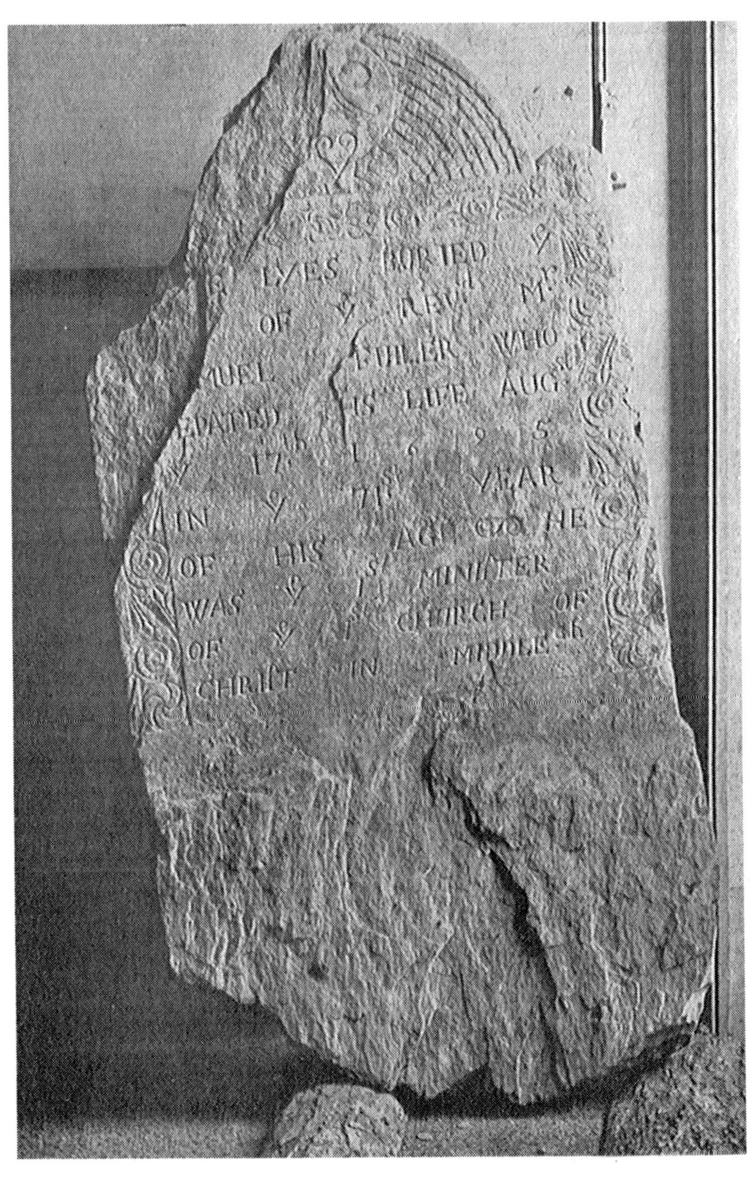

REV. SAMUEL[2] FULLER'S GRAVESTONE AT MIDDLEBOROUGH, MASS.

[See page 256]

THE MAYFLOWER DESCENDANT

Vol. XVIII OCTOBER, 1916 No. 4

HOPKINS — SNOW NOTES

By George Ernest Bowman

Under the general title "Hopkins — Snow Notes", we shall print, from time to time, abstracts from the numerous notes made by the Editor, from original records and documents, relating to the descendants of Nicholas and Constance[2] (Hopkins) Snow of Eastham, Mass. Constance[2] Hopkins came over in The Mayflower with her father, Stephen[1] Hopkins, and her stepmother.

In this first article we give exhaustive abstracts of all records, in the Barnstable County, Mass., Registry of Probate, relating to the estate of Mark Snow[3] (*Constance*[2] *Hopkins, Stephen*[1]), of Eastham, and the estate of his widow, Jane (Prence) Snow. There are no original documents in the probate files.

Mark Snow's first wife, Anna[2] Cook (*Josiah*[1]), was not a descendant of Francis[1] Cooke, the Mayflower Passenger.

Mark Snow's second wife, and widow, was Jane Prence, a daughter of Gov. Thomas and Mary (Collier) Prence.

By the first wife there was only one child, Anna. By the second wife there were eight children: Mary, Nicholas, Elizabeth, Thomas, Sarah, Prence, Elizabeth, Hannah.

The births of Mark Snow and his wife Jane, his two marriages, the death of his first wife, and the births of all his children, copied from the records of Eastham, will be found in our third, fifth and seventh volumes.

Mark Snow of Eastham made his will 23 November, 1694, and it was probated 16 January, 1694/5; but his inventory was taken one week earlier, on 9 January, 1694/5. He died, therefore, between 23 November, 1694, and 9 January, 1694/5.

Widow Jane Snow of Harwich made her will 21 December, 1703. It was probated 2 July, 1712; but her inventory was taken four days earlier, on 28 June, 1712. The account of her son Nicholas, as executor, states that he cared for his mother, at his own house, "from ye 26th of october to ye Latter End of May following", and thus proves that she died at the end of May, or very early in June, 1712.

There are a number of errors and omissions in the copies of these two wills, printed in the "New England Historical and Genealogical Register," Volume XLVII, pages 85 and 186. Two of these errors should receive especial attention.

When Jane Snow signed her will, she did so by making her mark; but she did not make a cross, as printed in the "Register". She signed the will by her initials "J S", as stated in the abstract here printed.

Another error of especial importance, in the "Register", was in printing "Mary" Sparrow as the name of the first witness to Jane Snow's will. The name in the record is "Marcy" Sparrow. The name Mercy was frequently pronounced "Marcy", and many times it is so spelled on the old records.

The two witnesses to Jane Snow's will were Mercy (Cobb) Sparrow, the wife of Richard Sparrow[4] (*Hannah Prence*[3], *Patience*[2] *Brewster*, *William*[1]), and her sister Martha Cobb, who later married Richard Knowles[5] (*Mercy Freeman*[4], *Mercy Prence*[3], *Patience*[2] *Brewster*, *William*[1]).

Abstracts of the two wills, etc., follow, the proper reference to the Barnstable County, Mass., Probate Records being stated in each case.

[Mark Snow's Will]

[Barnstable Co. Prob., 1 : 111] "Mark Snow of Eastham" made his will 23 November, 1694. Bequests were as follows:

To "my Son Nicolas a parcel of Land where his house Stands computed at twenty and Six Acres according to bounds Sett down in ye purchesers Book of Records with two acres of meadow Lying at ye head of Nameskekit according to Record as aforesd" also "one half of my Lott of Land Lying at Satuckitt between Jonathan Banges and ye Indian Bounds" also "one half of a parcel of meadow Lying in ye Township of yarmouth in a place Called ye blue meadow on ye South Side of ye Bass River"

To "my Son Thomas Snow ye other half of my Lott where his house Stands on that Side next ye Indian Rainge and ye one half of my meadow in yarmouth in ye before Specified meadow"

To "my Son Prince Snow after my wifes decease or widowhood my now dweling house and all ye Lands Adjoyning and fifteen acres of Land above ye Comon Roade according to bounds Specified in ye Record afore Sd" also "three Acres of meadow that Lyies below my now dwelling house according to Bounds Set down in ye before Specified Book of Records"

To "my Son Thomas Snow an Acre of Land at ye northermost end of my Lott in ye old fields Comonly So Called and another Small divition of Land Estimated at three quarters of an acre Lying in ye before Specified old fields at Satuckett between Ensign Bangs and Thomas Freeman"

To "my Son Prince Snow ye Remainder of my Lott of Land in ye before Specified Indian fields after my wifes decease"

To "my Sons Nicholas and Thomas my Lott of Land Containing three acres of Land according to Record Lying betwen John Freemans pasture and ye Common Road"

To "my Son Prince after my wifes decease an acre and an half of meadow Lying between James Cole and Stephen Hopkins in Nameskeket meadow according to bounds Specified in ye before Specified Records:"

"All my Lands that Lye undevided after my wifes decease I give and bequeath to my three Sons Nicholas Thomas and Prince to be equally divided between them:"

To "my Loving wife Jane Snow all my whole personal Estate After my debts and Funeral Charges are paid"

"I doe Appoint my Loving wife Jane Snow my whole and Sole Executor"

To "my Son Prince Snow my muskit and Catusbox * and Cutlas and one pistol:"

To "my Son Thomas Snow my Back Sword and one pistol:"

To "my grand child Jonathan Snow my Carbine:"

The witnesses were Samuel Knowles, Thomas Crosby, Jr., and Jonathan Sparrow. "Capt Jonathan Sparrow Samuel Knowles & Thomas Crosby" made oath to the will on 16 January, 1694/5, before Barnabas Lothrop, Judge of Probate. The will was recorded 9 April, 1695.

[p. 110] On 16 January, 1694/5, "at Eastham ye will of Mark Snow Late of Eastham deceased was proved" and administration granted to "ms Jane Snow Relict of Sd deceased"

* Cartouch or cartridge box.—*Editor.*

[p. 112] On 9 January, 1694/5, Jonathan Bangs and Israel Cole took the inventory. The real estate was: "house and Land" £30; "four Acres of Land" £4, 10s.; "fifteen acres of Land" £6; "nine acres of Land" £8; "twenty Six acres of Land" £11, 14s.; "two acres meadow" £3; "thirty Acres of Land" £15; "four acres meadow" £4; "four acres and three quarters Land" £4, 10s.

On 16 January, 1694/5, Jane Snow made oath to this inventory "of her husband Mark Snow deceased" before Barnabas Lothrop, Judge of Probate. The inventory was recorded on 10 April, 1695.

[Widow Jane Snow's Will]

[3: 271] "Jane Snow Widow of Herwich" made her will on 21 December, 1703. Bequests were as follows:

To "my son Nicholas Snow my bason and your & a small brass kittle and one spit"

To "my son Thomas Snow one Copper kittle"

To "my son Prince Snow my Great Iron Kittle"

"my Cattle my Will is that they be Eaquiely Divided among all my Children"

"I Give to to Anne Attwood a puter Wine Cup & a Dram Cup & a sucking bottle"

"I Give my Cabinet unto my Grandchild Jane Nickerson"

"I Give my Little Trunk unto my Grandchild Jane Snow:"

"my will is that ye Rest of my movable Estate be eaquielly Divided betwixt my Two Daughters Mary and Sarah"

"my will is that Debts and Funerall Charges be paid out of my stock of Cattle;"

"I Do appoint my son Nicholas Snow: & my Brother Jona^t^ Sparrow for to be my Executors"

The will was signed by the initials "J S" as her mark. The witnesses were "Marcy Sparrow" and "Martha Cobb"

On 2 July, 1712, "Mercy Sparrow and Martha Late Martha Cob and Now Martha Knowles" made oath to the will, and administration was granted to "Nicholas Snow Sone of ye Deceased one of ye Executors In ye Same Will Named (the other beind Deceased)"

[p. 273] The inventory "of Jane Snow Widow Relict of Mark Snow of Harwich Deceased aprised at Eastham" on 28 June, 1712, by Nathaniel Freeman and Richard Godfree, "being appointed thereto by ye Executor" No real estate is mentioned.

[p. 274] On 2 July, 1712, Nicholas Snow, executor of the will "of Jane Snow his Mother Late of Harwich Deceased" made oath to the inventory.

On 23 September, 1712, an addition was made to the inventory.

Among the items in an undated "accompt of Nicholas Snow Execu^tr^ of all and singuler ye Goods and Chattels of Mrs Jane Snow of Eastham his mother Deceased", recorded following the addition to the inventory, are: "To house Room and providing firewood and Tendance for Sd Deceased from ye 26th of october to ye Latter End of May following" £2; "To Removing her houshold stuff and Goods from her own house to ye Sd Executors" £1; "To procuring a nurse in time of sickness & other Trouble" £3; "To plums shuger bisket Rum & other Distiled Lickurs used In her sickness" 7s., 6d. "To Prince Snow In part of pay for a Cow" £1, 8s., 7d.

PLYMOUTH COLONY VITAL RECORDS

(Continued from page 171)

1677 Heer followeth Divers other Registers which might have bin more methodically as I Could Desire because the order of Court hath not bin attended in bringing in the Regesters of the Townes as might have bine; and ptely alsoe in that I have bine Interupted therin by the troubles of the late warr

A Coppy of the Marriages beirthes and burialls of sundry p[r]sons p[r]sented from the Record att Barnstable
Jane the wife of Anthony Annible buried about December 1643
The said Anthony Marryed with Anne Alcocke 1 of March 1645
his son Samuell Borne about the 2[ccond] of January 1646
his son Ezek: *
his Daughter Desire about the begining of October 1653
Abraham Blush his Daughter Sarah Borne 2[cond] of Decemb: 1641
his son Joseph the 5th of Aprill 1648
hee buried his wife Anne 16 may 1651
and Marryed with hannah Barker vid:
his son Abraham Borne about 16 October 54
hee buried his wife Hannah about the 16th of March 1658
And marryed with Allice Derbey vid: 4 January 1658

* This entry was left incomplete.

Joseph Benjamine; and Jeremiah* Lumbert 10 June 1671*
Nicholas Bonham and Hannah Fuller Marryed January the 1 1658
his Daughter Hannah borne the 8th of October 1659;
Mary the 4th of October 1661
Thomas Burman and Hannah Annible Marryed March first 1645
his Daughter Hannah borne about the end of May 1646
his son Thomas about the middest 1648:
Samell about the end of July 1651
Desire about the end of May 1654
Mary the middest of March 1656
Mehittabell the begining of September 1658
Trustrum the begining of August 1661
Samell Bacon and Martha Foxwell Maryed the 9th of May 1659
his son Samell borne the 9th of March 1659:60
his Daughter Martha the sixt of January 1661
Austine Beirse his Daughter Mary borne 1640
Martha 1642
Presilla 10th of March 1643
Sarah the 28th of March 1646
Abigaill the 18th of December 1647
Hannah the 16th of Novmber 1649
Joseph the 25th of January 1651
Hester the 2cond of October 1653
Lydia the [*latt end* †] latter end of September 1655
Rebecka September 26 1657
his son James the latter end of July 1660
[p. 47] Nathaniel: Bacon and Hannah Mayo [*Mayo* †] marryed the 4th of Decem 1642
his Daughter Hannah Borne the the 4 of Sept: 1643
his son Nathaniell the 5th of February 1645
Mary the [*4th* †] 12th of August 1648
Samuell the 25th of February 1650
Elizabeth the 28th of January 1653
Jeremiah the 8th of May 1657
Mercye the 8th of february 1659
James Cleaguehorne and Abigaill Lumbert Marryed the sixt of January 1654
his son James borne the 29th of January 1654
Mary borne the 28th of October 1655
Elizabeth borne Aprill the 1658
Sarah the third of January 1659
Robert the 27th of october 1661
mr Henery Cobb his son John Borne Att Plymouth the 7th of June 1632

* The bride's name should be "Jemima", and the date should be "1661". See Mayflower Descendant, 2: 214, also Ninth Report of Boston Record Commissioners, page 81.

† Words in italics were crossed out, in the original record.

his son James borne att Plymouth the 14th of January 1634
his Daughter Mary borne att Scittuate March the 24 1637
his Daughter Patience att Barnstable about the 19th of March 1641
Gershom the 10th of January 1644
Eliezer [*the* *] the 30th of March 1648
his wife Patience buried the 4th may 1648
hee Married with Sarah Hinckley the 12th of December 1649
his Daughter Mehittable borne in Septem: 1651 and buryed the 8th of March 1652
Samell borne the 12 of october 1654
Sarah the 15th January 58 and buryed the 25th of January 1658
Jonathan the 10th of Aprill 1660
John Chipman his Daughter Hope borne august the 13th 1652
his Daughter Lydia the 25th of December 1654
his son John the 2cond of March: 56:57: and Died the 29th of May following
Hannah the 14 January 1658
Samuell the 15th of Aprill 1661
Willam Crocker his son John Crocker borne the last of May 1637
his Daughter Elizabeth the 22cond Septemb 1639
Samell the 3 of July 1642
Job the 9th of March 1644
Josiah the 19th of Sept: 1647
Eliezer the 21 of July 1650
Joseph 1654
hee buried his Daughter Elizabeth may 1658
his son John Crocker married with Mary Botffish November [*the 29* *] 1659
Elizabeth [*of the* *] Daughter of the said John borne october 1660
John Davis and hannah Lynnitt Married the 15 of March 1648
his son John borne about the Middest of January 1649
Samell the middest of December 1651
his Daughter Hannah and Mary the 3 of January 1653
his son Joseph and Benjamine June 1656
Symon the Middest of July 1658
Dolar the begining of October 1660
[p. 48] Edward Fitsrandalls Daughter Hannah borne Aprill 1649
Mary the last of May 1651
his son John the 7th of October 1653
Joseph the [*fift* *] first of March 1656
Thomas the 16th of August 1659
Hope the 2cond of Aprill 1661
Richard Foxwell his Daughter Mary borne the 17th of August 1635
Martha the 24 of March 1638
Ruth the 25 of March 1641
Samell Fuller senir his son Thomas borne the 18th of May 1650
his Daughter Sarah the 14th of Decem: 1654

* Words in italics were crossed out, in the original record.

Item a Child borne 8th February 1658 and buryed 15 Dayes after;
Roger Goodspeed and Allis Layton married December 1641
his son Nathaniell Borne October 6 1642
John the middest of June 1645
his Daughter Mary the latter end of July 1647
Benjamine the sixt of May 1649
Ruth the 10th of Aprill 1652
Ebenezer [*latt end**] Latter end of December 1655
Elizabeth in May 1658
John Gorum his Daughter Desire borne att Plymouth the 2cond of Aprill 1644

these borne at Marshfid { Temperance the 5th of May 1648
James the 28th of Aprill 1650
John 20th of February 1651 }

Att Yarmouth
Joseph Borne the 16th of February 1653
Jabez the third of August 1656
Mary the 20th of January 1658
Lydia the [*20th**] 11th of November 1661
his Daughter Desire Marryed† att Barnstable the 7th of October 1661
Samell Hinckley his son Samuell borne the 4th of July 1642
his son John the 24th of May 1644
hee buried Sarah his wife agust 19 1656
and Married with Bridged Botffish Decemb 15 1657
Mr Thomas Hinckly Married with Mary Richards the 4th of December 1641
his Daughter Mary borne the 3 of August 1644
Sarah the 4th of November 1646
Melletiah 25 of December 1648
Hannah the 15th of aprill 1651
his son Samuell the 14th of February 1652
Thomas the 5th of December 1654
Bethshuah the 15th of May 1657
Mehittable the 24th of March 1658:59
hee buried Mary his wife the 25th June 1659
And Married Mary Glover viz: the 16 march 59:60
his Daughter Admire borne 28 January 1661 and buried the 16th of february 1661
his son Ebenezer borne the 22cond february 1662
Thomas Huckens Marryed with Mary wells 1642
his Daughter borne about the 4th of July 1644 and buryed the 28th of the same Month July 1644
his Daughter Mary borne the 29th of March 1646
Elizabeth the the 2cond of february 1647 And buryed the 28th of December 1648

* Words in italics were crossed out, in the original record.

† The name of the husband was not entered. She married John Hawes. See Mayflower Descendant 5: 72 and 177.

his wife [*buried**] Mary buried the 28 July 1648
And hee Married with Rose Hollier viz: the 3 of November 1648
his son John borne about the 2cond of August 1649
[p. 49] Thomas the 25 of Aprill 1651
Hannah the 14th of October 1653
Joseph the 21 of February 1655
Deborah Hillies Daughter of the said Rose by her husband Hugh Hillies borne att Yarmouth october the 30th 1643
Samell Hillies att Yarmouth about the 30th of July 1646
James Hamblen his son [*his son**] Bartholmew born Aprill 1642
John the 26th of June 1644
Sarah the 7th of November 1647
Eliezer the 17th of March 1649
Israell the 25th of June 1655
John [*Hathewey**] Haddawey and Hannah Hollett Married the first of July 1656
his first borne son about October 57 and buried ten Dayes after
his son John Borne about the 16th of Augst 1658
Trustrum Hull his Daughter Mary borne the latter end of September 1645
Sarah the latter end of March 1650
Joseph in June 1652
John the latter end of March 1654
Hannah February 1656
John Jenkens and Mary Ewer were Marryed the [*2cond of february**] the 2cond of february 1652
his Daughter Sarah Borne the 15th of November 1653
Mehitable the 2cond of March 1654:55
Samuell the 12th of September 1657
John the 13th of November 1659
Ralph Jones his son Shuball borne the 27th of August 1654
Jedadiah the 4th of January 1656
John the 14th of August 1659
Gorge Lewis Junir Marryed with Mary Lumbert December 1654
[*Mary**] his son Gorge Borne the latter end of September 1655
Mary the 9th of May 1657
Sarah the 12th of January 1659
Thomas Lewis and Mary Davis Marryed the 15th of June 1653
his son James borne the last of March 1654
his son Thomas the 15th of July 1656
Mary the 2cond of November 1659
James Lewis and Sarah Lane Marryed October 1655
his son John Borne att the Latter end of October 1656
Samuell the 10th of Aprill 1659
Thomas Lumbert senir; his son Jededia borne the 20th of September 16[*worn off*]
Benjamine the 26th of Augst 1642

* Words in italics were crossed out, in the original record.

[p. 50] David Linnitt and Hannah Shilley marryed the 15th of March 1652
his son Samuell borne the 15th of December 1655
Elisha the 1 of June 1658
Hannah the 15th of December 1660
Barnard Lumbert his Daughter Martha borne The 19th of September 1640
Jabez the 1 of July 1642
Jabez Lumbert Married to Sarah Darbey the first of December 1660
his first borne son borne the 18th of February 1661 and Died the same Day;
Joseph Laythorp Married with Mary Ansell the 11th of December 1650
his son Joseph borne the 3th of December 1652
Mary the 22cond of March 1654
Benjamine the 25th of July 1657
Elizabeth the 18th of December 1659
John the 28th of November 1661
Joshuah Lumbert and Abigaill Linnett Marryed the latter end of May 1650
his Daughter Abigaill borne the 6th of Aprill 1652
Mercye the 15th of January 1655
Jonathan the 28th of Aprill 1657
Joshua the 16th of January 1660
Thomas Laythorp his Daughter Mary borne 4th of October 1640
Hannah the 18th of October 1642
Thomas the 7th of July 1644
Melletie the 2cond of November 1646
Bethya the 23 of July 1649
his Daughter Mary Marryed* the 20 Novemb: 1656
Gorge Lewis senir his son John Borne Att Scittuate the 2cond of March 1637
Ephraim the 23 of July 1641
Sarah the second of february 1643
John Martin Marrid to Martha Lumbert the 1 of July 1657
his son John Borne about the Middle of June 1658
Gorge borne in the first weeke in October 1660
Elisha Parker and Elizabeth Hinckley Married the 15 July 1657
his son Thomas borne the 15th of May 1658
Elisha about the begining of November 1660
Robert Parker Marryed with Sarah James The 28th of January 1656 [*1646* †]
his Daughter Mary borne the 1 of Aprill 1658
The son Samuell the latter end of June 1660
[*John Phinney Married with Elizabeth Bayley*‡]

* The name of the husband was not entered.

† Crossed out in the original record, and 1656 entered in the same hand and ink.

‡ Crossed out in the original record. See fourth entry following.

[p. 51] John Phinney and Abigaill Coggen Married the 10th of June 1650:
And his wife Abigaill buried the 6th of May 165[3*]
And his wifes son Thomas Coggen Buried the 26 of January 1658
The said John Phinney Marryed to Elizabeth Bayley the 26 of June 1654
his son Jonathan born August 14 1655
Robert the 13th of August 1656
Hannah the 2cond of September 1657
Elizabeth the 15th of March 1658:59
Josiah the 11th of January 1660:
Moses Rowley and Elizabeth Fuller marryed the 22cond of Aprill 1652
his Daughter Mary borne the 20th of March 1653
his son Moses the 10th of November 1654
A Child that Died the 15th of August 1656
Shuball and Mehittabl January 11 1660:
Henery Tayler and Lydia Hatch marryed the 19th of December 1650
his Daughter Lydia borne the 21 of June 1655
his son Jonathan the 20th of Aprill 1658
Robert Davis his Daughter Deborah borne [*the in June* †] in January 1645
Mary in May 1648
Andrew in May 1650
John first of March 1652
Robert in August 1654
Josias in September 1656
Hannah in September 1658
Sarah in October 1660

Presented to the Court this sixt of March 1661(62)
Pr me Thomas Hinckley

(*To be continued*)

FORM FOR A BEQUEST

I GIVE and bequeath to the Society of Mayflower Descendants, a corporation organized under the laws of the Commonwealth of Massachusetts, the sum of .... dollars.

*See Mayflower Descendant, 11 : 130.

† Words in italics were crossed out, in the original record.

THE WILLS OF OBADIAH AND THOMAS BOWEN

BY THE EDITOR

THE wills of Obadiah Bowen and Thomas Bowen, both of Swansea, Mass., with all other records or documents on file relating to their estates, found in the Bristol County, Mass., Registry of Probate, at Taunton, are here printed at the expense of Mr. Herbert Bowen, of Detroit, Mich.

The only original papers now in the files, relating to the estate of Obadiah Bowen, are the executor's bond and the inventory.

Obadiah Bowen's will was twice recorded, in Book II, page 290, and in Book III, page 1. At the end of the record in the third book is a note, in the same hand as that record, referring to the record in the second book.

The original will of Thomas Bowen is still preserved in the probate files. The only other paper remaining is the bond of the executrix.

The proper reference, to the record, or to the original document on file, is given with each copy or abstract presented.

[OBADIAH BOWEN'S WILL]

[2:290] In the Name of God Amen the Eleventh day of Decemb^r one Thousand seven Hundred & Eight I Obadiah Bowen of Swanzey in ye County of Bristol in New England Yeoman being Grown Ancient & weake of body Yet of sound mind & memory blessed be God for the same And being willing & desirous to set my house in Order & settle my outward Estate which the Lord in mercey hath Lent me I Do make this my Last will & Testam^t In manner & form following Viz^t: Imprimis I Commit my soul into the hands of God who gave it hopeing through grace to Receive the Remission of all my sins And through the Mirrits of my Blessed Saviour Jesus Christ to be made pertaker of the Inheiritance of ye saints in Light And my Body to be Decently buried according to the discresio of my Executors of this my Last will and Testament hereafter Named And as touching such worldly Estate wherewith it hath pleased

God to Bless me in this life I give Demise and Despose of the same in the following manner and form

My will is that all my Just Debts which I owe to any person or persons whatsoever be be duely payd by my Execut^r out of my Estate in time Conveinient after my Decease

Imp^ms I give to my well beloved son Samuel Bowen of Cohansey Ten pounds silver money at the fifteen peny weight and seventeen pounds of the like money I give to my said son Samuel Bowen and my Daughter hannah Brooks Equally to be divided betwixt them I do also give to my daughter hannah Brooks my bed and beding

Item I give to Lidia Mason a Cow

Itt: I give & bequeath unto my Grandsons Aron Bowen & Daniel Bowen sons of my son obadiah Bowen Deceased to them and Each of them for Ever All y^t my Right & Interest of and in the lands both divided and undivided scittuate Lyeing & being within the Township of Attleborrough in the County of Bristol afores^d Equally to be divided between them :

Item I give unto my Grandson Nathan Bowen son of my s^d son obadiah Bowen to him the said Nathan Bowen for Ever All that my two Divissions of lands in Rehoboth the one being allready laid out & the other now due to be layd out by ye selectmen of Rehoboth afores^d that land wch is allready layd out being somewhat distant from Blisses saw mill . and allso all my Right of fresh meadow vizt two peices of fresh meadow the one lyeing at a place called the great meadow the other somewhat distant from s^d meadow

Itt I give and bequeath unto my son Joseph Bowen his heires and Assignes for ever All that my Division or Divisions of land layd out adjacent to said Josephs lands within the Township of Rehoboth afores^d and allso the whole of all my undivided lands throughout the Commons of undivided lands both in the township of Rehoboth & Swanzey aforesaid

Itt I give and bequeath unto James Bowen & Hezekiah Bowen forever Respectively all that my lot of land of land lyeing & being in Rehoboth afores^d Contayning Twenty acres it being Recorded to william Bowen in said Rehoboth land Records And to all other of my Relations not herein mentioned that should under any Tollerable pretence Claime any portion of my Estate left I give one shilling allso in full sattisfaction to them all: And whereas there is Amongst my household stuff four pewter platters that were given to me in my infancy when I was Baptized I do now give one of s^d platters to my Grand Daughter Katherine Bowen And one of them to my Grandaughter Sarah

Bowen and one of them I give to my Granddaughter Allice Bowen and the fourth & last platter I give to my Grand daughter Elizabeth* Bowen . that is to say to each of them a Platter

Item I Give to my Grand daughter† a smale iron Kettle

Itt I give and bequeath to my son Thomas Bowen all the Rest of my Estate not yet disposed of And ffinally I do hereby make Constitute Appoint & ordain my said son Thomas Bowen to be my sole Executor of this my last will and Testament & doe allso Charge him to see it [p. 291] Punctually and duely performed according to the purpose & true meaning thereof And I do allso hereby Revoke and utterly null & make void all former wills & Testaments by me at any time made Either by word or wrighting to be of no Effect or Use But this my last will & Testament to stand firm & good In witness whereof I the said obadiah Bowen have hereunto subscribed my name and affixed my seale with my own hand given and published and Declared the day & year first above written

Signed sealed and Delivered Obadiah Bowen (S)
In the presence of us
Caleb Eddy
John Paddock
John Devotion

Bristol ss: october 14th 1710 then Caleb Eddy and John Paddock Junr two of ye wittnesses of the within written will of Obadiah Bowen above Named Came before me Nathal Paine Esqr Judge of the Probate of wills & granting Administrations within the County aforesd & made Oath that they were present and did see the said Deceased signe seal publish & declare this Instrumt as his will and Testamt & that he was of a Disposeing mind when he so did and that they together with John Devotion the othe other witness set their hands as witnesses at the same time

John Cary Regr Nathl Paine

Entered Novr 29 1710 By John Cary Regr:

[From original bond] On 14 October, 1710, "Thomas Bowen of Swanzey in the County of Bristol" as "Executor . . . . of his late Father obadiah Bowen of Swanzey Deceased" with "Joseph Bowen & James Bowen of Rehoboth" gave bond for £300, "Currant Money". The bond bears the autograph signatures of "Thomas Bowen", "Joseph bowin" and "James Bowen", also of "Caleb eddy" and John Cary as witnesses.

* Recorded as "Mary" in Vol. III, p. 2.

† The name was omitted.

[From original inventory] An Inventory of the Estate of Obadiah Bowen late of Swanzey Deceased Apprized by us the subscribers hereof october the 4th day Anno Domini 1710:

Imp^rs his wearing Cloathes both woollen & Linning	05	10	0
his Bookes two Bibles old &c:	00	12	00
one Sword 5s	00	05	00
one feather Bed & boster a pillow 2 pair of shet & a pair blankets and Coverlids	08	00	00
A pair of old Curtaines	00	10	0
one feather Bed & beding	07	00	0
Three bedsteeds at	01	08	0
A Table & Nine Chaires & 3 Chushings : at	01	13	6
A Cubbard 40s A Chest 8s	02	08	0
3 pewter plattrs a plate 2 Cupes and warming Pann & one pewter bason	01	00	0
A pair of stilliard	01	00	0
5 wooden bowles & a tray & Churn	00	09	6
in silver money at 15d weight	17	00	0
one Iron pott & 2 iron Kettles at	01	05	0
hack tongs a pair of Pothook Candlestick	00	05	0
one old Brass Kettle & skillet	00	08	0
two Chaines 12s Horss Chaines 6s old Iron at 10s a share & Coulter 6s	01	14	0
one old hand saw 2s bark shave & beaming Knifes 7s	00	09	0
An old wheel and a hammer — with Real	00	04	0
more silver money 13£ 7–2d in ye house 5£ 5–0: abroad	18	12	2
Tubs & barills & old Lumber	00	05	0
his lands in Attlebororough divided and undivided	40	00	0
his lands & meadows in Rehoboth given to Nathan bowen	20	00	0
lands & Rights to land in Rehoboth & Swanzey given to his son Joseph Bowen at	15	00	0
Twenty acres given to James an Hezekiah Bowen	05	00	0
	149	18	2

Caleb eddy
John Carey prisers

since brought in by the Exer:

Octbr 14:1710 An old horss	1	5	0
frying pan Cops Ring & staple	0	6	0
a bill from Robt Cartter	2	0	0

Thomas Bowen Exer of the last will and Testament of obadiah Bowen late of Swanzey deceased Appeared this fourteenth day of october 1710 Before Nathal Paine Esqr Judge of Probate of wills &c within the County of Bristoll & made Oath the Inventory on ye other side Containes the whole of the Estate that the sd Deceased Dyed seized of & is come to his knowledge & that when he knowes of any more he will reveal it that it may be of Record herewith

John Cary Regr Nathl Paine

Bristol ss In the second Book folio 291 Novembr 29:1710 the above and within written was Entered By John Cary Regr

[3:57] On 16 October, 1711, "Samuel Bowen of Cohanze In the County of Salem in the Province of West New Jerzey" gave power of attorney to "Isaac Ayars of Cohanze aforesd late of Rhod Island" to receive from "Thomas Bowen of Swanzey .... New England" everything "Due by will from his & my Honrd Father Obadiah Bowen Senr Deceased". The witnesses were William Porter and Sarah Wheaton. On 24 October, 1711, Samuel Bowen acknowledged the instrument, before Abraham Porter and Woollo Dalbo, Justices of the Peace for "the County of Glossester & of Province of New Jerzey".

On 16 November, 1711, Isaac Ayars of Cohanzey, as attorney for Samuel Bowen, receipted to Thomas Bowen, executor, for £18, 10s., "in full of a Legacie" in will of Obadiah Bowen. The witnesses were Nathaniel Millerd and John Cary. The power of attorney and receipt were recorded 16 November, 1711.

[3:76] On 16 October, 1711, "Timothy Brooks & Hannah Brooks his wife of Cohanse .... west New Jerse" gave power of attorney to "Our well beloved Brother John Brooks of Rehoboth .... New England" to receive from Thomas Bowen of Swanzey everything "due by will from his and our Honrd Father Obadiah Bowen Senr Deceased". Hannah signed by a mark. The witnesses were Samuel Bowen, Isaac Ayars and Nicholas Johnson. On 24 October, 1711, Samuel Bowen and Isaac Ayars "did Testify this to the Act and Deed of the persons whose hands are to the seals" before Abraham Porter and Woollo Dalbo, Justices of the Peace for Gloucester County, New Jersey.

On 10 March, 1711/12, John Brooks of Swanzey, as attorney for Timothy and Hannah Brooks, receipted to Thomas Bowen, executor, for £8, 10s., in money, "& one bed & beding in full of a Legacie .... unto s^{d} Hannah Brooks". The witnesses were Jonathan Peck and John Cary. The power of attorney and receipt were recorded 10 March, 1711/12.

[3:95] Bristol ss In Bristol May the 12:1712:

The accompt of Thomas Bowen of Swanzey in the County of Bristol Executor of the last will and Testament of Obadia Bowen Late of said Swanzey Deceased

Imp^{rms} the said Accomptant Chargeth himself with the Estate Left by the s^{d} Deceased Obadiah Bowen Contained in an Inventory upon Record Amounting to the sum of 153$^{£}$ 09^{s} 02^{d}

The Accomptant further desireth allowance for such & so much of the Estate as he hath payd in Legacies to severall of the Children and Grand Children of the s^{d} Dec^{d} Obadiah bowen given & bequeathed in his last will and Testament

Payd unto Isaac Ayres for the use of Samuel Bowen of Cohanse as by Receipt the sum of 18–10–00

payd to John Brooks for the use of Timothy Brooks and Hannah his wife as p^{r} Receipt 08–10–00 & one bed and beding a Legacie given s^{d} Hannah

payd to Joseph and Lidia Mason one Cow as p^{r} Recipt

Delivered to Jacob Chase one pewter platt^{r} give to his wif Allice, as p^{r} Receipt

Certain lands given to Joseph bowen Accepted of by him as p^{r} his Receipt

Certain lands given unto James and Hezekiah Bowen by them Accepted as by their Receipt

Certain lands given to Daniel and Aron Bowen by them Accepted as by their Receipt

Delivered to Mary Bowen Alias Bush as p^{r} her Receipt a pewter platter given to her in and by s^{d} will

Delivered to Abigail Bowen for the use of her Daughter Sarah Bowen one platter as by her Receipt

Delivered to Ephraim Smith for the use of his wife Mary a smale Iron Kettle

the Rest of the Estate given to the Executor as by the s^{d} will may appear

Bristol ss By Natha^{l} Paine Esqr Judge of Probate &c

Thomas Bowen Executor as abovesaid presented the above written accompt of his Administration upon the Estate Left by his s^{d} Father Obadiah Bowen and Made Oath that it Containes a Just and true accompt of his said Administration so far as he hath proceeded therein which I do Accordingly allow and approve off and order the same to be off Record.— Bristol May the 12:1712

Jurr^{t} Coram Natha^{l} Paine

Entered May 14:1712 By John Cary Regist^{r}

[3:96] On 1 January, 1710, Lydia Mason and Joseph Mason receipted to Thomas Bowen for "one Cow given to me by will: By my Honrd Father"

"January ye 6:1711 this is to signify that Allice the Daughter of Joseph Bowen the wife of Jacob Chase hath Rec^{d} a pewter platt^{r} which was given to her by her Honored Grandfather in his last will". Signed by Jacob Chase.

"october ye 24th 1710. Then Rec^{d} of Thomas Bowen a Certain pewter platter which my hon^{d} Grandfather gave me in and by his will". Signed by the mark of "Mary Bowen Alias Mary Bush".

These three receipts were recorded 24 May, 1712.

[Thomas Bowen's Will]

[From original will] "Thomas Bowen of the Town of Swanzey . . . . yeoman; being grown Aged" made his will 25 December, 1730. Bequests were as follows:

To "my beloved wife Thankfull all my housold goods and Stoke of Cattle and my movable Estate fully to be at Her Dispose During har Life for her Support and to help my two Daughters Namly Mary and Hannah wives of Gilbert and Charles Seamans and what Remains of Sd goods or Chatles after my wifes Decease shall be Equally Devided to my sd two Daughters or their heirs: Excepting the Housold goods that I Have in possesion: that I gave to my Daughter Marcey Luther Deceasd which good I give to my grand Child Lydia Luther: Daughter of my sd Daughter Marcey at the age of Eighteen years"

To "my Daughter Katheren Curtice one Cow or the vallue of a good Cow in money"

"I have given to my Eldes Son Josiah Bowen Lands by a Deed of gift"

"I have given to my Son Isaac Lands by a Deed of gift"

"I have given to my Son Stephen Lands by a Deed of gift"

"I have given to my Son Samuel one Hundred and fifty pound in Currant money and he has Recived sd money"

"I have given to my Son Nathaniel a Deed of gift of my house and Land where I now Dwell"

"and I have given to my Son Richard one Hundred pounds in money Received by him"

To "my Son John one Hundred pounds in Currant bill of Credit to be paid by my Executrix"

To "my Grand Son Constant Luther the Sum of three pounds money"

To "wife Thankfull the use and profite of the one half of a peice of Salt meadow Lying between the meadow of my Son Samuel and my Son Nathaniel on New meadow river in Swanzey During her Life and after her Decease to my Son Stephen"

"I make . . . . my well beloved wife Thankfull Bowen my Sole Executrix"

The witnesses were Thomas Wood, Jr. (who signed by a mark), Rebecca Wood (who signed by a mark) and Joseph Mason.

On 21 June, 1743, Thomas Wood and Joseph Mason made oath to the will, before Nathaniel Blagrove, Judge of Probate.

The will and testimony are also recorded, Book 10, pages 287 and 288.

[10:283] On 21 June, 1743, the will was proved and letter of administration was granted "To Thankful Bowen of Swanzey .... Widdow" on the estate "of your Husband Thomas Bowen Late of Swanzey .... yeoman Deceased"

[From original bond] On 21 June, 1743, "Thankful Bowen widdow & Sole Executrix .... of Thomas Bowen Late of Swanzey .... yeoman Deceased" gave bond for £500. The bond was signed by a mark. The witnesses were Stephen Paine and William Richmond.

PLYMOUTH, MASS., VITAL RECORDS

(*Continued from page 146*)

[Vol. 2, p. 1] The Children of Samuell Bartlett Esqr, and Elizabeth his wife. Continued from page 120. First Book.

4th Lothrop Bartlett Born, Aug^st^ 7 . 1755. Thirsday, half an hour After 7 Clock A M Deceased June 13th 1756

5th Hannah Bartlett, Born . April ye 11th 1757 Monday, about 1 Clock A M

6 . Isaac Bartlett, Born Octr 5th 1759, on Fryday, about half after 2 aClock P.M

The Child of Joseph Silvester, and Susannah his Wife

Joseph Silvester, Born July 15 . 1755.

The Children of Thomas Davis and Mercy his Wife

1 Sarah Davis, born June 29th 1754. Dec^d^ Novr 10 . 1821 in Plym^o^

2 Thomas Davis born June 26 . 1756 Deceas'd, at Boston, January 21st 1805

3 William Davis born July 13th 1758 Dec^d^ January 6 . 1826 . in Plym^o^

4 John Davis born Jan^ry^ 25th 1761

5 Samuel Davis born Mar: 5th 1765

6 a Daughter born Aug^st^ 7th & deceas^d^ ye 14th Aug^st^ 1766

7 Isaac Davis . born . Octob: 7th 1771

8 Wendell Davis born Febr^ry^ 13 1776.

The Children of William Bartlett, & Mary his Wife

1. Hannah Bartlett, Born Novr 8th 1752.
2. William Bartlett, Born, Aug^st^ 9. 1754.
3 a Daughter not named. Born July Deceased July
4 Samuell . Bartlett . Born July . 24th 1757
5. Judah Bartlett . Born December 14 . 1759 . deceased May 27 : 1791
6. Amasa Bartlett . Born June . 23 . 1763.
7 Mary Bartlett . Born Novemb^r^ 16th 1765
8 Sarah Bartlett . Born July . 30th 1768
9 Thomas Bartlett . Born Jan^ry^ 9th 1770

10 Nathaniel Bartlett . Born June . 28th 1772
Mrs Mary Bartlett above named the mother of the Above family Deceasd July 16th 1785
[p. 2] The Child of the Revd Mr Elijah Packard . and Mary . his Wife
1. Abigail . Packard Born Aprill ye 18th 1755
The Children of Joshua Totman, & Joanna, his wife
1. Joshua Totman Born, June 3 . 1753
2. Betty Totman, Born Janry 9 . 1756.
3. Elkanah Totman Born Augst 18 . 1758.
4. Thomas Totman Born Decr 24th 1760.
The Child of Mary Ward.
1 James Beeten Born Janury 8th 1761
The Chilldren of Samuel Sherman . & Experiance his Wife
1 Samuel Sherman Born Decr 1st 1751. Died Novr 9th . 1818.
2 Elijah Sherman Born Octr 29th 1753
3 Lydia Sherman . Born . Octr 16th 1755
[p. 3] The Children of Ebenezer Churchell Junr & Jean his Wife
1. Ebenezer Churchell Born, Octr 5 . 1755.
2. Timothy Churchell Born Janry 21 . 1757
3 John Churchell . Born Febry 4th 1759 . Deceasd August 23rd 1760
4 Jean Churchell . Born Janry 6 . 1761.
5. John Churchell, Born June 24 . 1763.
6. Martha Churchell born January . 10 . 1767 . Saturday.
The Chilld . of . Nathaniell Holmes . And Lydia His Wife
1. Nathaniell Holmes Born Decr 16th 1755.
The Children of Mr Elkanah Watson & Patience his Wife
1. Marston Watson Born May 28th 1756.
2. Elkanah Watson Born Janry 22 . 1758 . at 12 aClock, Sabbath Day.
3. Priscilla Watson Born Sepr 30 . 1760
4 Patty Watson Born October ye 16 . 1762
5 Lucia Watson Born Novemr ye 11 . 1765
[p. 4] The Children . of Ebenezer Silvester, & Mary his Wife
1 Ebenezer Silvester, Born June 18th 1756 . Deceasd April 24th 1760
2 Lemuel Silvester Born May 24th 1758
3 Caleb Silvester Borne June 17th 1760
4 Joseph Silvester Born Augst 15th 1763
5 Solomon Silvester Born Octobr 17 : 1764
The Child of Ebenezer Churchell Junr & Jean his wife
Timothy Churchell Born Janry 21 . 1757. Entd page . 3rd
The Child of John Wall, & Ruth Wall, his Wife
Ruth Wall . Born June 25th 1756.
[p. 5] The Children of Thomas Silvester, & Martha, his Wife
1. Thomas Silvester, Born, Febry 11th 1750/1
2. Sarah Silvester Born June 5 . 1753.
3. Hannah Silvester Born March 4 . 1756.
The Children of Samuell Elles, & Lydia his Wife
1. Sarah Elles . Born March 10 . 1755.

2. Nathaniel Elles, Born Jan^{ry} 30 . 1757.
The Chilldren of James Shurtleff . & Faith his wife
1 Lydia Shurtleff born June 16th 1735 Deceas^{d} Augst 19th 1764
2 Elizabeth Shurtleff born Feb^{ry} 15th 1736/7
3 Hannah Shurtleff born Jan^{ry} 11th 1739/40
4 Molley Shurtleff born April 1741 Deceas^{d} May 1742
5 Faith Shurtleff born March 25th 1745
[p. 6] The Child of Seth Barnes Junr, & Elizabeth, his Wife
Elizabeth Barnes, Born Decr 25th 1754.
The Children of Edward Burt & Elizabeth his wife

1.	Tamson Clark . born	Decr 28 . 1817.
2.	Silas Hathaway	Feby 21 . 1820
3.	Benjamin Thomas	Mar: 5 . 1822
4.	John E. Burt	Decr 27 . 1823
5.	Charity S. Burt	Feby 17 . 1826
6.	Charlotte H	Mar: 29 . 1828.
7.	Elizabeth C	Sep^{t}: 25 . 1830
8.	William B	June: 6 . 1832
9.	Almira Burt	Augt 31 . 1833 . deceased Sep^{t} 20 . 1833
10.	Eunice D. Burt*	Decr 8 . 1837
11.	Adoniram Burt*	July . 29 . 1836 . died June 7 . 1837
12.	Thomas B. Burt.	Feby . 15 . 1839.

The Children . of . Jacob Tayler & Jemimah his Wife
1 Jemimah Tayler Born Aprill 11th 1757.
2. Mary Tayler Born May 19th 1759.
3 Joannah Tayler Born August ye 11 . 1761
4. Jacob Tayler, Born, May 15th 1763.
5. Edward Tayler Born Septe^{r} 5^{t} 1765
6 Sarah
7 Elizabeth
8 Lucy
The Children . of . John . Washburn Junr & Lydia his Wife
1 John Washburn . Born . Decr 28th 1755
2 Abial . Washburn . Born Novr 21st 1757.
3 Benjamin Washb^{n} Born Aug: 14th 1761
4 Prince Washburn Born Sep^{t} 9th 1763
5 Lydia Washburn born Octr 1st 1765
6 Thomas Washburn born Decr 16th 1767
[p. 7] The Children of Silvanus Morton & Mary his Wife
1 Abigail Morton Born June 10 . 1753.
2. James Morton Born Sep^{t} 3 . 1755.
Henry W. Green & Elizabeth his wife, their Children.
1. Henry T. Green born 1833, 19th April.
2 Harriet Elizabeth 1838 . 31st . Dec^{r}.
The Chilldren of . Alezander Roberson & Abigail his Wife
1 Alexander Roberson Born May 29th 1752
2 Micah Roberson Born Aprill 8th 1755

* Before these two entries is written "vice versa"

Children of Richard Green & Mary T. Green his wife
1. Rachel T. Green born 1828 . December 16
2. Mary Jane Green 1832 March . 12
3. Richard F Green Dec. 10 . 1833*
4. Charles G. Green Dec. 14 . 1834†
5. George Franklin 1836 . Ap^{l} . 8.
6. Edward Everett 1837 . Nov^{r} . 16.

[p. 8] The Chilldren of Benjamin Cornish Junr & Rhoda his Wife
1 Deborah Cornish Born June 25th 1753
2 Susannah Cornish Born March 4th 1755
3 William Cornish Born March 3rd 1757
4 Rhoda . Cornish . Born Jan^{ry} 16th 1759.
5 Stephen Cornish Born Decem^{r} 25th 1760
6 Nancey Cornish Born Decem^{r} 22nd 1762
7 Benjamin Cornish Born Jan^{ry} 25th 1765
8 Sarah Cornish Born
9 George Cornish born 1 Novr 1767
10 Lemuel Cornish born [‡] Deceas^{d}

The Children of Jonathan Morton, & Rebeckah his Wife
1 Cary Harris Morton Born July 18th 1750.
2 Jonathan Morton Born, Feb^{ry} 25th 1753 Deceased April 17 . 1753
3 George Morton Born Augst 15 . 1757.

The Children of Samuel Chandler & Jerusha, his Wife
1. Samuel Bartlett Chandler bor, 1832 . July 14.
2. David Lothrop Chandler 1834 . May . 16.
3. Everline Coleman " 1835 . Novr 2
4 John Brown Chandler 1837 . Octr 7.

[p. 9] The Children . of . William Barnes & Mercy his Wife
1 Abigail . Barnes Born August . ye 7th 1755.
2 Marcy . Barnes Born Dec^{r} . 15th 1757
3. William Barnes, Born Jan^{ry} 2 . 1760

The Chilldren of Richard Holmes & Mercy his wife
1 Elizabeth Holmes born Octr 15th 1764 Deceas^{d} Feb^{ry} 5th 1782
2. Richard Holmes born July 5th 1766
3 William Holmes born March 26th 1768
4 Lydia Holmes born Jan^{ry} 8th 1770
5. Polley Holmes born May 18th 1779

The Chilldren of Jesse Rider . & Bethiah§ his Wife
1 Bethiah Rider Born Feb^{ry} 21st 1755
2 James Rider Born Decemb^{r} 8th 1756

The Children of Leavitt T. Robbins & Lydia his wife
1. Lydia Johson born 1833 . December 21

* "1834 Decr 14" was first written, but it was crossed out with pencil, and "Dec. 10 . 1833" written, in a different hand and ink.

† "1833 . Decr 10" was first written, but it was crossed out with pencil, and "Dec. 14 . 1834" written, in a different hand and ink.

‡ Space was left for the date.

§ "Thomas" has been interlined above, in a modern hand.

2. Elizabeth Fuller 1834 . November 25
3. Leavitt Taylor 1837 . Septr 2
4. Lemuel Fuller 1839 . Jany 22.

[p. 10] The Children . of Thomas Morton . & Mary his Wife
1. Nathaniel Morton . Born Decr 7th 1754
2 Thomas . Morton . Born Jan^{ry} 15th 1757
3 William Morton Born Octob^{r} 13th 1759
4 Jesse Morton Born August . 8^{t} 1761
5. Mary Morton Born Septr 23rd 1763
6 Andrew Morton Born Septr 23rd 1765
7 Martha Morton Born Decr 21 1767
Twins 8 { Tabor Morton Born Jan^{ry} 8th 1770
Twins 9 { Andrew Morton Born Jan^{ry} 8th 1770

The Children of William C. Green & Marcia his Wife.
1. William Henry born 1830 Sept. 13th
2. Nathaniel Holmes born 1832 . April 6
3. Marcia Ann 1833 . July 20 deceased
4. Marcia Ann 1835 . July 14 deceased

The . Chilldren . of . Lemuel . Fish & Joannah his Wife
1 Jane Fish . Borne Decr 1st 1754
2 Lemuel Fish . Borne Octr 17th 1756
3 Deborah Fish Borne
4 Johannah Fish Borne Sep^{t} 29th 1760.
5 Samuel Fish Born July . 17 . 1762
6 Lucy Fish born [*] Deceas^{d}
7 Caleb Fish born
8 Lucy Fish born
9 Eliz^{a} Fish born
10 Mary Fish born
11 Lemuel Fish born May 12th 1779.

[p. 11] The Child of Robert Roberts, & Margaret, his Wife
John Roberts, Born July 28th 1757.

The Children of Nathan Bacon Robbins & Lucia his Wife
1. Lucia Rider Robbins . born . 1824 . Ap^{l} 11th
2. Mary Bacon Robbins, 1826 . Jan'y 13.

The Children of Nathan Bacon Robbins & Lucia his 2^{d} Wife
1. Hannah Tilden Robbins born 1831 . Sep^{t} 23d.
2. Nathan Bacon Robbins 1834 . July . 31.

The Children of Ichabod Shaw, & Priscilla his Wife
1. Priscilla Shaw Born Jan^{ry} 11 . 1758.
2. Mary Shaw Born Augst 2 . 1760.
3. Experience Shaw, Born, July . 1 . 1762.
4 Desire Shaw Born June 7 1765
5 Lydia Shaw born Augst 15th 1767
6. Ichabod Shaw born Novr 21st 1769
7. Southworth Shaw born Feb^{ry} 3rd 1772 Deceas^{d}
8 Lucy Shaw born June 2nd 1773
9 Southworth Shaw born July 28th 1775

* Space was left for the date.

10 Sarah Shaw born May 4th 1778.
11 Nansey Shaw born Jan^{ry} 4th 1781 Deceased
12 John Atwood Shaw born April 18th 1783
13 Samuel Shaw . born . Septemb: 22 1785 Deceased
[p. 12] The Children of Caleb Stetson & Abigail his Wife
1. Caleb Stetson Born August 12 . 1755.
2. Bradford Stetson Born May 20 . 1757.
Children of Orrin Bosworth & Jane his wife, viz
1. Jane Taylor, born, 1831 . May 5.
2. Orrin Waterman, 1835 . Decr 8
The Child of Orrin Bosworth & Betsey his 2d wife
3. Hannah Elizabeth born 1838 Augt 4th
The Children of Zacheus Churchell, & Mary his Wife
1. Elezabeth Churchell Born Jany 24 . 1755
2. Zacheus Churchell Born Decr 1 . 1757
3 Mary Churchell Born Novr 24 . 1758
4 Ephraim Churchell Born Sep^{r}
The Children of Bourn Spooner & Hannah his wife.
1. Nathaniel Bourn Spooner, born 1818 . Feby 2^{d} *Should be 1815.*[*]
2. William Thomas Spooner, born 1817 April 25
3. Charles Walter Spooner born 1824 . Ap^{l} 27.
4. John Adams Spooner . born 1826 . Augt 27
5. Edward Amasa Spooner born . 1830 Jany 7.
Marmion Born at New Orleans Aug. 13 . 1819.
[p. 13] The Children of George Watson Esqr and Elizabeth his Wife.
1. Mary Watson Born April 15 1754
2. George Watson, Born July 24 1757 . Deceased Augst 10th 1757
3 Sarah Watson, Born March 23 1759
4 Elizabeth Watson Born August 29 1764 Deceased September 14 1764
5 Elizabeth Watson Born Feb^{ry} 19th 1767
Mrs Eliz^{a} Watson Mother of the Above Family Deceas^{d} Feb^{ry} 19th 1767
The Child of Lemuel D Holmes & Polly his wife viz
Mary Antoinette Holmes, born January 6th . 1837.
The Chilldren of Nathaniel Foster, & Abigail His Wife,
1 Hannah Foster . Born June 15th 1749 Deceas^{d} Sep^{t} 18th 1750
2. Sarah Foster Born Sep^{t} 10th 1750
3 Nathaniel Foster Born Sep^{t} 28th 1751
4 Abigail Foster Born Mar: 9th 1753
5 Gershom Foster Born July 6th 1754
6 Hannah Foster Born Octr 1st 1755
7 Betty Foster Born Aprill 1st 1757.
See his Children by his first wife Lib^{r} 1st page 172.
The Children of Amasa Bartlett & Esther his wife,
1. Amasa S. Bartlett, born 1834 . August 5th
2. Mary Ann Bartlett 1838 . Feby 9th

(*To be continued*)

[*] The words in italics are in a different hand and ink.

UNRECORDED BARNSTABLE COUNTY DEEDS

ABSTRACTS BY THE EDITOR

(*Continued from page 134*)

THE abstracts presented in this issue were made in April, 1909, from original deeds owned by Mr. Oliver Doane, of East Orleans, Mass.

These three deeds were recorded in the Barnstable County Registry of Deeds, in 1764, but had not been re-recorded after the fire in 1827.

[HIGGINS TO FREEMAN AND COLE]

"I Zaccheus Higgins of Eastham .... Yeoman" for £56, 8s., 11d., "to me .... paid by Jonathan Freeman & Joseph Cole Jur yeomen & James Cole Labourer all of Eastham" sold to them "two third parts of all that parcel of upland for Quanty & Quallity which was the upland of the Estate of Seth young Late of Eastham Desd which parcel of upland I purchased of the s[d] Joseph Cole Jur by one Deed Bearing Date July Twenty Six 1763 To Have & To Hold .... for Ever (viz) one Third part of the whole of S[d] Land to the Said Jonathan Freeman .... & one Sixth part of the whole of S[d] Land .... to the S[d] Joseph Cole Ju .... & one Sixth part of the whole of S[d] Land to the S[d] James Cole"

The deed was dated 27 July, 1763, and signed "Zaccheus Higgin". It was witnessed by "Elisha Young jur" & "Isaac Sparrow" and was acknowledged by the grantor, at Eastham, on 16 August, 1763, before Jonathan Doane, Justice of the Peace. It was recorded 20 March, 1764, in Barnstable County Deeds, Book 30, folio 52, by Solomon Otis, Register, and has not been re-recorded, since the fire in 1827.

[JOSEPH COLE, JR., TO JAMES COLE]

"I Joseph Cole: Ju[r]: of Eastham .... yeoman: for" £5 "to me .... paid by Jeams Cole of Eastham .... yeoman" sold to him "all that my Rite in a parcel of Land lying to the westward of a place called the slash and Joining to Jonathan mayos Land which I boutght of Nathanel mayo in partnership with Zaccheus higgens as may be seen by a Deed from Nathanel mayo to Zaccheus higgens & Joseph cole ju[r] bairing Date June the Twenty fifth" 1762 "to which Deed Reference being had for Boundarys .... to have and hold"

The deed was dated 31 January, 1764, and signed "Joseph Cole Jur". It was witnessed by "Joseph Higgins" & "James Young" and was acknowledged by the grantor, on 6 February, 1764, before John Freeman, Justice of the Peace. It was recorded 20 March, 1764, in Barnstable County Deeds, Book 30, folio 52, by Solomon Otis, Register, and has not been re-recorded, since the fire in 1827.

[Freeman — Higgins — Cole — Division]

"whereas we Jonathan Freeman Zaccheus Higgins Joseph Cole Jur & James Cole all of Eastham .... Yeoman holding as Proprietors in Common a Parcil of Land situate in Eastham abve said being the Estate of Seth Young late of Eastham Decasd lying on the Northward side of the way that leads from Leiut Richard Sparrows to the Meeting House adjoining on the Easterly side to the Land of the above S[d] Zaccheus Higgins or the westerly side to the Land of Moses Higgins and Freeman Higgins y[e] Jonathan Freeman owning one third of S[d] Land y[e] S[d] Zaccheus Higgins owning one third of S[d] Land y[e] S[d] Joseph Cole Jur and James Cole owning in equil proporetion the other third part of Said Land and we having agreed to Divide S[d] percel of Land .... have therefore .... Divided Said Parsil of Land as follows: the S[d] Jonathan Freeman to have .... for his third .... the first or westermost Lot in sd Division Bounded as follows begining at a stone set in the Fence in the range of the Land of moses Higgins being the northwest corner Bound of S[d] Lot thence runing northeast on a straite line thirty one Poles to a stone sit in the Fence marked F H being the Northeast Cornor Bound of S[d] Lot thence southerly Eighty two Poles and five feet to a stone in the Ground marked F H by the Fence and way above s[d] thence westerly by S[d] Fence and way twenty Poles and Six feet to the Land of Freeman Higgins thence Notherly Seventy Six Poles in the Rainge of S[d] Higginses land to the first specified Bound: in Consideration whereof S[d] Jonathan Freeman doth hereby .... Quitclame to the other two third hereafter expressed: in which Division y[e] Zacheus Higgins is to have .... for his third part of S[d] Land the middle or second Lot Bounded as follows viz begining at a stone set in the Fence marked F H being y[e] S[d] Freemans North East cornor Bound thence runing northeasterly by S^{d} Fence twenty seven Poles and Six Feet to a stone set in the Ground by S^{d} Fence marked H C thence runing southerly Ninety Six Poles and Seven Feet to a stone set in the Ground marked H C by the above s^{d} Fence and Cart way thence runing westerly by s^{d} Fence and way twenty Poles & Six Feet to a stone in the Ground being the above s^{d} Freemans southeast cornor Bound thence Notherly in S^{d} Freemans range Eighty two Poles and five feet to the first specified Bound In Cosideration whereof ye Said Zaccheus Higgins doth hereby . . . . Quitclame to the other two thirds of S^{d} parcil of Land: in which Devision ye S^{d} Joseph Cole Jur with his Sone James Cole are to have . . . . the third or Easterly Lot Bounded as follows viz begining at stone set in the Ground by the Fence on the Notherly End of S^{d} Parcil of Land being the above S^{d} Higginses Northeast Cornor Bound marked H C thence runing Southerly in S^{d} Higgines Range Ninety Six Poles and Seven Feet to a stone set in the Ground marked H C by the above S^{d} Fence and Cart way thence Easterly by sd Fence and way twenty Poles and Six Feet to a stone in the ege of a Swomp being the southwest cornor Bound of S^{d} Higgines other Land adjoining on the Easterly side of S^{d} Lot thence runing Notherly across S^{d} Swomp in the S^{d} Higgines range to the way that leads from Richard Sparrows to Thomas Snows thence runing by S^{d} way as the Fence now stands Northwesterly to the first specified Bound in Consideration whereof ye Joseph Cole Jur & James Cole do . . . . Quitclame to the other two Lots of S^{d} Land: and also with regard to the Fence that Incloseth S^{d} Parcil of Land we . . . . have agreed . . . . as Follows viz each Proprietor shall maintain the Fence at the Northward and southward end of his Lot ye owner of ye first or westorly Lot shall maintain that Part of the Petition fence on the westerly side that appertaines to S^{d} Parcil of Land: the owners of the second and third Lots shall maintain in Proportion to their Interest in s^{d} Land that Part of the Petition Fence on the Easterly side that Apartaines to S^{d} Percil of land so long as we the above s^{d} Proprietors improve s^{d} Parcel of Land in a general Field and provided we the above S^{d} Proprietors should hereafter Separate our several Lots in S^{d} Division by Fence we do hereby detirmin both for our selves our Heirs and Assigns that ye owners of ye first and third Lots shall make a sufficient Fence both on the Eastward and westward side of ye middle or second lot two thirds of the way in Length of S^{d} Lot each of them on that side to which they adjoin which Fence when Finished shall be proportiond and maintaind by Each proprior according to his Interest in S^{d} Land:"

The deed was dated the "twenty fourth* Day of February in ye fourth year of his Majestyes Reign Anddomoney—1764" and was signed by "Jonathan Freeman", "Zaccheus Higgins", "Joseph Cole Jur" and "James Cole". The witnesses were Isaac Sparrow and Simeon Higgins.

The deed was acknowledged by the four grantors, "on the 6th* day of febuary 1764", before "John Freeman Justice Peace", and was recorded 27 June, 1764, in Barnstable County Deeds, Book 29, folio 104, by Solomon Otis, Register. It has not been re-recorded, since the fire in 1827.

THE WILLS OF ANTHONY AND MATTHEW SPRAGUE OF HINGHAM, MASSACHUSETTS

By the Editor

Anthony Sprague of Hingham, Mass., married at Plymouth, 26 December, 1661, Elizabeth Bartlett[3] (*Mary*[2] *Warren, Richard*[1]), and had eleven children: Anthony, Benjamin, John, Elizabeth, Samuel, Sarah, James, Josiah, Jeremiah, Richard, Matthew. Three of these children, Benjamin, John and Elizabeth, died in 1690. Seven of the sons, and the daughter Sarah, were mentioned in their father's will, which was made 21 July, 1716, and probated 12 October, 1719.

Matthew Sprague[4] (*Elizabeth Bartlett*[3], *Mary*[2] *Warren, Richard*[1]), the youngest son, married at Hingham, 13 September, 1716, Sarah Fearing, and had five children: Sarah, Israel, Margaret, Lydia and Noah. The son Israel died young. The three daughters and the son Noah were mentioned in their father's will, which was made 8 August, 1764, but was not probated until 8 July, 1783, about a month after he died.

Exhaustive abstracts of all records, and original documents on file, in the Suffolk County, Mass., Registry of Probate at Boston, relating to the estates of Anthony Sprague and his son Matthew Sprague, are here printed, at the expense of Mr. William T. Macfarlane, of Bridgeport, Conn., a descendant of Matthew Sprague, through his daughter Margaret, who married Isaiah Hersey.

*These two conflicting dates are printed as written on the original deed. 24 February, 1764, was Friday, therefore, it is not probable that "6th" was an error for "26th", as the latter date was Sunday.

The original will of Anthony Sprague is still in the files, and is in excellent condition. The original refusal of the son Samuel to act as one of the executors, and the original account of the son Josiah as executor are still in the files.

The original will and the original inventory of Matthew Sprague are in the files. The will is in two pieces and badly worn; but nothing of importance is lost, as shown by a comparison with the record.

The proper reference, to the original document or to the record, is given with each of the following abstracts.

[ANTHONY SPRAGUE'S WILL]

[From original will] On 21 July, 1716, "Anthony Sprague of Hingham in the County of Suffolk .... yeoman" made his will. Bequests were as follows:

To "my Son Anthony Sprague my best sute of apparel to Complate his Portion I having dun for him formerly"

To "my grand Son Anthony Sprague Son of my S^d^ Son Anthony Sprague my hors Sadle and bridle"

To "my Son Richard Sprague two Cows to Complate his portion I having don for him formerly:"

To "my son James Sprague .... all the house that he now dwells in: and all the Land on the west Side of the Cart way that leadeth from my house to the Town So far as it Coms to a dich about Twenty rods above the bridg that lyeth Cross the river (Exepting the barn and bearn yard and land the bearn stands on as it is now fenced in)"

To "my Sons Samuel Sprague and Mathew Sprague .... my dwelling house barne and bearn yard and Land the bearn Stands on my orchard and all my land on the north East Sid of the Cart way above S^d^ untill it Coms to the ditch above said"

To "my Sons James Sprague Samuel Sprague and Mathew Sprague .... all my Salt marsh Lying in the Township of Hull to be equaly devided betwen them:"

To "my Said two Sons Samuel Sprague and Mathew Sprague .... all that my peice or parcel of meadow Called briery meadow to be equely devided betwen them:"

To "my Son Josiah Sprague .... the house and Bearne where he now dwells also the one half Part of all my Land and meadow Called the old pasture being part of the Third devizion of Coneyhasset upland and he shall have it on the South west

Side thereof also all that my peice of Salt marsh at a place Called Gulf Island:"

To "my Son Jeremiah Sprague .... the one half of my fresh meadow Lying on the South sid of the fresh river that devids the third devizion from the Common land and he shall have it on the East side thereof also all that Lot in the third devizion that I purchesed of Stephen Stodder also the house where he now dwells with the Land adjoyning Containing by Estamation ten acres"

To "my Sons namely Samuel James Josiah Jeremiah and Mathew Spragues .... all the remander of my Lands in the Third devizion above S^d^ as also all my Land in the undevided Commons in Hingham afores^d^ to be aquely devided betwen them:"

To "my daughter Sarah Bate five pounds in bills of Credit of this province to be paid her by my Exec^rs^ out of my movable Estate"

To "my Son Samuel fifteen ponds to be paid him out of my movable Estate by my Exec^rs^"

"my mind and will is that my Sons above S^d^ that I have given my home Lands and third devizion to Shall have free liberty to pass and repass at all times hereafter for them and theire heirs or assigns throug the home lands as the way now goeth with Carts or otherways as they shall have occation as also through the Third devizion where the way now is"

"I give and bequeath the resedue and remainder of my Estate not heretofore in this my will disposed of unto my Seven Sons"

"I do hereby Nominat and appoint my two Sons namly Samuel Sprague and Josiah Sprague Executors of this my Last will and Testement:"

The witnesses were: Samuel Thaxter, Israel Fearing and Samuel Thaxter, Junior.

"Suffolk Ss By the Honble Samuel Sewall Esqr Judge of Probate &c

"The within written Will being presented for Probate by Josiah Sprague one of the Executors within named Samuel Thaxter and Samuel Thaxter jun^r^ made Oath" to the will, "and that they together with Israel Fearing (now in remote parts) set to their names as witnesses .... Samuel Sewall."

The will was also recorded, 21:493.

[From original document, without date] "To the Hon^rbl^ Samuel Sawell* Esqr Judg of Probate for ye County of Suffolk:

* An error for "Sewall."

"Sr my father Anthony Sprague Late of Hingham Decd having appoind me the Subcriber one of the Executors of his Last will and Testament

"These are to Informe your honor that my famely being very Sick as also other dificult Sircumstances which I labour under I have thought: fit to refuse that trust: and pray that Administration may be granted to the other Executor mentioned in the will.

witness Samll Sprague"

Samll Thaxter

Samll Thaxter Junr

[21:496] "An Inventory of the Personal Estate of Anthony Sprague of Hingham lately deced apprised by the Subscribers September 24th 1719

Imprimis Wearing Apparel	£14	5	
Money £4, 11, 6 Books and Arms £1, 11	6	2	6
A feather Bed and Furniture belonging to it	15	5	
Sheets, Pillow bears, Napkins and Other Linnen	3	13	6
New Cloath Buttons and Trimming	3	1	6
Pewter platters, Plates Porringers Potts Basons &c	2	16	
Brass, Kettles Skillets Spoons Mortar & Warming pan	2	4	
Iron, Vizt Pot Kettle, Racks, Andirons, Spit, Driping pan firepan, Tongs Gridiron &c	4	12	6
Candlesticks, Smoothing Iron, Flax comb, Shears Sickles Spade Grindstone Augers Wedges &c	3	6	
Earthen Ware and Glasses	1		
Tables, Chest Cupboard, Stools Boxes Chairs &c	4	19	6
Tubs Dishes Hogsheads Barrels & Lumber	5	5	10
A Timber Chain and Other Chains Hoops & Boxes &c	3	19	
A Horse £10 3 Cows £12	22		
2 heifers two year old £6 half a Bull 2 yrs Old £1, 7	7	7	
8 Sheep and 5 Lambs at 9s ℔ peice	5	17	
2 Grown Swine £2, 13 two large Piggs £1, 12	4	5	
13 Geese £1, 6 A Hive of Bees wth Honey 18s	2	4	
A Small Chest 3s Leather Spatterdashes 2s 6		5	6
	£112	8	10

Thomas Sayer, Jacob Beale, Abraham Leavitt"

"Josiah Sprague Executor presented the above written and made Oath, that it contains a true and perfect Inventory of the Personal Estate of his Father Anthony Sprague", at Boston, 12 October, 1719, before Samuel Sewall, the Judge of Probate.

[21:492] On 12 October, 1719, "the Will of Anthony Sprague late of Hingham .... Yeoman deceased" was probated at Boston, and administration granted "unto his Son Josiah

Sprague (Samuel Sprague the other Executor declining that trust) one of the Executors in the same Will named"

[From original document] "The accompt of Josiah Sprague Executor of the last Will .... of his Father Anthony Sprague late of Hingham Husbandman deceased

"The said Accomptant Chargeth himself wth all .... Personal Estate .... Specifyed in an Inventory thereof by him Exhibited .... on the 12th day of October 1719 amounting to 112 8 10

"And the said accomptant Prays allowance as follows Viz^t^

Paid Col: Thaxter a Debt	5	7	
To Sarah Bates in full for her Legacy	5		
To Caleb Bates and his wife a Legacy	30		
To Henry Gannet for digging the Grave		4	
For a Bushel of Corn		4	
To Jeremiah Tewer a Debt		18	
To Elisha Levett a Debt		10	
For Proving Recording & Copy of the Will &c	1		6
To Ephraim Jones a Debt	1	3	3
To ambrose Low a Debt		4	10
To Hezekiah Joy for ringing the Bell		1	
To Benjamin Garnet for weaving		1	8
To Thomas Sayer		3	0
	44	17	3
To Benj^a^ Loring for Rates		8	4
To Abraham Levitt	0	3	6
To Richard Sears	0	1	6
To Joseph Lewis a Debt	0	17	
To Jacob Beal	0	6	
To Jeremiah Sprague a Debt	0	3	
[*To your Accomptant a Debt upon Book*	*5*	*0*	*0**]
To Sundry Expences in coming 3 times to Boston with Witnesses to prove the Will	3		
To your Accomptants time & trouble	2	0	0
For drawing allowing & recording this acc^t^		10	6
Errors Excepted	52	7	8

℘ Josiah Sprague"

This account was allowed, by Samuel Sewall, Judge of Probate, at Boston, 11 July, 1720.

This account was also recorded, 21 : 773.

[Matthew Sprague's Will]

[From original will] "Matthew Sprague of Hingham in the County of Suffolk .... yeoman" made his will on 8 August, 1764, "being far advanced in years". Bequests were as follows:

* This entry has been crossed out.

To "my three Daughters namely Sarah Gilbart, Margret Hearsey, & Lydia Stowell, Three feather Beds Viz Two in the Back Rom in my now Dwelling House & one in the Chamber, to be Equally divided between them w^{c} togather with what I have Already given them I Judge to be their Sufficient portion; especialy considering I have by the Providence of God been taken of from my Labours for near Twenty years past and the Only Assistance I have had towards my Support, has been from the Care & Labour of my only Son."

To "my Only Son Noah Sprague all the Residue & Remainder of my Estate Real & personal to him and His Heirs and Asigns for ever; he paying my Just Debts & funarel Charges & I do hereby appoint him my s^{d} Son Noah Sprague Sole Executor to this my last will"

The will was signed by a mark. The witnesses were Benjamin Lincoln, James Fearing and Thomas Jones.

The will was proved at Boston, 8 July, 1783, before Oliver Wendell, Judge of Probate, on the testimony of two of the witnesses, James Fearing and Thomas Jones. The other witness, Benjamin Lincoln, died before the will was presented for probate.

The files also contain a certified copy of the will, signed by William Cooper, Register.

The will was also recorded, 82:479.

[82:478] On 8 July, 1783, "the Will of Matthew Sprague late of Hingham . . . . yeoman Deceased" was probated at Boston, and administration granted to "his Son Noah Sprague Sole Executor in the same Will Named"

[From original document] On 8 July, 1783, Benjamin Cushing, Esq., Shubael Fearing and Nathaniel Gilbert, all of Hingham, were appointed to take the inventory. It was taken on 11 September, 1783.

His wearing apparel	£1	10	0
Books 15^{s} one square table 6^{s} one oval D^{o} 4^{s}	1	5	
one Chest 4^{s} one Joint stool 6^{d} 1½ doz: Chairs 18^{s}	1	2	6
a Bed boalster & 2 pillows in the foreroom	2	15	
a Bed stead Cord & under bed 10^{s} 1 Coverlet 6^{s}		16	
a Small bed boalster & two pillows in ye bedroom	2	5	
Bed stead under bed & Cord		6	
1 Coverlet 3^{s} pewter 25^{s} 6 a Brass Morter 2^{s}	1	10	6
2 p^{r} Steelyards 18^{s} Glass ware 4^{s} a Stone jugg 1^{s} 6	1	3	6
a Warming pan 8^{s} 3 Hakes & 1 Hook 18^{s} 2 p^{r} andirons 24^{s}	2	10	
2 p^{r} tongs One fire pan & 1 slice 4^{s} 3 Gridirons 3	0	7	

a p^r Bellows		1	6
a Tobacco Knife drawing knife & Sickle		4	
an Augur Gimlets Chopping knife, Spit & Scuers		6	
3 Small Bells 9^s a press iron 1^s 6 old iron 32^s	2	2	6
3 Small Looking Glasses 14^s 2 Cloth Brushes 3^s	0	17	
Sundries of wooden ware & Basketts 5^s		5	
1 Brass kettle 24^s 1 D^o 6^s 1 Iron pot 8^s 1 D^o 5^s 1 D^o 2^s 5^d	2	5	5
a Dish Kettle 3^s a Sauce pan 2^s Sundry tubbs & wooden ware 3^s	0	8	0
Sundrys of wooden & Earthen Diary ware 22^s a Chest in the Diary 2^s	1	4	
a Grind stone 3^s two Clock Reels 6^s Close stool 2^s		11	
3 Funnels 2^s a Garter loom 3^s Sundries of old wooden ware 4^s		9	
a Bed & Boalster in the west room 50^s	2	10	
Bedstead under bed & Cord 6^s 1 Coverlet 3^s		9	
5 Chests & a Small trunk 30^s two small Boxes Locket &c 8^s	1	18	0
Hat case 1/6 Saddle & pillion 12^s a Hitchel & Stool 24^s	1	17	6
a Samp Morter 1^s 4 9 p^r Sheets 48^s pillow Cases & Napkins 18^s	3	7	4
2 p^r Sheep Shears 3^s a Quiltng frame 2^s 4 Corn Basketts 4^s	0	9	0
a Cheese press 2^s a meal Chest 3^s 2 Meal bags 6^s		11	
Sundry of old wooden ware in the Chamber		13	
a Winnowing fan 4^s 1 p^r Woolen Blankets 4^s		8	
3 Cyder Barrels 6^s old Lumber in ye Cellar 12^s		18	
3 Powdring tubbs 18^s Cart & Wheels 72^s	4	10	
Yokes & Irons belonging therto 10^s Horse Gears 12^s	1	2	0
foot Carried Over	41	18	9
5 Chains 60^s 4 Hoes a Spade & Iron Barr 10^s	3	10	
2 Hay forks & 1 Dung fork 2^s 2 Rakes 2^s flax break 1^s		5	
½ Tun English hay 40^s 2½ Tuns fresh D^o 75^s	5	15	0
Beatle & Wedges 4^s Knives & forks 4^s	0	8	
5 M Hemlock Shingles	2	10	
	£54	6	9

Real Estate

The Mansion house	10	0	0
Barn	20		
2 Acres land adjoining the house @ 16 p^r Acre	32		
8 Acres by the Bridge	102	0	0
4 Acres at Brier meadow @ 7 .. 10	30		
27 Acres in y^e third Division @ £6	162		
	£410	6	9
A yoke of Oxen	10	10	
3 Cows @ $3^£$ 18^s	11	14	

1 two year old Heifer	4	00	
2 yerlings @ 36s	3	12	
1 Calf	1	4	
10 Sheep & Lambs	2	14	
3 Swine	3	0	0
	£447	0	9

This may certify the Judge of Probate .... that ye Exacutor of Mathew Sprague being an Invalid & unable to attend ye Office for making Oath to ye Inventory above was duely sworn to this Inventory before me

Benja Cushing Just: peace

The inventory is endorsed: "Mathew Spragues Inventory Novemr 4. 1783. Recorded Lib 82 page 415"

The inventory was recorded in Book 82, and page 831, as now numbered.

THE SETTLEMENT OF JAMES WOOD'S ESTATE AND THE WILL OF GEORGE HOLMES

By the Editor

James Wood of Middleborough, Mass., married Experience[3] Fuller (*Rev. Samuel*[2], *Dr. Samuel*[1]) at Middleborough, on 12 April, 1693*, and they had at least seven children, one daughter and six sons, as shown by the settlement of the father's estate. If there were any others, they died without issue, before the settlement of the estate. The known children were: Lydia (who married George Holmes), Jonathan, Benjamin, Barnabas, Abel, Ichabod and James; but no records of their birth dates have been found.

On 5 May, 1721, James and Experience (Fuller) Wood sold land formerly the property "of Our Honoured Father Samuel Fuller deceased", and both grantors acknowledged the deed on 16 April, 1725. Both James and Experience must have died before 21 December, 1728, when Jonathan Wood was appointed administrator of his father's estate, and Experience probably died before her husband, since there is no mention of her name in the probate proceedings.

* Pilgrim Notes and Queries, 3:122.

The daughter, Lydia Wood^4, was married to George Holmes, at Plymouth, 5 February, 1718/19*, by Rev. Ephraim Little, and had two children, George Holmes^5, who married Lydia West^6 (*Bethiah Keen*^{5}, *Josiah*^{4}, *Abigail Little*^{3}, *Anna*^{2} *Warren*, *Richard*^{1}), and Richard Holmes^5, who apparently died before his father.

George Holmes, the father, died between 11 February, 1746, the date of his will, and 4 March, 1746, the day it was probated. His widow, Lydia (Wood) Holmes, was still living on 8 January, 1768, when she acknowledged the release she had given her son George Holmes, of her rights in the dwelling and land of her deceased husband.

In the following pages we print, at the expense of Mr. John W. Churchill of Plymouth, a descendant of George and Lydia (West) Holmes, exhaustive abstracts of all records, and original documents on file, in the Plymouth County, Mass., Registry of Probate, relating to the estates of James Wood and his son-in-law George Holmes. Exhaustive abstracts are also given of two deeds by James and Experience (Fuller) Wood, and of a deed by Lydia (Wood) Holmes.

The proper reference, to the original document on file, or to the record, is noted for each abstract.

[James and Experience Wood to Jacob Tomson]

[Plym. Co. Deeds, 19:46.] "We James Wood & Experience Wood his Wife of ye Town of Middleborough . . . . For & In Consideration of One Lot of Land Containing fourty five Acres be it more or less being in number the One Hundred Sixty Sixth Lot in ye South Purchase in Middleborough afores^d Conveyed & by Deed of Exchange Confirmed unto Us by Capt. Jacob Tomson of ye Town of Middleborough aforesaid . . . . do Bargain Exchange . . . . & Confirm from us ye s^d James Wood & Experience Wood his Wife . . . . Unto him ye s^d Jacob Tomson . . . . One third Part of that whole Share of Land both Divided & Undivided, which did originally belong unto the Right of Our Honoured Father Samuel Fuller deceased lying & being in the Purchase of Land called ye Sixteen Shilling Purchase & also in Assawamsett Neck in the Township of Middleborough afores^d"

The deed was dated 5 May, 1721, and signed by James and Experience Wood.

The witnesses were John Tomson, Jr., Abigail Tomson, Jr., and Lydia Tomson.

* Mayflower Descendant, 14:38.

The deed was acknowledged by James Wood and Experience his wife, on 16 April, 1725, before Samuel Prince, Justice of the Peace. It was recorded 15 June, 1725.

[JAMES AND EXPERIENCE WOOD TO SON JAMES]

[Plym. Co. Deeds. 37:159] "We James Wood and Experience Wood his Wife of the Town of Middleborough . . . . for . . . . the Love and good affection which We bear unto our Son James Wood jun^r Together with other good Causes and Considerations . . . . Confirm from Us the said James Wood and Experience Wood . . . . unto him Our said Son James Wood jun^r . . . . A Certain Lot of Land Containing fourty and five acres be it more or less lying and being in the Purchase of Land called the South Purchase in the Township of Middleborough aforesaid, and is in Number the one hundred Sixty Sixth Lot in said Purchase, and lyeth in the fifth Division [p. 160] Division; and is bounded at the West South West End thereof by the Range between the fourth and fifth Divisions from a Stake and a Heap of Stones about it at the End of a Valley, North North West fourty five Pole in Breadth to a Stake with a Heap of Stones about it, and from these two Aforementioned Boundaries the Ranges on Each Side of the said Lot run East North East half a Mile in Length unto the Range between the fifth and Sixth Divisions, as may appear upon the Record of the aforesaid Purchase: Which said Lot of Land did originally belong unto Capt. Jacob Tomson of said Middleborough, and was lately Conveyed . . . . from him unto us by a Deed of Exchange under his Hand and Seal:"

The deed was dated 5 May, 1721, and was signed by "James Wood Sen" and Experience Wood, and acknowledged by both, on that date, before Jacob Tomson, Justice of the Peace. The witnesses were John Tomson, Jr., Abigail Tomson, Jr., and Lydia Tomson.

The deed was recorded 12 August, 1745.

[JAMES WOOD'S ESTATE]

[Plym. Co. Prob., 5:406] On 21 December, 1728, "m^r Jonathan Wood of middleboro" was appointed administrator of the estate of "your Father James Wood Late of middleboro . . . . lately dyed Intestate".

[From original bond] On 21 December, 1728, Jonathan Wood, as administrator, with Peter Bennet and William Thomas, as sureties, all three being of Middleborough, gave a bond of £150. William Thomas signed by a mark. The witnesses were Matthew Lemote, who signed by a mark, and Mary Winslow.

[From original inventory] On 7 March, 1728/9,* "Peter Bennet", "James Soul" and "Jacob Tomson" took the inventory, "at Middleborough", as follows:

Imprimis : all his moveable Estate : at	36	13	6
his homestead land with the buildings thereon : at :	65	00	0
his two acres and a half of meadow ground lying at the foot of Luke Shorts land at	05	00	0
the twenty acres of land lying in the purchase called the South purchase given by deed to his Son Jonathan at :	08	00	0
the 166 lot in the aforesaid South purchase given by deed to his Son James at :	15	00	0
Total	129	13	6

On 7 March, 1728/9, Jonathan Wood, administrator, and the three appraisers made oath to the inventory, before Isaac Winslow, Judge of Probate.

There is also a contemporary certified copy of this inventory in the files. The inventory was recorded, 5 : 579.

[5:470] On 24 May, 1729, "Barnabas Wood Blacksmith Benjamin Wood House Carpenter both of Plimpton Abel Wood Labourer of Plimouth .... & Georg Holmes of Plimouth .... afores^d^ Cordwainer & Lidia his wife which S^d^ Barnabas Benjamin Abel & Lidia are the Children of James Wood late of Middleborrough afores^d^ deceased", for "twenty pounds money & divers other good Causes & considerations us thereunto moveing have .... forever Quitted our & Each of our respective Claims unto Jonathan wood of Middleborrough afores^d^ husbandman & son of the S^d^ James Wood deceased .... all that our Interest or part of all Such Right .... whatsoever that our worthy father James Wood .... yeoman Deceased had or of Right ought to have in the South purchase in the Township of Middleborough afores^d^ .... with all housing or Appurtenances to the S^d^ James Wood in his life time belonging within the S^d^ purchase as also all the [p. 471] Interest we or each of us have or may have (as heirs to the S^d^ James Wood) in the Personall Estate our S^d^ father died Possest of or of right was due or owing to our S^d^ father (he the S^d^ Jonathan Wood paying the Just debts due from our S^d^ father)"

* In recording this date, the "9" was omitted, by error of the Register.

This quitclaim was signed by Barnabas Wood, Benjamin Wood, Abel Wood, George Holmes and Lydia Holmes (Lydia signing by a mark), and all acknowledged the instrument, the day it was made, before Nathaniel Thomas, Justice of the Peace.

[7:126] "I James Wood of Plymouth . . . . Labourer Have recieved my full Part or Portion in the Estate of my Hon[d] Father James Wood . . . . Deceased from the Hands of my Brother Jonathan Wood administrator . . . . and I do . . . . Quit Claim any Right or Title the s[d] Estate unto my s[d] Brother . . . . Excepting what I have Given to [p. 127] to me from my Honoured Father by vertue of a Deed of Gift". This receipt was dated 14 March, 1729/30, and acknowledged 14 April, 1735, at Plymouth, before Josiah Cotton, Justice of the Peace. The witnesses were Thomas Harlow and Hannah Morton.

[From original document] "The settlement of the housen and lands and Reall Estate of James Wood late of Middleborough . . . . deceased the personall Estate being all disposed of in paying debts and Charges: The sd settlement made and done" by Isaac Winslow, Judge of Probate, on 15 March, 1736, "And it being Represented . . . . to me that the sd Reall Estate cant be devided to and amongst all the Children . . . . without great predijuce to and spoiling of the same the sd Reall Estate being prised at ninety three pounds the whole of the sd housen and lands being and lying in Middleborough aforesd is therefore settled upon Jonathan Wood the eldest son of the sd deceased . . . . he paying to the other children their proportionable parts therof in maner following viz To Benjamin Wood of Middleborough one of the sons of the sd deceased" £15, 10s., "which is his share of the sd Estate"; "To the Children of Barnabas Wood late of Middleborough aforesd deceased who was one of the sons of James Wood aforesd deceased" £15, 10s., "which is their share of the sd Estate"; "To Abell Wood of Rochester one of the sons of the sd deceased" £15, 10s., "which is his share of the sd Estate"; "To Ichabod Wood of Rehoboth one of the sons of the sd deceased" £15, 10s., "which is his share of the sd Estate"; "To Ledia Holems the wife of Gorge Holmes of Plimoth and one of the daughters of the sd deceased the sum of fifeteen pounds ten shillings which is her share of the sd Estate"; "James Wood one of the sons of the sd deceased haveing formerly received his full part and proportion of the sd Estate hath therefore not any thing now settled on him"

There is also a copy of this settlement, in the files. The settlement was not recorded.

[Will of George Holmes]

[Plym. Co. Prob., 10:361] "George Holmes of Plimouth .... Cordwainer" made his will 11 February, 1746, "In the 20th year of his Majestys Reign"

Bequests were as follows.

To "wife Lydia Holmes the Sole use and improvement of all my Estate both Real and Personal .... Dureing the time that She Shall remain my widdow (Excepting Such a part of House Shop & land which I Gave the improvement of to my son George Holmes as may Appear by Lease to him Dated November the 1st 1744 .... and allso Excepting what of my Estate I have in this will otherwise Bequeathed"

To "my said wife Two of my best Feather Beds with all Suitable Beding & furniture Needfull for sd two Beds with the two Bedsteads, and allso .... my Brass Kettle"

[p. 362] To "my son George Holmes junr my Horse Cart & Sled, and all ye tackling belonging to them, and all the Shoe makers Lasts in my Shop"

"if my said wife Should again Marry Then I Give .... to her forever all my household stuff, that Shall be then Remaining with her and also fifty pounds money of the old tenour"

To "my said Son George Holmes .... after the decease or second Mariage of my said wife Debts and Legacies first being paid, all my Estate both Real and personal"

"Stephen Churchell of Plimouth aforesaid Gentleman, and my said wife Lydia" to be executors.

The witnesses were Samuel Bartlett, William Sergeant and Samuel West.

On 4 March, 1746, "This will being Presented by Lydia Holmes Execx Abovenamed for Probate The abovenamed Stephen Churchell the other Execr .... Renounceing the Executorship, Samuel Bartlett William Sergeant & Samuel West made Oath" to the will, which was approved, and letter of administration was issued to Lydia Holmes the widow.

There are no original papers in the files, relating to this estate.

[Widow Lydia Holmes to son George]

[Plym. Co. Deeds, 54:16] "I Lydia Holmes of Plymouth .... Widow, For divers good Causes & Considerations moving, and for five Shillings money in hand paid by George Holmes of Plymouth .... Cordwinder .... Do by these Presents quit all my Right of Dower of Thirds in the Dwelling House and Land in Plymouth which my Husband George Holmes late of Plymouth deceased with all my Right & Title to him the said George Holmes"

The deed was dated 10 March, 1765, and signed by a mark. The witnesses were Perez Tillson and Lydia Holmes.

The deed was acknowledged 8 January, 1768, before John Cotton, Justice of the Peace, and was recorded 14 January, 1768.

MOSES³ SOULE'S ESTATE

By the Editor

Moses³ Soule (*John*², *George*¹) of Duxbury, Mass., married, first, Mercy Southworth⁴ (*Mary Pabodie*³, *Elizabeth*² *Alden*, *John*¹); but the date of the marriage does not appear on the records. He married, second, at Duxbury, Sarah Chandler of Duxbury, on 15 January, 1729/30. All of the children were by the first wife.

Moses³ Soule was living on 9 May, 1748, when a list was drawn up of the Proprietors of the Second Division of Commons in Duxbury and Pembroke, who were qualified to vote. He died, intestate, between that date and 25 January, 1748/9, the day his eldest son, Isaac⁴ Soule of Pembroke, was appointed administrator.

The only original papers, relating to the settlement of the estate, now remaining in the files in the Plymouth County, Mass., Registry of Probate, are the letter of administration and the bond of the administrator.

Exhaustive abstracts of all records, and documents on file, relating to this estate, are here printed at the expense of Mrs. Herschel Bartlett, of St. Joseph, Mo., a descendant of Moses³ Soule through his son Barnabas⁴ Soule, and a member of the Massachusetts Society of Mayflower Descendants.

The proper reference is given with each of the following abstracts.

[Moses³ Soule's Estate Settled]

[From original document] On 25 January, 1748, administration was granted "To Isaac Sole of Pembrooke . . . . yeoman" on the estate of "yoʳ Father Moses Soule late of Duxborough . . . . Yeoman Deceased" [Also recorded, 11 : 125.]

[From original document] On 25 January, 1748, "Isaac Soul" of Pembroke, yeoman, as administrator, with "Thos Josselyn" and David Stockbridge, both yeomen of Hanover, as sureties, gave a bond of £1000. The witnesses were Daniel Lewis, Jr., and Briggs Alden. [The bond was not recorded.]

[11 : 176] On 25 January, 1748, "Messrs George Partridge Samuell Seabury & Samuell Alden all of Duxborough", yeomen, were appointed to appraise "all the Estate which Moses Soul Late of Duxberough afores^{d} yeoman Deceased, Dyed Seisd of .... Mem^{o} apprise also w^{t} ye s^{d} Moses Advanced to any of his Children by Way of Settlement In His Life Time."

On 15 February, 1748, the inventory was taken at Duxbury, by the three appraisers. "Note the Inventory Was Taken In the old Ten^{r}"

[p. 177] Imprimis To Cash In old Ten^{r} Bills	80	16	
To Wareing apparrel Both Mens & Womans	283	14	6
To 1 Fowling Peice & Powder Hornes	4		
To 1 Bead N° 1 & Furneture	73	19	
To 1 Bead N° 2 & Furneture	36	19	
To 1 Ditto & Furneture	48	5	
To Table Linin & Towels	1	15	
To Iron Household Stuff	21	7	
To Brass Ditto	6	3	
To Pewter & Tin £9 : 18s. Earthen & ston Ware £2 : 4 : 6^{d}	12	2	6
To Bible & other Small Books	3	18	2
To Glass Ware 32s Wooden Dishes & Trays 23s 6	2	15	6
To old Cask 47s Chests Boxes & Tables £8 .. 14s	11	1	
To Chair & Cushings 60s a Parcel of fethers 85s	7	5	
To Wool yarn Worsted & Starch	12		6
To 1 Padlock & 12^{lb} Tallow	3	6	
To Sundry Provisitions	36	5	
To 2 Baskets with yarn	1	14	
To 3 Seickels & a Percel of old Iron	2	8	
To axes & Hoes 30s Spining Wheels 40s	3	10	
To 152^{lb} Tobaco	17	7	
To Farming Tools & Tackling	27	8	
To Bass Lines & P^{s} Rope & meal Bagg	1	2	
To old Saddle & old Chest	2	5	
To one thousand of Shingles	4		
	705	6	2^{d}
To 1 Broom 1 fishing lead & Some Small things		13	
To 1 Pilyon & Cloath	1		
To 2 Pr Card		12	
To 1 Lace Pillow & Bobins 10s		10	
To $4\frac{1}{2}$ Load Hay £45 .. 0s 2 Small Swine £7 : 15s	52	15	
To 10 Sheep £22 : 0s 1 P^{r} of oxen £62 : 0s	84		

	£	s	d
To 4 Cows £66 . . os 1 Pr Money Scales 15s	66	15	
To 1 Lott of Wood Land Laying Near Jonathan Petersons, Containing about 38 acres	620		
To one Lott of Wood Land Lying Near Nathll Brewsters Containing about 36 acrees	315		
To 1 Lott of Land to ye Northward of Nathll Brewsters Containing about 10 acres	130		
To 1 Lott of Land Lying Near Island Crick Pond Containing about 29 acres	660		
To 1 Ps Land Joyning To Plymo Road Containg about 7 acres	70		
To 1 Ps of Land Where Mr Soul formerly Dwelt Joyning to George Partridges	500		
To 1 Ps Meadow at a Place Commonly Called Common Island	320		
To one Half of an Island of Salt Marsh Commonly Called Hammer Island	200		
To 1 Bond on John Keen Dated May 9th 1743	38		
To Interest on sd Bond	6	5	5
To 1 Note of Hand one John Hunt Dated Septr 10th 1748.	100		
To 1 Do of Hand on Peleg Sprague Dated Novr 15 . 1748.	24		
	3189	10	5

The above Inventory Was Taken at Doxborough by us the Subscribers Febry 15th 1748. } George Partrage, Samuell Seabury, Samll Alden

an accot of What we find ye Deced advanced to Sundry of His Children by Way of Settlement in his Life Time

		£	s	d
Viz 1 Bead Given To Jno Hunt	21 : 12			
1 Bead & Bolster Given to Jedediah Soul	8	29	12	
	old Tenr	£3924	8	7

Apprisers Sworn March 22nd 1748.

[11 : 505] Province of the Maassachseh Bay Plimouth Ss To Mr Samuel Seabury Gerge Partidge Abraham Samson Jonathan Peterson all of Duxborough and Daniel Lewis Esqr of Pembrooke all in the County of Plimouth Greeting

You are hereby Impowered and Directed to take a veiw and make a Just and Eqwal Division of the Estate that Moses Soul Late of Duxborugh aforesad yeoman Deceased died Seizd of into Tew Equal pach or Shares & assign to Isaac the Eldest Son Two tenth parts to Cornelius Soule One tenth part to Barnabeas Soule One towth* part to Abigail Soule Daughter and

* This is clearly an error of the record. It should be "tenth".— Editor.

only Child of Ichabod Soul One tenth part to Gideon Soule one tenth part to Jedediah Soule One tenth part . to Ruth Soule one tenth part to Else the wife of Barnabas Perry one tenth part to Deberah Hunt one tenth part and you are to assign & Set of the Same by meet & bownds So that, Each of Said heirs may hold thair parts or Shaers as aforesaid in Severalty & you are to make return hereof under your hands & upon your Oath unto my Selfe as Soon as you Can Given under my hand & the Seal of ye Court of Probate the 7th deay of august Anno Domni 1750*

John Cushing

Persuant to an order from the Honorabl John Cushing Esqr Judge of Probate of Wills & Granting of Administration & within & for the County of Plimouth hereto anexed Impowering and Directing us the Subscribers to Take a veiw & make a Just & Equall Division of the real Estate that Moses Soul Late of Duxborough in the County aforesaid Yeoman Deceased Died Seized of into ten Equall parts or Shairs & assigns to Isaac ye Eldst Son two tenth partes to Cornelius Soul one tenth Part, to Barnabes Soul one tenth part, to Abigal Soul Daughter & only Child of Ichabod Soule one tenth part, To Gideon Soule one tenth parte, to Jedediah Soul one tenth Part, to Ruth Soule one tenth part, to Else the Wife of Barnabas Perry one tenth part, to Deborah Hunt wife of John Hunt one tenth part, and to assigne & Set of ye Same By Meets & Bounds &c, as by said order or Warrant appears, Having veiwed ye S^d^ Real Estate have & do assign & Sett of their Severall Parts or Shears as Follows viz —

[p. 506] We do assign & Sett of to S^d^ Isaac Soule for his two Tenth parts or Shars as follows viz about four acres & Three quarters more or less of Salt Meadow & flats Lying in Duxborough aforesaid at a Place Colled Common Island and is bounded a fallows viz Begining at a Stake Standing Just below a turn in the Creek which S^d^ turn in s^d^ Creek Runs Easterly, S^d^ Stake Standing ten rods from a Stake Standing by S^d^ Creek Masured On a Line Runing near South 12 Degreas West or North 12 Degreas East Sd Last Mentioned Stake being the Bounds between the said medow the S^d^ Moses Soul died Seized of & ye meadow of William Barns and from the first Mentioned Stake the bounds of S^d^ Isaac Soule Meadow or Shear of Madow hereby Set of to him runs South Seventy Eight ½ Degreas East by a Range of Stakes To a Creek and thence down S^d^ Creek to the River & thenc up the River to the

*This year probably is an error of the record for 1749. Compare the dates of the actual division, and of the oaths of those who made the division. — Editor.

Mouth of the first Mentioned Creek & thence up S[d] Creek to the Bounds or Stake first mentioned also one Peice of upland & Swamp Lying in Duxborough aforesad being part of the 17th Lot in the first Divison of The Commons of Duxborough aforesd Containing about Ninteen acres more or Less Bounded as follows viz begining at the Easterly Corner of S[d] Lot by keens Brook thence Runing North Sixty one Degreas West in the Northerly Range of S[d] Lot ninty one & a half Rods to a Stake & Stons Standing ninteen rods & two feet measured in S[d] range from the North Cornar of S[d] Lot and from S[d] Stake & Stons it Runs South Thirty Seven Degrees West thirty Eight rods to a Stake & Stons thence South Sixty one Degrees East to Keens Brook aforesed thenc down S[d] Brook to the place first Mentioned Which we do assign & Sett of to Said Isaac for his two tenth parts or Shears

2[ly]. We do assign & Sett off to S[d] Cornelias Soal for his Tenth parte or Shere as fallows viz about twenty Seven acres & thre quarters more or Less the way Passing through the Same being inCluded & Considered it being part of the Eighteenth Lot in Number Lying in Duxborough afores[d] s[d] Eighteenth Lot being part of y[e] Second Division of ye Commonns of Duxborough & Pembrooke S[d] Twenty Seven acres & three quarters more or Lese is bounded as follows viz begining at a pitch pine Sappling marked by y[e] Side of a way S[d] pitch Pine Sappling Standing in y[e] South Westerdly range of S[d] lot & ninteen rods & Seventeen Links Distant from a Stake Standing in y[e] Edge of a Cedar Swamp S[d] [p. 507] Ninteen Rods & Seventeen Links being Measured in S[d] range and from S[d] Pitch pine Sappiling it runs north thirty tow Degreas Easterly to the north earstly range of S[d] Lot to a Stake and Stons Standing in the range of the Land of Nathanil Breuster & ninteen rods & twenty Links from the North west Corner of S[d] Lot mesured in the North Easterly range thairof and From the first mentioned Stake & Stons it runs South Sixty Degrees Easterly by S[d] Brewsturs Land about fifty Eight rods to the north East Corner of S[d] Lot thence South forty four Degres Westerly thirty Seven rods thence South thirty Eight Degrees westerly 47½ rods to a Stake & Stons thence north fifty Eight Degres Westerly forty Eight rods & Eight Links to the place first mentened which we do assign & Sett of in full for S[d] Cornelius his tenth part or Share

3[ly] We do assign & Set of to S[d] Barnabas Soul for his tenth Parte or Shair as fallows viz about Sixteen acres of Land more or Less beeing Parte of the Second lot in y[e] Division of y[e] Commons aforesd and is Bounded as follows viz bgining at a

Stake & Stons Standing in ye range Between ye first & Second Lots Sd Stake & Stons Standing Twenty tow rods distant from ye most Southerly Corner of Sd Second Lot & from Sd Stake & Stons it runs north fifty one Degrees & a quarter East by ye Land hereafter Sett of to ye aforesaid Jedediah Soul twenty five Rods & three quarters to a Stake & Stons thence North Forty Degres Westerdly by ye Land hereafter Sett of to The aforesed Deborah Hunt unto Island Creek Pond Thence by Sd Pond to ye Corner betwen ye Sd first & Second Lot thence South forty Degrees Easterly in ye range betwixt ye first & Second Lot aforsad to ye Stake & Stons first mentioned which we Do assign & Sett of in full for Said Barnabus His tenth part or Shair

4ly We do assign & Sett off to Sd abigal Soule Daughter & only Chilld of Ichabod Sowle for her tenth part or Shear as follows viz about ninteen acers more or Less of upland being part of ye 17th Lot in ye first Diviseon of ye Commons of Duxboraugh aforeSd & Lyeth in Sd duxborugh and is bounded as follows viz begining at ye Southerly Corner of ye Land before Sett of to [p. 508] Isaac Soul in Sd 17th Lot & from thence it runs South 37 Degrees West forty Seven rods to ye Southerly range of Sd Lot to a Stake & Stons Standing Ninteen rods & two feet distant from ye Southerly Corner of Sd Lot mesured in Sd range & from thence South Sixty one degres East to Keens Brook thence down Sd Brook to ye Land before set off to Sd Isaac Soul thence North Sixty one degrees West By ye Land Sett of to Sd Isaac Soul to ye place First mentined which we do assign & Sett of to Sd Abigal as hir Tenth part or Shair in Full

5ly. We do assign & Sett off to Sd Gideon Soul for His Tenth part or Shair as follows viz about Twenty five acres of upland & Meadow more or less Lying in duxborough aforesd being part of ye Farm on Which Sd Moses Soul Deceased formerly Dwelt and is Bounded Northerly by a Line as it is now Staked out Runing Perralal with ye Southerly Line of Mr George Partridges Homested & thirteen rods distant Therefrom measured at right angles Easterdly by a Creek and ye Bay Southerly by ye meadow & Land of Christopher Wadswortts westetly by ye head of ye Sd old Lot on which Sd moses Soul formerly dwelt Which we do assign & Sett off to Sd Gideon in full For his Tenth part or Share

6ly We do assign & Sett off to Sd Jedediah Soul for His tenth part or Share as follows viz about Three acres of Salt meadow Lying in duxborough aforesd at a place Called Common Island & is Bounded Southerly by ye medow on Sd Island befour Sett of To Isaac Soul north Easterly by a Creek & north Westerly partly by the meadow of willams Barns & part by a Creek till it Coms to y[e] meadow before Sett of to S[d] Isaac Soul also about Seven acres and a half of wood Land more or Leser lying near Benjamin Pryers in S[d] Duxborough being formerly part of y[e] Lot on wheich S[d] Benj[a] now dwells and is Bounded as by record appars also about two acres & a half of upland being part of y[e] Second Lot afoursd & is Bounded as follows viz begining at y[e] Southerly Corner of y[e] Land before sett off to y[e] aforesd Barnabas Soul thence runing North fifty one degres & a quarter East fifty rods to y[e] South [p. 509] Easterly Corner of S[d] Second Lot to a Red oake tree marked South 40 degrees Easterly Eight Rods to a Red oak tree Marked thence South fifty one Degres & a quarter West Fifty Rods to y[e] South Westerly Range of S[d] Second Lot thence North 40 Degres Westerly Eight rods To y[e] place first mentioned, & also one other Peice of upland Containing about four acers & a Quarter more or Less being part of y[e] Eighteenth Lot Before mentioned & is Bounded as follows viz begining at a Stake & Stons Standing in y[e] North Westterly by range of y[e] aforesd 18th Lot Twenty Rods & a half Distant from y[e] Westerly Corner of S[d] Lot being a Stake in y[e] Edge of a Cedar Swamp and from y[e] first mentioned Stake & Stons it runs North thirty two Degreas East thirty three & a half Rods in S[d] ranges to a Stake & Stons thence South 58 Degrees East 17 Rods & 17 Links to a read oak marked By y[e] way Side thence y[e] Same Cours to y[e] Land before sett of to Cornelius Soul thence South 30 two Degreas Wes 33 rods & a half by y[e] Land Sett of to S[d] Cornelius To a red oake marked thence north fifty Eight degrees Westerdly to y[e] place first Mentioned which we do assign & Sett of in full for S[d] Jedediah Soul his tenth part or Share

7[ly] We do assign & Set off to S[d] Ruth Soul For her Shear or tenth part as follows viz, about three acres & a quarter more or Less of Salt medow & Sedge flat lying in S[d] Duxborough at a place Called Hammer Island bounded as follows viz, Southerly by a range of Stakes Standing Seventeen rods & twenty four Links Distant from y[e] northerly End y[e] meadow of M[r] Joshua Soul of S[d] Duxborough measured at right angles S[d] Stake ranging north fifty Seven & a half degres West or South fifty Seven & a half Degrees East aCross S[d] Island & parallell to S[d] Joshua Souls Line & from S[d] Line y[e] other part of S[d] meadow & flat is Bounded North Easterly & North Westerly by y[e] river also about ten acres of Land mour or Less Lying in S[d] Duxbowrough to y[e] northward of Nathanil Brewster Commonly Called y[e] Kentish Lot bounded as by record appears also about three acrs more or leser of upland in ye aforesaid 18th Lot bounded North Easterly by ye Land of Nathanial Brewster South Easterly by ye Land befour Sett off to Cornelas Soule South Westerly by ye Land before [p. 510] Set of to S^d Jedediah Soul & North Westerly By the North Westerly bounds of S^d Eighteenth Lot which we do assign & Sett off in full for S^d Ruth Souls Shear

8^ly We do assign & Sett off to S^d Else ye wife of Barnabas Perry for hir tenth part or Share as follows viz about three acres and a half of Salt meadow & Sedge flate lying on ye afor S^d Hammer Island Bounded Southerly by the meadow of Joshua Soul northerly By the Medow & Sedge flate before Sett of to S^d Ruth Soul Easterly & westerly by the River, also about Thirteen accres or Less of upland & maedow being part of the Place on which the afoursd Moses Soul Formerly Dwelt & is Bounded northerly by the Land of the afours^d Gorge Partrige Easterly by The Land & medow of Christopher Wadsworth Southerly by the Land & meadow Before Set of to Gideon Soul afores^d & Westerdly By the hed of S^d old Farm and also about two acres & a half more or Lesser of upland being part of The afores^d Eighteenth Lot & is Bounded north Easterly by the Land before Set of to Jedediah Soul South Easterly by the Land before Set of to Cornelius Soul South westerly by the South westerly Range of S^d Lot from pitch pine tree marked by a way north fifty Eight Degreas west 19 Rods & Seventeen Links to the Southerly Corner of S^d Lote & the north west Side theirof is Bounded by the north westerly Side of S^d Lot which we do assign & Set of to S^d Else in full for her Shear or or tenth part

9^ly We do assign & Sett off to S^d Deborah Hunt for her Tenth part or Share as fallows viz about fourteen acres More or Less of upland being part of the aforsaid Second Lot & is Bounded as follows viz north Easterly by the north Easterly Bound of S^d Second Lot South Easterly by the Land Before Set of to Jedediah Soul South Westerly by the Land before Set of to Barnabas Soul & north westerly by Island Creek Pond which we do assign & Sett off to S^d Deborah Hunt for her full Shear or Tenth part as Witnes our Hands ye twenthty third Day of august A D 1749

Sam^ll Seabury — Jonathan Peterson
Gorge Partreadge — Dan^ll Lewis Ju
Abraham Samsons

[p. 511] Plimouth Ss Sepr 4 . 1749 The within named Samuel George abraham Jonathan & Daniel perronally appearing Made Oath that the afore going was a Just & Equal Division & Partition of the Estate of Moses Soul Late of Duxbeurgh Deceasd according to the beest of thair Judgmants and I do hereby Confirm ye Same John Cushing Judge of Probat

[12:411] To the Honourabel John Cushing Esqr Judge of Probate &c For the County of Plimouth The Account of Isaac Soule Administrator on the Estate of Moses Sole Late of Duxborough Yeoman Deceased Is Humbly Offerd for Allowance viz: This Accountant Charges himself with the Personal Estate of the Deceasd as Containd In the Inventory Old

Tenour	£705	6	2
Also By Sundreys Come to Hand Since the Inventory was Taken: viz			
3lb of Hemp 9s 1 pr of Spectacles 5s	0	14	
To 300 of board Nails	1	4	
To a Bell a Beatle Ring and Wedge	1	15	0
To a Pr of Old Worsted Combes	2	10	0
Allso By Sundrey Debts Received Due to Said Estate: viz:			
of Abijah Sprague 13/6 Of John Chandler 10/	1	3	6
of Amaziah Delano 13/ of Benjm Pryor: 4 . 13 . 9	5	6	9
of Abner Weston 30/ of Joshua Soule 3£	4	10	0
of Joseph Chandler 12/ of Nathll Brewster 25/	1	17	0
To a Debt Due to the Estate from the Administrator	9	16	0
To a Debt Recd of Kenelm Baker	2	0	0
To Ditto of Dea Arnold 20/	1	0	0
	£736	16	5
The Accont prays that 2 Shares and a quarter In Duxborough Beach May be Added			
2ly This Accountant prays Allowance for the following Disbursments: viz:			
paid Jonathan Chandler 20/ To Judith Chandler 33/4	2	13	4
To William Brewster 2/6 To Mr Veazie £3 . 5 . 0	3	7	6
paid John Pryor 10/ Peleg Sprague £4 . 10	5	0	0
paid Doctr Thomas 18/ paid Doctr Harlow £2 . 18	3	16	
paid Abraham Samson	1	6	6
To John Hunt 49 . 5 . 0	49	5	0
To paid Jedediah Soule	23	0	0
To the Administrators Time and Trouble In the Admr & to Cash pd ye Judge	28	15	0
	117	3	4

Errors Excepted Pr Isaac Soule

Plimo Ss Decr 2 . 1751 This Account Haveing ben Sworn to Is Allowed

Pr John Cushing Judge of Probate

THE CHILDREN OF BENJAMIN AND RUTH BARTLETT

BY GEORGE ERNEST BOWMAN

BENJAMIN BARTLETT[4] (*Benjamin*[3], *Mary*[2] *Warren*, *Richard*[1]), of Duxbury, married Ruth Pabodie[3] (*Elizabeth*[2] *Alden*, *John*[1]) of that town, in December, 1676 or 1678.* The births of only two of their children, Robert and Priscilla, are found on the town records. The names of the other seven, Sarah, Rebecca, Ruth, Mercy, William, Deborah and Abigail, have been determined by a study of the probate and land records.

Many inaccurate and conflicting statements have been printed about this family. It is, therefore, important that such errors should be corrected, and that the facts, shown by a critical examination of the original records, should be printed, for the protection of descendants.

Justin Winsor's History of Duxbury, published in 1849, says that Benjamin Bartlett married Ruth Pabodie in September, 1672; but the town records prove that they were married in December, 1676 or 1678, as already shown.

Winsor gives to Benjamin and Ruth a list of nine children; but he omits the son William (mentioned in his father's will) and includes a son Benjamin. No mention of a Benjamin, son of Benjamin and Ruth (Pabodie) Bartlett, has been found on the records; and since we can prove that Benjamin and Ruth had nine children, the number given in Winsor's list, it is probable that Winsor unintentionally substituted the name Benjamin for the name William.

William T. Davis, in his "Ancient Landmarks of Plymouth", published in 1883, evidently copied Winsor's list of the children, including the doubtful Benjamin; but he added the son William, omitted by Winsor. Davis also included a daughter Elizabeth; but he corrected this latter error in an appendix to the 1899 edition of his book.

Mrs. M. L. T. Alden, in "Putnam's Monthly Historical Magazine", V:81, 82, and VI:69, and in "New England Historical and Genealogical Register", LII:56, not only copied Winsor and Davis in giving the unproved Benjamin; but added other, and more serious, errors. Only a few of her errors can be considered in this article.

* The day of the month was omitted. The last figure of the year is uncertain; but it must have been either 6 or 8.— See Mayflower Descendant, 8:232.

Mrs. Alden says that the widow Ruth (Pabodie) Bartlett died 27 August, 1740; but the division of Benjamin Bartlett's real estate shows that Ruth died before 27 March, 1725.

Mrs. Alden says that Benjamin Bartlett's will mentioned his daughters, Priscilla, Deborah, Abigail, Sarah Bradford, Rebecca Bradford and Ruth Murdock, and also mentioned "Mercy, daughter of son William, decd." This statement must have been made after a very superficial examination of the will, a portion of which plainly reads as follows: "my Daughters; viz. Sarah Bradford, Rebecca Bradford: Ruth murdoch, mercy Turner, Priscilla Deborah and Abigail . and also my Grand Daughter Ruth Bartlett y[e] Daughter of my Son William Dec[d]". Mrs. Alden, therefore, omitted the daughter Mercy Turner, and also changed the name of William's daughter (Benjamin's granddaughter) from Ruth to Mercy. A careful abstract of this will was printed in our last issue.*

Mrs. Alden's paragraph, of thirteen lines, about William Bartlett† contains but one correct statement—that he died before his father. He was not born "about 1674", at least two years before his parents were married. He had no daughter Mercy. His sister Mercy (not his daughter) married John Turner. William Bartlett did not die until 1716 or 1717, therefore "the widow, Hannah Bartlett of Duxbury" who married Thomas Delano in 1699 (not 1698, as Mrs. Alden gives it) was not William Bartlett's widow. She was the widow of his uncle, Ebenezer Bartlett[4] (*Benjamin*[3], *Mary*[2] *Warren*, *Richard*[1]). William Bartlett married at Plymouth, 5 July, 1716, Sarah Foster, who survived him and married, second, Nathan Thomas, and, third, Jedediah Bourne, whom she also survived.

As only two birth dates are known, we cannot be sure of the order in which the children of Benjamin and Ruth (Pabodie) Bartlett were born; but the order in which they are named in their father's will is the same as in the two deeds printed in our last issue; and they are given in that order in the following list. It is interesting to note that five of the eight children married descendants of Mayflower Passengers.

Children of Benjamin and Ruth (Pabodie) Bartlett

Robert Bartlett, born 6 December, 1679; died before December, 1717, without issue.

Sarah Bartlett, born about 1681, died 3 April, 1761; married, 27 November, 1701, Israel[3] Bradford (*William*[2-1]), who was born about 1677, and died 26 March, 1760.

* Mayflower Descendant, 18:178, 179.

† Putnam's Monthly Historical Magazine, VI:69.

Rebecca Bartlett, married, 27 November, 1701, John[4] Bradford (*John*[3], *William*[2-1]), who was born 29 December, 1675, and died 27 March, 1724.
Ruth Bartlett, married John Murdock, who was born 8 June, 1691, and died 17 September, 1756.
Mercy Bartlett, born about 1694, died 6 October, 1757; married, 5 August, 1714, John Turner[5] (*Benjamin*[4], *Mary*[3] *Brewster*, *Jonathan*[2], *William*[1]), who was born 1 January, 1692/3, and died 20 March, 1778.
William Bartlett, died in 1716 or 1717; married, 5 July, 1716, Sarah Foster. Had one child, Ruth, who died young.
Priscilla Bartlett, born in January, 1696/7, died 7 July, 1758; married, 31 December, 1718, John[3] Samson (*Stephen*[2], *Henry*[1]), who was born 17 August, 1688, and died 26 January, 1770.
Deborah Bartlett, died after 25 October, 1750; married, 19 December, 1723, Josiah Thomas, who died after 28 March, 1748.
Abigail Bartlett, born about 1703, died 30 August, 1776; married, 30 August, 1728, Gamaliel[4] Bradford (*Samuel*[3], *William*[2-1]), who was born 18 May, 1704, and died 24 April, 1778.

THE WILL OF EDWARD SOUTHWORTH OF DUXBURY

Communicated by Miss Ethel Bradford Davis

Edward Southworth of Duxbury, son of Constant and Elizabeth (Collier) Southworth, married Mary Pabodie[3], daughter of Elizabeth[2] Alden (*John*[1]). This marriage took place, at Duxbury, on 16 November, 1671,* not in 1669, as stated in the Southworth Genealogy, published in Boston in 1905.

Mary (Pabodie) Southworth was alive 11 December, 1727, when her husband's will was probated; but the date of her death is not known.

Edward Southworth made his will 11 June, 1719, and died before 7 November, 1727, when the witnesses were sworn. The will was probated 11 December, 1727. The original will and the original bond of the executors are still in the files of the Plymouth County, Mass., Registry of Probate. The abstracts here presented were made from the original documents.

The present writer is a descendant of Edward and Mary (Pabodie) Southworth, through their son Thomas Southworth, who married Sarah[3] Alden (*Jonathan*[2], *John*[1]).

* Duxbury Vital Records, in Mayflower Descendant, 8: 232.

[Edward Southworth's Will]

[From original will] "Edward Southworth of Duxborough" made his will 11 June, 1719. Bequests were as follows:

To "my eldest son Thomas Southworth that Farm of land whereon he now Dwelleth with ye housing thereon with two small points of medow lying at ye foot of the s^d land on the southerly side of the mill Brook and six acres of medow be it more or less lying by Blue-Fish-River and Joyning to ye medow of Cp^t Alden also half my medow lying at a Place Called Pine Point with half Barren-hill lying at a place Called North hill and half my swampy and medow land there except three acres of medow Called ye upper medow and also one half of a place Called great wood Island . all which s^d lands and medow is lying & being within the township of Duxborough aboves^d"

To "my son Constant Southworth my Mill and all my land on both sides ye s^d Mill brook to ye southward of my Barn, except what is above given to my son Thomas Southworth with about an acre of medow be it more or less lying upon both sides of ye s^d mill brook and also all my medow lying on ye Northerly side of the s^d mill brook or River, till it comes to a creek which is ye partition betwixt my s^d medow & John Chanlers, except a small parcel of medow on ye North side ye s^d mill brook Called ye Peck hole medow, which s^d land & medow with ye priviledges & appurtenances thereto belonging are lying & being within ye s^d town of Duxborough"

To "my son Benjamin Southworth my land at North hill now within ye Pasture so Called from a Red oak tree marked which is a Corner bound betwixt Robert Stanford and my self at ye head of ye neck or point of woods & from thence on a streight line near Northeast till it Comes across ye swamp taking in all ye land which I bought of ye s^d town of Duxborough with one half of ye aboves^d Barren hill & half ye swampy and medow land there with three acres of medow there Called north Hill upper medow also my salt medow Called ye Cutt medow with half my medow lying at Pine Point also a piece of fresh medow lying at a place Called Phillips Brook which I bought of John Washburn all which lands and medows are lying in Duxborough aboves^d"

To "my son John Southworth my now Dwelling house with all my adjacent land down to my Barn with my medow lying by Duck hill Called Bumpu's neck with a small piece of medow Joyning to ye medow of John Chanler at Duck hill also a piece of fresh medow Called Lindals medow lying on ye Northerly side of Greens-Harbour brook which s^d house & lands & medows are lying in s^d Duxborough"

To "my s^d^ sons Constant Southworth & John Southworth my neck of medow lying in s^d^ Duxborough betwixt the Cutt River and Goteham River which was formerly sold by Governour Josiah Winslow to Mr William Paybodie & Mr John Washburn and also my Grist mill and aboves^d^ Peck hole medow which s^d^ mill and medows are being within ye s^d^ town of Duxborough and I give them with all ye priviledges and appurtenances thereto belonging to my s^d^ sons Constant Southworth & John Southworth to be equally Divided between them"

"I give my half purchase right of lands lying at West Canaog in ye Government of Rhoad Island which I formerly bought of Mr William Paybodie the one half to my four forenamed sons equally among them & the other half to my three Daughters. viz. Mercy ye wife of Moses Soule Elisabeth ye wife of Samuel Weston & Priscila Southworth equally among them"

To "my s^d^ Daughters Elisabeth & Priscila my forty acre lot of land belonging to ye first division of ye Commons in ye township of Duxborough aboves^d^"

To "my Grand son Cornelius Soul my whole share in ye upland in ye second Division of ye Commons belonging to ye towns of Duxborough and Pembroke in ye County aboves^d^"

"my will is that my s^d^ Daughter Priscila Southworth shall have free liberty and priviledge of Dwelling in my aboves^d^ Dwelling house above given to my s^d^ son John & also all ye use benefit and Income of my aboves^d^ Peck hole medow and also pasturage procured & allowed Convenient for two Cows by all my four abovenamed sons equally among them all during ye time she shall Continue unmarried"

"my will is that through all the Lands herein given to my four forenamed sons a convenient way be allowed by them to each other for their passing to and improving each one of them their Respective proprieties"

To "my s^d^ son John Southworth half my Point of upland lying at ye s^d^ North hill and below ye s^d^ Pasture fence with half of my lower medow there with all my lower part of ye upper medow there with the place there called the Island of upland with ye swampy land belonging thereto s^d^ lands & medows are in the s^d^ town of Duxborough"

"my will is that the swampy and medow land with the medow at North hill within willed to my s^d^ sons Thomas & Benjamin be taken to be ye upper part of the s^d^ upper medow"

To "my Deer & loving wife Mary one third part of all ye profits and incomes and benefit of all ye housing lands medows. &c, herein given to my four fore named sons. viz. Thomas Southworth Constant Southworth Benjamin Southworth & John Southworth during y[e] whole term of her natural life"

"my will is that y[e] land before given to my son John Southworth adjacent to my now Dwelling house down to my Barn. &c. shall extend a little below s[d] Barn and shall be bounded as followeth. viz. y[e] southeast end of it from a white oak tree marked standing by y[e] mill pond a little lower down stream than s[d] Barn and from thence Running on a streight line near Northeast to another white oak tree marked standing near y[e] end of a swamp and near y[e] range of y[e] land of Moses Simons which s[d] line shall be y[e] partition betwixt y[e] lands of my s[d] sons Constant and John"

"I give my afores[d] Barn to my s[d] sons Constant Southworth and John Southworth equally between them & my will also is that my son Constant Southworth shall have a convenient & direct way from his own land to s[d] Barn"

"all y[e] Rest and Residue of my Estate which shall not be disposed of at my Decease I give .... to my .... wife Mary for her to use or dispose of as she shall se cause and what shall remain thereof undisposed at her Decease I give to my s[d] son John Southworth and my s[d] Daughter Priscila Southworth equally between them"

"wife Mary & my s[d] son Thomas Southworth Executrix and Executor"

The witnesses were Elnathan Weston, Philip "Dilano", and John Wadsworth. The three witnesses, "all of Duxborough", made oath to the will, 7 November, 1727, before Isaac Winslow, Judge of Probate.

"The Will of mr Edward Southward late of Duxborough .... deceased" was probated at Marshfield, 11 December, 1727, and administration granted "unto Mary Southward Relict Widdow of the sd deceased and Thomas Southward eldest son of the sd deceased".

The will was also recorded, Volume V, page 360.

[From original document] On 7 November, 1727, "Mary Southward Thomas Southward and Ellathan Western all of Duxborough" gave a bond of five hundred pounds, "the above named Mary Southward and Thomas Southward" having been appointed executors.

The bond was signed by Mary Southworth, who wrote her initials "M S" as her mark, and by "thomas southworth" and "Elnathan Weston". The witnesses were John Partridge and "Cornelius Soul".

The bond was not recorded.

PLYMOUTH COLONY WILLS AND INVENTORIES

(*Continued from page 188*)

[ROBERT ROLLOCK'S ESTATE]

[p. 12] "Joseph Burge aged about 30 yeares Doe testify that I heard Robert Rollocke say that hee Did Intend to Marry with his Land Lady this fall when Mr Freeman Came to the Court or as hee went home; and Did Intend to take a Frend or two with him and bee married; this his speeh to mee was about a month or six weekes before hee Died" Sworn before Thomas Southworth, Assistant, at Plymouth, 28 October, 1669.

"This Deponant* saith, being aged about 45 yeares That about seaven weekes agoe .... That Robert Rollocke now Deceased spake to him to buy a good hatt; I said to him for what; and hee said to be married in this fall to his Land Lady;" Sworn before Josias Winslow, Assistant, 28 October, 1669.

[p. 13] The inventory "of Robert Rollocke late of Sandwich Deceased" was taken 15 September, 1669, by Richard Bourne, Nathaniel Fish, Thomas Tobey and John Ellis, Ellis signing by a mark. It was presented at Court at Plymouth, 29 October, 1669, "on the oath of Mistris Sissillia Fish of Sandwich aforsaid widdow;" No real estate was mentioned.

"Att the prising .... Mistris Fish Did say to the prisers .... That the breeches above said vallued ten shillings was given by Robert Rollock to her son John Fish; somtime before his Death; and likewise that Robert Rollocke Did give to her a wastcoat cloth for her selfe out of the" 5¼ yards "of Kersey above prised; witnes to this Edmund Freeman Junir:"

[WILL OF JOHN RICHMOND, SR.]

[p. 14] "John Richmond of Taunton" made his will 14 December, 1663. Bequests were as follows:

To "my eldest son John Richmond my Purchase heer in Taunton;"

"my lands .... at Squamicott which is halfe a share or purchase; first I give .... to my son in law Willam; Paule and Mary his wife and to theire Children forty acrees of the Land att Squamicott .... and .... unto my younger son Edward Richmond; and to his son Edward after him forty acrees of the Land att att Squamicott; alsoe .... unto my son in law Edward

* The name of the deponant was omitted from the record.

Rew and to Sarah his wife the fourth p^r^te of my halfe share of Land which is att Squamicott alsoe . . . . unto my eldest son John Richmond; and to his son Thomas after him the Remainder of my lands att Squamicott;"

To "son John Richmond my Mare" but the first foal is to go to John's son Thomas.

To son John all debts that are due, he to pay all debts owed by the estate.

To "eldest son John Richmond the Mare or sixteen pounds which I layed out for the Lands wherin my son John now Dwelleth; alsoe . . . . all my goods which is in my eldest sons house;"

To "my son in law Edward Rew and Sarah his wife all my goods which are now in my son Edward Rews house; except a paire of sheets and a hamacke; which sheets I give . . . . unto my Daughter Mary the wife of Willam Paule; and the hamacke I give unto my son in law Willam Paule;"

To "son John Richmond my Cow to Defray funerall Charges;"

To "son Edward Richmond all my wearing apparrell;"

To "son John Richmond all my writings in my Chist; which are in my son in law Edward Rews house;"

"I . . . . appoint my eldest son John Richmond Exequitor . . . . and appoint Shadrach Wilbore with . . . . son John Richmond; to see this Last will . . . . p[r]formed"

The will was signed by a mark. The witnesses were Joseph Wilbore and Shadrach Wilbore. It was probated at Plymouth, 29 October, 1669, both witnesses being present. "althoe it was made as the Date first * above expresseth; yett it was not recorded untill the Date last mentioned by reason of an obstruction that fell in the way;"

[p. 15] "A true inventory of the estate of John Richmond seni[r]: of Taunton Deceased the 20th of March 1663, or 64, being aged about 70 yeares apprised by us Joseph Wilbore and Willam Harvey on the fift of Aprill; 1664 in the house of Edward Rew;" The total in Rew's house was £29, 5s. In "his son John Richmons hands" personal estate £19, 15s., 3d. His "Rights to Lands and Devisions heer in Taunton" £10.

The inventory was exhibited at the court, at Plymouth, 29 October, 1670, "on the oath of John Richmond Juni[r]:"

On 11 April, 1664, "Edward Richmond of Newport on Rhode Iland" receipted to Shadrach Wilbore and John Richmond for his share of the estate. John Macomber and William Langley witnessed the receipt.

* 14 December, 1663.

[George Hall's Will]

[p. 16] "Gorge Hall of Taunton" made his will 16 October, 1669, and it was exhibited to the court, at Plymouth, 1 March, 1669,* on the oath of Richard Williams. Bequests were as follows:

To "my wife During widdowhood; The p^r^te of my Dwelling house; that p^r^te which I built Last; and the Garden Joyning to it; and halfe my new barne; and halfe the staule against the barne; Item I give her that I bought of Benjamine Wilson lying between Richard Williams and that which was Nicholas Harts; which is eight acrees which lyeth on the North syde of the great River;" also "the Land that is called by the Name of Cobbs Necke" also "the land That I broke up in the Necke that John Hall hath; and one acree more If shee want it" also "att broad Cove a Carriage of hay: halfe in Samuells and halfe in Josephs (if shee Doth want it) for her selfe; This is my wifes Dureing her widdowhood; after to be Disposed as followeth; and I make her my exequitrix,"

To "my son John Hall the Necke of Land Called by the Name of Jone Wyates bed; and the Land the house stands upon; and the 4 acrees that Reacheth against Tabetts Land and the Necke Called by the Name of Cobbs necke and 76 acrees by the great River; att the further syde of Thomas Deans Land on the east syde"

To "my son Samuell Hall my great Lott: viz: all my land there Lying from the great River to James Leanards Land; the one syde is against Hesekiah Hores Land; and the other syde against Mr Pooles Lands and twenty two acrees against the great River on the west syde of Thomas Deanes:" also "my twenty acrees: and the meddow belonging to it att the three mile River Called Romford; and halfe my meddow att Broad Cove;"

To "my Daughter Charity six pound;"

To "my sonne Joseph Hall my homlott which is eight acrees two acrees wherof I bought of Willam Harvey and six acrees over the great River;" also "that which I bought of Benjamine Wilson which is eight acrees upon the North syde of the great River; The east syde against Richard Williams" also "halfe my meddow att broad Cove; Samell is to p^r^te it equally and Joseph is to Choose the halfe hee will have; and I Give him my Purchase and ten acrees from the towne of my Devision;"

To "my grandchildren to each of them forty shillings"

* This is in old style. In new style it would be 11 March, 1670.

To "my Daughter Sarah twenty pounds; and if shee Doe not match to her Mothers mind shee is to have but sixteen pounds;"

To "the Church in Taunton forty shillings to buy Cupps;"

To "Willam Evens twenty shillings"

To "my son John My new Purchase;"

To "my Daughter Mary forty shillings;"

To "my son Samuell six acrees of Land That is Due to mee from the Towne and three acrees of swampe;"

The witnesses were Richard Williams and Walter Deane.

[p. 17] The inventory of "Gorge Hall of Taunton .... yeoman, Deceased october 30th 1669" was taken 8 February, 1669/70, by Richard Williams and Walter Deane, and exhibited at Court, at Plymouth, 1 March, 1669/70, on the oath of "mistris Mary Hall Widdow". A "share in the Iron workes" was valued at £30. No real estate is mentioned.

[Inventory of Widow Gartherew Hurst]

[p. 18] The inventory of "Gartherew Hurst widdow Deceased" was taken 30 May, 1670, by Ephraim Tinkham and William Crow, and exhibited at court, at Plymouth, 7 June, 1670, on the oath of John Cobb. No real estate is mentioned. "Halfe a Cow in Gershom Cobbs hands" was valued at £1, 10s.

"Grandmother Hurst Debtor" (apparently to John Cobb, as he presented the inventory, and no one else is named) for "finding of her Corne for six yeare" at 20s. per year, other supplies for five years, and "5 yeares washing Dressing of Diett and other trouble att: 20s: a yeare" to 26 June, 1668. "June: 1670: Disbursed since 1668" several items, and "one yeare and an halfe Diett and tendance 08 00 00"

[Nathaniel Goodspeed's Inventory]

[p. 19] The inventory of Nathaniel Goodspeed of Barnstable, deceased, was taken 23 May, 1670. On 2 July, 1670, "Elizabeth the Relict of the above said Nathaniel" made oath to the inventory, and "Roger Goodspeed the father of the above said Nathaniel: acknowlidged .... that he gave .... the said Nathaniel: 5 acrees of upland and one acree of Marsh which was in his posession before his Decease" both before Thomas Hinckley, Assistant.

[Capt. William Hedge's Will]

[p. 20] "Willam Hedge seni^{r}: in yarmouth" made his will 30 June, 1670, and the will of "Captaine Willam Hedge of yarmouth" was probated, at Plymouth, on 11 August, 1670, on the oaths of "Capt Mathew Fuller and John Davis" two of the witnesses. Bequests were as follows:

To "son Abraham Hedge this now my Dwelling house; with all the houshold stuffe in the Parlour; as beding Curtaine Curtaines bedsteed and all the moveables therunto belonginge . . . . and all my land that belongeth to my Dwelling house and alsoe all my lands both upland and meddow that I have in the prime feild"

To "son Elisha Hedge my necke of land and medow belonging therunto provided that hee pay his brother my son Willam: five pounds"

To "son Willam forty pounds in Debts and my best suite of Clothes and my best hatt"

To "son John fifty pounds and my next suite of Clothes and my brasse muskett and my rapier and belt and two mares and; two Colts"

To "son Elemuell fifty pounds and two mares and two Colts"

To "Daughter Sarah Mathews five pounds"

To "Daughter Elizabeth Barnes five pounds"

To "Daughter Mary Sturgis forty pounds"

To "Daughter Marcye fifty pounds"

To "my beloved sister Brookes thirty pounds that is of mine in Verginnia that is Due to mee from Brother Brookes Deceased likewise . . . . my sister Brookes shall have her livelyhood amongst my Children soe Longe as shee Continews a widdow"

"I make my beloved son Elisha my sole exequitor . . . . alsoe I . . . . appoint . . . . Mr Thomas Thornton Mr Edmond Hawes and Richard Tayler tayler; the overseers of this . . . . Will"

"And Wheras Blanch my Wife hath Dealt falcly with mee in the Covenant of Marriage in Departing from mee; therefore I Doe in this . . . . Will . . . . give her twelve pence; and alsoe what I have received of hers . . . . shalbe returned to her againe"

The witnesses were Mathew Fuller, John Gray and John Davis.

[p. 21] The inventory of "Capt: Willam Hedge of yarmouth" was taken, 15 July, 1670, by Thomas Howes and John Thacher, and exhibited at court, at Plymouth, 11 August, 1670. No real estate is mentioned. "Elisha Hedge Conceiveth" that "Joseph Hollott", shoemaker, and William Griffith are alsoe indebted to the estate.

[WILLIAM BASSETT'S INVENTORY]

[p. 22] The inventory of "Willam Bassett of Sandwich late Deceased" was taken by Richard Bourne, Thomas Dexter and James Skiffe, 9 August, 1670, and exhibited at court, at Plymouth, 11 August, 1670, "on the oath of mistris Mary Bassett Widdow". No real estate is mentioned. Among the items are: Cattle "att Jacob Burges" and "att Saconesset"; "the boate"; "owing from the English to the widdow", money due "from Leiftenant Ellis".

(*To be continued*)

EARLE — WESTGATE NOTE

By the Editor

In our seventeenth volume, on pages 62 and 63, we printed an agreement, dated 3 March, 1731/2, of the heirs of Mary (Wilcox) Earle, the widow of John Earle of Tiverton, R. I., and the daughter of Daniel Wilcox, of Tiverton, by his wife Elizabeth[3] Cooke (*John*[2], *Francis*[1]). This agreement shows that Mary's daughter Elizabeth had married George Westgate of Warwick, R. I.

The marriage of George Westgate and Elizabeth Earle and the births of their five children were all entered on page 67 of the first book of the town records of Warwick, R. I. A literal copy of the marriage record, transcribed by the Editor, from the original at Warwick, is here printed.

"George westgeate of warwick and Elisabeth Earl of Tiver Town Came into Portsmouth ye 5th Day of octb^r^ Anno Domini 1727 with Certeficates of their being Lawfully Published and was Then Lawfully married by me Joseph Brownwell Justice"

The five children were: George, born 1 September, 1728; John, born 1 February, 1730/1, about 4 o'clock, P.M.; Priscilla, born 8 September, 1732, about 3 o'clock, A.M.; Mary, born 7 January, 1734/5; Earl, born 26 February, 1735/6.

The marriage record plainly shows that Elizabeth Earle was from Tiverton, R. I. She was not "of Portsmouth", as stated in Arnold's "Vital Record of Rhode Island", Volume I, Part I, page 129. The original record also shows that the marriage took place in Portsmouth, R. I. It did not take place in Warwick, as would be inferred from a reading of Arnold's statement.

In "Ralph Earle and His Descendants", pages 27 and 36, the statement is made that Elizabeth (Earle) Westgate married, second, on 14 November, 1757, Capt. John Adams, of Warren, R. I. It is true that the marriage of a widow Elizabeth Westgate to Capt. John Adams is found on the Warwick records; but the proof that she was not the widow of George Westgate is conclusive, and no attempt has been made to identify her. George Westgate was still alive eight years after this marriage of Capt. John Adams.

That Elizabeth (Earle) Westgate died before her husband is shown by an original lease, dated 10 June, 1764, now owned by Miss Jennie L. Westgate, of Haverhill, N. H., who recently presented photographs of the document to the Massachusetts Society of Mayflower Descendants, and called attention to the error of the Earle genealogy. This lease proves that both Elizabeth (Earle) Westgate and her youngest son Earl Westgate died before the date of the instrument. It was signed by Joseph Gifford, by Elizabeth (Gifford) Westgate, widow of Earl, by John Westgate, oldest brother of Earl, and by George Westgate, Sr., father of John and Earl. George Westgate, Jr., the only other son of George and Elizabeth (Earle) Westgate, was one of the witnesses.

An exhaustive abstract of the lease and its endorsements follows:

[JOSEPH GIFFORD AND ELIZABETH WESTGATE TO JOHN WESTGATE]

"This Indenture of Lease Made" 10 June, 1764, "between Joseph Gifford of portsmouth In the County of Newport in the Colony of Rhode Island . . . . Blacksmith and Elizabeth Westgate of the Town County & Colony aforesaid Widow and Raleck of Earl westate* Late of said portsmouth Deceased on the one part: And John westgate of Tiverton In the County and Colony aforesaid Cordwainer on the other part Witnesseth that they the said Joseph Gifford and Elizabeth Westgate for" £10, "to them . . . . paid and secured by the said John Westgate and for other good Causes . . . . hath Demised set & to farm Letten & by these presents Doth Demise set & to farm Let unto the above Named John Westgate His Executors & assigns one fifth part and one third of one fifth part of all that Land which hath been set of to the heirs of Elizabeth Westgate Deceased by the

* Sic.

men thereunto appointed as may .... appear by their Return on Record special Referance thereunto being had for the perticuler bounds Quantity & manner of the whole of said Lands Lying: &c: With free Ingress Egress and Regress unto upon & from said Lands &c: To Have And to Hold .... During the full term of Eighteen years next Ensuing from & after the Day of the Date hereof .... and It is Covenanted and aGread betwen the said perties that the said John Westgate shall pay all Rates and Taxes that Shall be Lawfully Levied on the above Letten premisses During sd term And .... the said John Westgate his Executors & assigns .... shall and may .... During the above s[d] term peaceably & Quietly .... occupie possess & Enjoy .... all & Every of the above Letten premisses without the Let suite Trouble molestation Interruption or Eviction of them the said Joseph Gifford & Elizabeth westgate .... & of all & Every other person or persons whatsoever Lawfully Claiming or to Claime any Right to or to any part of the above Letten premisses from by or under them or any of their procurements And at the Expiration of this present Lease the peaceable possession of all the abovesd premises is Immediatly to be surrendered up to them the said Joseph Gifford and Elizabeth westgate their heirs or assigns and then the fee simple therof By a further agreement between the parties to these presents is Directly to be Conveyed to the Said John Westgate his heirs & assigns for Ever . the which said agreement will fully appear by one Certain obligation and the Conditions thereunder written bearing Even Date with these presents special Referance thereunto being had .... And George Westgate Seanyer Doth hereby freely willing give yield up & Surrender all his Right title Intrest possession property Claim & Demand whatsoever In or to all the above Letten premisses unto his son the said John westgate his Executors and assigns for & During the term above mentioned"

The lease was signed by Joseph Gifford (by a mark), "Elisabeth Westgate", "John Westgate" and "George Weastgeate". The witnesses were "George Weastgate Jn[r]" and Restcome Sanford.

"Joseph Gifford Elizabeth Westgate John Westgate and George Westgate the subscribers the within Written Instrument personally appeared In Tiverton" on 7 September, 1765, and acknowledged it, before Restcome Sanford, Justice of the Peace.

"Tiverton September the seventh A D 1765 then Received the within Written Instrument and the Same Is Recorded on the 396th page in the first book of Land Evidence
N° 1: P[r] Restcome Sanford Town Clark"

NOTES BY THE EDITOR

THE GRAVE OF REV. SAMUEL^{2} FULLER. The illustration facing page 193 is from a photograph presented to this Society in 1906, and described in a note on page 256 of the October, 1906, issue of "The Mayflower Descendant", as follows. "REV. SAMUEL^{2} FULLER'S GRAVESTONE. Mr. Joseph E. Beals has recently presented to this Society a photograph of the gravestone of Rev. Samuel^{2} Fuller (*Dr. Samuel*^{1}), the first pastor of the First Church of Middleborough, Mass. This stone originally stood in the Nemasket Hill Cemetery, but was replaced, some years since, by a granite block. The old stone now rests in a closet of the present church edifice, built at The Green in 1828. A portion of the stone has been broken off, but the inscription can be readily completed. In the following copy the missing parts are supplied in brackets: [HER]E LYES BURIED Y^{e} [BODY] OF Y^{e} REV^{d} M^{r} [SA]MUEL FULLER WHO [D]EPATED THIS LIFE AUGst Y^{e} 17th 1695 IN Y^{e} 71st YEAR OF HIS AGE HE WAS Y^{e} 1st MINISTER OF Y^{e} 1st CHURCH OF CHRIST IN MIDDLE^{gh}"

Mr. Beals resided in Middleborough until his death in 1909. As his guest, the Editor visited the grave of Rev. Samuel^{2} Fuller, in the Nemasket Hill Cemetery, at Middleborough, in 1905 or 1906.

Especial attention is called to the location of this grave because the Fuller Genealogy, published by William H. Fuller of Palmer, Mass., in 1910, erroneously states, on page 15, that Rev. Samuel^{2} Fuller was buried at Plymouth, Mass. The copy of the inscription there printed is also inaccurate; and the erroneous claim that Rev. Samuel^{2} Fuller's wife was Elizabeth Brewster is repeated.

Rev. Samuel^{2} Fuller married Elizabeth (——) Bowen, widow of Thomas Bowen, of Rehoboth.

HANNAH (COOK) ATKINS. Isaiah Atkins and Hannah Cook were married 12 November, 1724, according to the records of Truro, Mass.; and the births of nine children are found on the same records. The marriage record does not give the residence of either of the contracting parties, or the names of their parents; and this Hannah has been erroneously claimed as the daughter of William^{4} Cooke (*Jacob*$^{3-2}$, *Francis*^{1}) of Kingston, Mass.

Isaiah Atkins married Hannah Cook^{5}, daughter of Josiah Cook^{4} (*Deborah*^{3} *Hopkins*, *Gyles*^{2}, *Stephen*^{1}) of Eastham.

William^{4} Cooke's daughter Hannah married Nathan Wright^{4} (*Adam*^{3}, *Hester*^{2} *Cooke*, *Francis*^{1}) of Kingston.

On 12 July, 1737, William Cooke of Kingston conveyed land to his daughter Hannah, wife of Nathan Wright, cordwainer, of Kingston. [Plym. Co. Deeds, 31 : 114.]

On 26 January, 1776, Hannah Wright of Kingston, then a widow, sold to David Lucas, of Kingston, a part of the land "which was given me by my Father William Cook" [Plym. Co. Deeds, 64 : 218.]

INDEX OF PERSONS

INDEX OF PLACES